COMPUTER
BOOK SERIES
FROM IDG

Microsoft® Office® For Wi... For Dummies®

Microsoft Office Shortc...

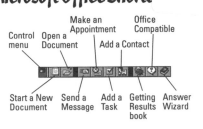

Control menu · Open a Document · Make an Appointment · Add a Contact · Office Compatible

Start a New Document · Send a Message · Add a Task · Getting Results book · Answer Wizard

Microsoft Access form and datasheet view toolbars

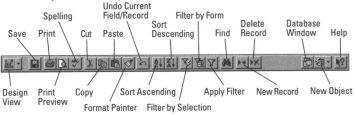

Save · Print · Spelling · Cut · Paste · Undo Current Field/Record · Sort Descending · Filter by Form · Find · Delete Record · Database Window · Help

Design View · Print Preview · Copy · Format Painter · Sort Ascending · Filter by Selection · Apply Filter · New Record · New Object

Microsoft Access design view toolbar

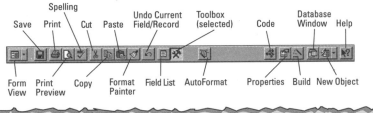

Save · Print · Spelling · Cut · Paste · Undo Current Field/Record · Toolbox (selected) · Code · Database Window · Help

Form View · Print Preview · Copy · Format Painter · Field List · AutoFormat · Properties · Build · New Object

IDG
BOOKS
WORLDWIDE

Microsoft Schedule+ toolbar

Today (selected) · Go to Date · Print · Copy · Insert New Appointment · Recurring · Reminder · Tentative

Open · Cut · Paste · Undo · Delete · Edit · Private · Timex Watch Wizard

... For Dummies: #1 Computer Book Series for Beginners

COMPUTER
BOOK SERIES
FROM IDG

Microsoft® Office® For Windows® 95 For Dummies®

Cheat Sheet

Microsoft Excel Standard and Formatting toolbars

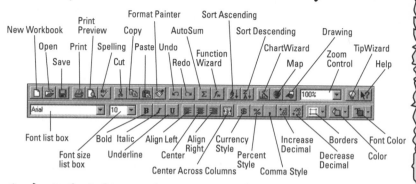

New Workbook, Print Preview, Format Painter, Sort Ascending, Sort Descending, Drawing, Open, Print, Copy, AutoSum, ChartWizard, Zoom Control, TipWizard, Save, Spelling, Paste, Undo, Function Wizard, Map, Help, Cut, Redo

Font list box, Bold, Italic, Align Left, Align Right, Currency Style, Increase Decimal, Borders, Font Color, Font size list box, Underline, Center, Percent Style, Decrease Decimal, Color, Center Across Columns, Comma Style

Microsoft Word Standard and Formatting toolbars

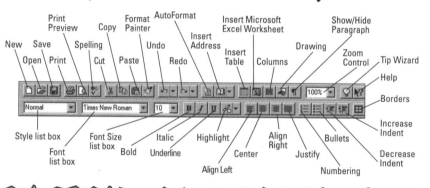

Print Preview, Copy, Format Painter, AutoFormat, Insert Microsoft Excel Worksheet, Show/Hide Paragraph, New, Save, Spelling, Undo, Insert Address, Drawing, Zoom Control, Open, Print, Cut, Paste, Redo, Insert Table, Columns, Tip Wizard, Help, Borders, Increase Indent

Style list box, Font list box, Font Size list box, Bold, Italic, Underline, Highlight, Center, Align Left, Align Right, Justify, Bullets, Numbering, Decrease Indent

Microsoft PowerPoint Standard and Formatting toolbars

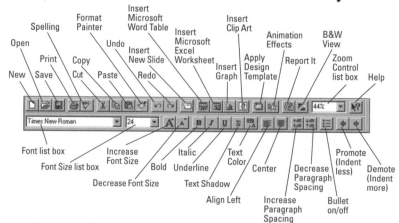

Spelling, Format Painter, Insert Microsoft Word Table, Insert Clip Art, Insert, Animation Effects, B&W View, Open, Undo, Insert Microsoft Excel Worksheet, Apply Design Template, Report It, Zoom Control list box, Print, Copy, Insert New Slide, New, Save, Cut, Paste, Redo, Insert Graph, Help

Font list box, Increase Font Size, Italic, Text Color, Center, Promote (Indent less), Font Size list box, Bold, Underline, Decrease Paragraph Spacing, Demote (Indent more), Decrease Font Size, Text Shadow, Align Left, Increase Paragraph Spacing, Bullet on/off

MICROSOFT®
OFFICE
FOR WINDOWS® 95 FOR
DUMMIES®

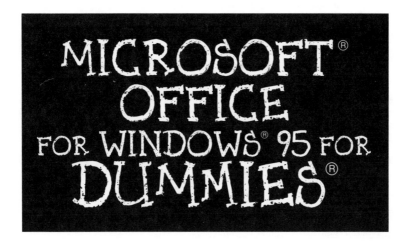

MICROSOFT® OFFICE FOR WINDOWS® 95 FOR DUMMIES®

by Roger C. Parker

IDG Books Worldwide, Inc.
An International Data Group Company

Foster City, CA ♦ Chicago, IL ♦ Indianapolis, IN ♦ Braintree, MA ♦ Southlake, TX

Microsoft® Office For Windows® 95 For Dummies®

Published by
IDG Books Worldwide, Inc.
An International Data Group Company
919 E. Hillsdale Blvd.
Suite 400
Foster City, CA 94404

Library of Congress Catalog Card No.: 95-79923

ISBN: 1-56884-917-6

Printed in the United States of America

10 9 8 7 6 5 4 3 2

1A/RR/QT/ZW/IN

Distributed in the United States by IDG Books Worldwide, Inc.

Distributed by Macmillan Canada for Canada; by Computer and Technical Books for the Caribbean Basin; by Contemporanea de Ediciones for Venezuela; by Distribuidora Cuspide for Argentina; by CITEC for Brazil; by Ediciones ZETA S.C.R. Ltda. for Peru; by Editorial Limusa SA for Mexico; by Transworld Publishers Limited in the United Kingdom and Europe; by Al-Maiman Publishers & Distributors for Saudi Arabia; by Simron Pty. Ltd. for South Africa; by IDG Communications (HK) Ltd. for Hong Kong; by Toppan Company Ltd. for Japan; by Addison Wesley Publishing Company for Korea; by Longman Singapore Publishers Ltd. for Singapore, Malaysia, Thailand, and Indonesia; by Unalis Corporation for Taiwan; by WS Computer Publishing Company, Inc. for the Philippines; by WoodsLane Pty. Ltd. for Australia; by WoodsLane Enterprises Ltd. for New Zealand.

For general information on IDG Books Worldwide's books in the U.S., please call our Consumer Customer Service department at 800-762-2974. For reseller information, including discounts and premium sales, please call our Reseller Customer Service department at 800-434-3422.

For information on where to purchase IDG Books Worldwide's books outside the U.S., contact IDG Books Worldwide at 415-655-3021 or fax 415-655-3295.

For information on translations, contact Marc Jeffrey Mikulich, Director, Foreign & Subsidiary Rights, at IDG Books Worldwide, 415-655-3018 or fax 415-655-3295.

For sales inquiries and special prices for bulk quantities, write to the address above or call IDG Books Worldwide at 415-655-3200.

For information on using IDG Books Worldwide's books in the classroom, or ordering examination copies, contact the Education Office at 800-434-2086 or fax 817-251-8174.

For authorization to photocopy items for corporate, personal, or educational use, please contact Copyright Clearance Center, 222 Rosewood Drive, Danvers, MA 01923, or fax 508-750-4470.

is a trademark under exclusive license to IDG Books Worldwide, Inc., from International Data Group, Inc.

About the Author

Roger C. Parker

More than 750,000 desktop publishers and software users throughout the world own books by Roger C. Parker. In addition to frequently contributing to a variety of publications, including *Graphic Solutions, Publish, Technique,* and *x-height,* Roger has written numerous books on desktop publishing and design.

Roger has conducted presentations throughout the world for organizations such as the Consumer Electronics Show, Apple Computer, Creative Seminars, the State Street Bank, Yamaha Audio, and the University of Illinois. During the past few years, Roger has been the keynote speaker and lead presenter at PageMaker conferences conducted throughout the United States. He is active with the Boston Computer Society.

Roger's recent books for IDG Books Worldwide include *Desktop Publishing & Design For Dummies, Harvard Graphics 2.0 For Windows For Dummies, WordPerfect 6.0 (DOS) Secrets* (with David Holzgang), *WordPerfect 6.0 for Windows Power Techniques,* and *Freelance Graphics 2.1 For Dummies.*

Welcome to the world of IDG Books Worldwide.

IDG Books Worldwide, Inc., is a subsidiary of International Data Group, the world's largest publisher of computer-related information and the leading global provider of information services on information technology. IDG was founded more than 25 years ago and now employs more than 7,700 people worldwide. IDG publishes more than 250 computer publications in 67 countries (see listing below). More than 70 million people read one or more IDG publications each month.

Launched in 1990, IDG Books Worldwide is today the #1 publisher of best-selling computer books in the United States. We are proud to have received 8 awards from the Computer Press Association in recognition of editorial excellence and three from Computer Currents' First Annual Readers' Choice Awards, and our best-selling *...For Dummies*® series has more than 19 million copies in print with translations in 28 languages. IDG Books Worldwide, through a joint venture with IDG's Hi-Tech Beijing, became the first U.S. publisher to publish a computer book in the People's Republic of China. In record time, IDG Books Worldwide has become the first choice for millions of readers around the world who want to learn how to better manage their businesses.

Our mission is simple: Every one of our books is designed to bring extra value and skill-building instructions to the reader. Our books are written by experts who understand and care about our readers. The knowledge base of our editorial staff comes from years of experience in publishing, education, and journalism — experience which we use to produce books for the '90s. In short, we care about books, so we attract the best people. We devote special attention to details such as audience, interior design, use of icons, and illustrations. And because we use an efficient process of authoring, editing, and desktop publishing our books electronically, we can spend more time ensuring superior content and spend less time on the technicalities of making books.

You can count on our commitment to deliver high-quality books at competitive prices on topics you want to read about. At IDG Books Worldwide, we continue in the IDG tradition of delivering quality for more than 25 years. You'll find no better book on a subject than one from IDG Books Worldwide.

John J. Kilcullen

John Kilcullen
President and CEO
IDG Books Worldwide, Inc.

IDG Books Worldwide, Inc., is a subsidiary of International Data Group, the world's largest publisher of computer-related information and the leading global provider of information services on information technology. International Data Group publishes over 250 computer publications in 67 countries. Seventy million people read one or more International Data Group publications each month. International Data Group's publications include: **ARGENTINA:** Computerworld Argentina, GamePro, Infoworld, PC World Argentina; **AUSTRALIA:** Australian Macworld, Client/Server Journal, Computer Living, Computerworld, Digital News, Network World, PC World, Publishing Essentials, Reseller; **AUSTRIA:** Computerwelt, PC TEST; **BELARUS:** PC World Belarus; **BELGIUM:** Data News; **BRAZIL:** Annuário de Informática, Computerworld Brazil, Connections, Super Game Power, Macworld, PC World Brazil, Publish Brazil, SUPERGAME, languages, Reseller World; **CHILE:** Computerworld Chile, GamePro, PC World Chile; **COLUMBIA:** Computerworld Colombia, GamePro, PC World Colombia; **CANADA:** CIO Canada, ComputerWorld Canada, InfoCanada, Network World Canada, Reseller World; **CHILE:** Computerworld Chile, GamePro, PC World Chile; **COLUMBIA:** Computerworld Colombia, GamePro, PC World Colombia; **COSTA RICA:** PC World Costa Rica/Nicaragua; **THE CZECH AND SLOVAK REPUBLICS:** Computerworld Czechoslovakia, Elektronika Czechoslovakia, PC World Czechoslovakia; **DENMARK:** Communications World, Computerworld Danmark, Macworld Danmark, PC World Danmark, PC World Danmark Supplements, TECH World; **DOMINICAN REPUBLIC:** PC World Republica Dominicana; **ECUADOR:** PC World Ecuador, GamePro; **EGYPT:** Computerworld Middle East, PC World Middle East; **EL SALVADOR:** PC World Centro America; **FINLAND:** MikroPC, Tietoverkko, Tietoviikko; **FRANCE:** Distributique, Golden, Info PC, Le Guide du Monde Informatique, Le Monde Informatique, Reseaux & Telecoms; **GERMANY:** Computer Business, Computerwoche, Computerwoche Extra, Computerwoche Focus, Electronic Entertainment, Macwelt, PC Welt; **GREECE:** GamePro, Macworld & Publish; **GUATEMALA:** PC World Centro America; **HONDURAS:** PC World Centro America; **HONG KONG:** Computerworld Hong Kong, PCWorld Hong Kong, Publish in Asia; **HUNGARY:** ABCD CD-ROM, Computerworld Szamitastechnika, PC & Mac World Hungary, PC-X Magazine; **INDIA:** Computerworld India, PC World India, Publish in Asia; **INDONESIA:** InfoKomputer PC World, Komputek Computerworld, Publish in Asia; **IRELAND:** ComputerScope, PC Live!; **ISRAEL:** PC World 32 BIT, People & Computers; **ITALY:** Computerworld Italia, Computerworld Italia Special Editions, Lotus Italia, Macworld Italia, Networking Italia, PC Shopping, PC World Italia, PC World/Walt Disney; **JAPAN:** Macworld Japan, Nikkei Personal Computing, SunWorld Japan, Windows World Japan; **KENYA:** East African Computer News; **KOREA:** Hi-Tech Information/Computerworld, Macworld Korea, PC World Korea; **MACEDONIA:** PC World Macedonia; **MALAYSIA:** Computerworld Malaysia, PC World Malaysia, Publish in Asia; **MEXICO:** Computerworld Mexico, GamePro, Macworld, PC World Mexico; **MYANMAR:** PC World Myanmar; **NETHERLANDS:** Computable, Computer! Totaal, LAN Magazine, Macworld, Net Magazine; **NEW ZEALAND:** Computer Buyer, Computerworld New Zealand, MTB, Network World, PC World New Zealand; **NICARAGUA:** PC World Costa Rica/Nicaragua; **NIGERIA:** PC World Africa; **NORWAY:** Computerworld Norge, Computerworld Privat, CW Rapport Klient/Tjener, CW Rapport Nettverk & Telecom, CW Rapport Offentlig Sektor, IDG's KURSGUIDE, Macworld Norge, Multimedia World, PC World Ekspress, PC World Nettverk, PC World Norge, PC World's Produktguide, Windows Spesial; **PAKISTAN:** Computerworld Pakistan, PC World Pakistan; **PANAMA:** GamePro, PC World Panama; **PARAGUAY:** PC World Paraguay; **P. R. OF CHINA:** China Computerworld, China Infoworld, Computer & Communication, Electronic Product World, Electronics Today, Game Camp, PC World China, Popular Computer Week, Software World, Telecom Product World; **PERU:** Computerworld Peru, GamePro, PC World Profesional Peru, PC World Peru; **POLAND:** Computerworld Poland, Computerworld Special Report, Macworld, Networld, PC World Komputer; **PHILIPPINES:** Computerworld Philippines, PC Digest, Publish in Asia; **PORTUGAL:** Cerebro/PC World, Correio Informático/Computerworld, Mac•In/PC•In Portugal; **PUERTO RICO:** PC World Puerto Rico; **ROMANIA:** Computerworld Romania, PC World Romania, Telecom Romania; **RUSSIA:** Computerworld Rossiya, Network World Russia, PC World Russia; **SINGAPORE:** Computerworld Singapore, PC World Singapore, Publish in Asia; **SLOVENIA:** MONITOR; **SOUTH AFRICA:** Computing S.A., Network World S.A., Software World; **SPAIN:** Computerworld España, COMUNICACIONES WORLD, Dealer World, Macworld España, PC World España; **SWEDEN:** CAP&Design, Computer Sweden, Corporate Computing, MacWorld, Maxi Data, MikroDatorn, Natverk & Kommunikation, PC/Aktiv, PC World, Windows World; **SWITZERLAND:** Computerworld Schweiz, Macworld Schweiz, PCtip; **TAIWAN:** Computerworld Taiwan, Macworld Taiwan, PC World Taiwan, Publish Taiwan, Windows World; **THAILAND:** Thai Computerworld, Publish in Asia; **TURKEY:** Computerworld Monitor, MACWORLD Turkiye, PC WORLD Turkiye; **UKRAINE:** Computerworld Kiev, Computers & Software Magazine, PC World Ukraine; **UNITED KINGDOM:** Acorn User, Amiga Action, Amiga Computing, Amiga, Appletalk, CD Powerplay, CD-ROM Now, Computing, Connexion, GamePro, Lotus Magazine, Macaction, Macworld, Open Computing, Parents and Computers, PC Home, PC Works, The WEB; **UNITED STATES:** Cable in the Classroom, CD Review, CIO Magazine, Computerworld, Computerworld Client/Server Journal, Digital Video Magazine, DOS World, Electronic, InfoWorld, I-Way, Macworld, Maximize, MULTIMEDIA WORLD, Network World, PC World, PUBLISH, SWATPro Magazine, Video Event, WebMaster; **URUGUAY:** PC World Uruguay; **VENEZUELA:** Computerworld Venezuela, GamePro, PC World Venezuela; and **VIETNAM:** PC World Vietnam   10/17/95

Acknowledgments

Although the author's name appears on the cover, books are team sports. The talents of many others contribute to a book's success.

In this case, from the IDG team, I'd like to acknowledge the contributions of fellow IDG author Wallace Wang, plus IDG's strong and supportive editorial team headed by Colleen Rainsberger and Barb Terry. I'd also like to acknowledge the support and encouragement of numerous other IDG folk: Senior Vice President and Publisher Milissa Koloski, Associate Publisher Diane Steele, Editorial Managers Kristin Cocks and Mary Corder, and Brand Manager Judith Taylor.

On the author's "team" I'd like to acknowledge the enthusiastic support of Margot Maley of Waterside Productions and, as always, the patience of my family: Betsy, Christopher, Zachary and — especially — Ryan.

In addition, I'd like to acknowledge the talents of the numerous programmers who conceived and executed the idea of packaging several no-compromise, easy-to-use programs into a single package that is flexible enough to satisfy either first-time or power users.

(The Publisher would like to give special thanks to Patrick J. McGovern, without whom this book would not have been possible.)

Credits

Contents at a Glance

Cartoons at a Glance

By Rich Tennant

page 239

page 209

page 286

page 225

page 131

page 171

page 328

page 47

page 311

page 9

Table of Contents

Introduction

●●

*A*long time ago, a single program cost several hundred dollars, looked entirely different from the other programs on your computer, and stored data in its own special file format. Not surprisingly, many people found computers frustrating, intimidating, and downright hostile to use. More than a few computers wound up collecting dust in a closet despite the owner's best intentions to master the electronic beast and join the ranks of the computer literate.

So to make computers easier to use (and also make a few bucks for themselves in the process), the folks at Microsoft developed their own word processor (Microsoft Word), spreadsheet (Microsoft Excel), presentation graphics program (Microsoft PowerPoint), scheduler (Microsoft Schedule+), and database (Microsoft Access).

Of course, buying all these programs individually might cost you more than the amount of your entire computer. As a slick marketing trick, Microsoft decided to sell as many programs as possible and blanket the world with Microsoft products. To this end, Microsoft bundled all of its top-selling programs into a single package and dubbed it Microsoft Office.

To learn all the programs in Microsoft Office, you can buy separate books for all of Microsoft's programs (*Microsoft Word For Windows 95 For Dummies, Access For Windows 95 For Dummies, Excel For Windows 95 For Dummies,* and so on) or you can just use this book. While this book won't make you an expert in using any single program, it will give you the basics of each program (well, enough to get by and fool your boss) and show you how to use Microsoft Office as a single entity rather than as a rag-tag collection of programs packaged together.

Who Should Buy This Book

Whether you already own and use Microsoft Office, are considering buying it, or have it installed on your computer and dread trying to figure out how to make the whole thing work by yourself, this book is for you no matter what your previous computer background may be.

- ✔ If you *haven't yet purchased* Microsoft Office, this book can show you all the neat things Microsoft Office can do for you when you finally decide to get a copy for yourself.

- ✔ If you're new to computers and *have already purchased* Microsoft Office (or your computer includes a preloaded version of Office), this book can get you started using each program with a reasonable level of proficiency so that your co-workers will start asking you for help with their own computers.

- ✔ If you're *familiar with earlier versions of Word or Excel* and are considering upgrading (or have recently upgraded) to the latest versions, this book will show you how to use each program's fancy new features.

- ✔ Finally, this book is for you if you want to work faster, produce better-looking documents and presentations, or share data between separate Microsoft programs.

In short, this book provides a foundation that you can put to work immediately and then build on later by browsing through the other books in the popular *. . . For Dummies* series.

How This Book Is Organized

To help you find what you need quickly, this book is divided into several parts, with each part covering a certain topic of Microsoft Office. Whenever you need help, just flip through this book, find the part that covers the topic you're looking for, read the information you need, and get back to work.

Part I: Getting to Know Microsoft Office

Even though Microsoft Office looks like a bunch of unrelated programs thrown together by Microsoft, it's actually a bunch of unrelated programs that have been tortured over the years into working together.

Besides sporting similar menus, icons, and keystroke commands, all of the programs in Microsoft Office also know how to share data in a single file. Rather than scattering separate Word, Excel, or PowerPoint files across your hard disk (and forcing you to keep track of them), Microsoft Office can store related documents in a single file called a *binder*.

One binder may contain your business-related documents (form letters, tax records, and proposal slide shows) and another may contain your personal information (diaries, household budgets, and bankruptcy legal forms). By using binders, you can get the benefit of using all the programs making up Microsoft Office without going mad trying to organize everything as well.

Part II: Working with Words

Microsoft Word (which shows you that even Microsoft has trouble coming up with original names once in a while) is fast becoming the most popular word processor on the face of the earth. Sure, you can use Word just to write letters, proposals, or apologies. But you can also use Word to create reports, brochures, or newsletters that combine spreadsheet data and charts from Microsoft Excel, artwork from PowerPoint, and addresses from Access.

Even if you can't type, don't like to write, or flunked spelling in second grade, you'll find Word an eminently useful companion to turn your $2,000 computer into your personal secretary. With Word's spelling checker, grammar checker, and outliner, you can turn your random thoughts into coherent words and sentences that even your boss can understand.

Part III: How to Excel at the Numbers Game

This part shows you how to design your very own spreadsheets using Microsoft Excel. Here you learn what the heck a spreadsheet is, how you can plop numbers and labels on it, how to create your own formulas so that Excel calculates new results automatically, and how to format the whole thing to make it look pleasing to the eye.

After you understand the basics of spreadsheet creation, the next step is to convert your raw data into eye-popping graphs, charts, and other colorful images that can amuse everyone from high-powered CEOs of Fortune 500 companies to children roaming around in a day-care center.

Part IV: Suddenly It's Show Time

Microsoft PowerPoint helps you create slide shows, overhead transparencies, and on-screen computer presentations that can either enhance your information or hide the fact that you don't have the slightest idea what you're doing in the first place.

Any time you need to make a presentation, let PowerPoint help you develop a dynamic presentation that includes: *visuals* (which can be 35mm slides, overhead transparencies, or screen images), *notes* (to help you rehearse your presentation), and *handouts* (to give your audience something to look at so that you don't have to keep talking all the time).

Part V: Keeping Track of Time with Schedule+

Everyone seems busy all the time. In today's fast-moving world where seconds count (and yet major corporations move with a glacial-like pace that makes arthritic mailmen look downright speedy), you may want to keep track of your tasks, appointments, and schedule so that you can effectively manage your time (while 90 percent of your peers wander aimlessly through the corporate landscape).

To help you accomplish this task, Microsoft Office includes Microsoft Schedule+, a program that combines the features of an appointment book, calendar, and to-do list in one screen. By fanatically managing your time with Microsoft Schedule+, you can plan your projects, ration out your time, and effectively squeeze every last productive second out of each day — unless, of course, you don't use your computer that day.

Part VI: Making the Most of Your Data

If you have the Professional edition of Microsoft Office, you have a bonus program called Microsoft Access. For those of you who like official definitions, Access is a relational database that lets you store and retrieve data, design reports, and actually create your own programs.

Because every business needs to store data, you'll find Access handy for saving names, addresses, and phone numbers as well as storing more esoteric information, such as part numbers, Internet addresses, or credit card numbers. If you need to save and retrieve information at a later date, Access can help you do it quickly and easily.

Chapters 17 and 18 show you how to make the most of your data by exchanging it between applications.

Part VII: The Part of Tens

Looks are everything — which explains why most people ignore Nobel Prize winning geniuses, yet get excited about the latest rumors of their favorite *Baywatch* television stars. To help you make the most of each program and create the most visually stunning and useful documents and presentations as possible, this part contains lots of shortcut tips, design tips, and integration tips that can make your time spent with Microsoft Office much more bearable (and even enjoyable).

Glossary

To communicate quickly without using a lot of words, every industry creates its own unique words that make absolutely no sense to anyone else. To help you decipher some of these terms, glance through the glossary in the back of this book. While not as comprehensive as the *Illustrated Computer Dictionary For Dummies* (also available from IDG Books Worldwide), you'll find definitions for most of the crazy words and phrases that the Microsoft Office manuals like to use from time to time.

How to Use This Book

You can use this book as a reference or as a quick tutorial. Unlike novels, this book isn't designed for someone to read from cover to cover (although you can if you want). Instead, just browse through the parts that interest you and ignore the rest.

If you plan to take full advantage of Microsoft Office, reading Part I first is a good idea so that you can understand how to store all your data in a single file (binder). But if you decide to stick to your old habits of scattering files all over the place and then wondering why you can never get anything done, feel free to skip Part I.

The other parts of this book are here for your reference and amusement as well. While you may not care about making presentations with PowerPoint at first, one day you may like to play around with it, just to see what it can do. To your surprise, certain programs that you thought you would never use may turn out to be more useful than you ever imagined. (Then again, they may really turn out to be useless after all, but you'll never find out until you try them.)

How much do you need to know?

Besides knowing how to turn on your computer and use a mouse, you should also have a basic understanding on how to use Microsoft Windows 95. (If you're just learning Windows 95 because Microsoft shoved it in the marketplace and everyone seems to be using it for no apparent reason, then you may want to buy *Windows 95 For Dummies* as well.)

Conventions

To avoid confusion later on (Microsoft has already sowed enough confusion in the computer industry), understanding the following terms is important:

✔ When looking at the screen, notice the blinking *cursor* and the *I-beam pointer*. Move the mouse. Notice that the I-beam pointer moves to follow the mouse's movement.

✔ *Clicking* refers to pressing the left mouse button once and letting go. Clicking is how you activate buttons in the toolbar, for example.

✔ *Double-clicking* refers to pressing the left mouse button twice in rapid succession. Double-clicking typically activates a command.

✔ *Dragging* selects items you want to move, delete, or format. To drag, place the I-beam pointer to the left of the item that you want to select, hold down the left mouse button, and move the mouse in the desired direction. When you release the mouse button, Windows 95 selects that item. You can tell when an item is selected because it appears in white against a black background.

✔ *Right-clicking* means clicking the mouse button to the right. (Some mice have three buttons, so ignore the middle button for now.) Right-clicking usually displays a shortcut menu on the screen.

Figure I-1 shows a typical Office window, and Figure I-2 shows a typical Office dialog box. The parts are labeled with the terms used in this book.

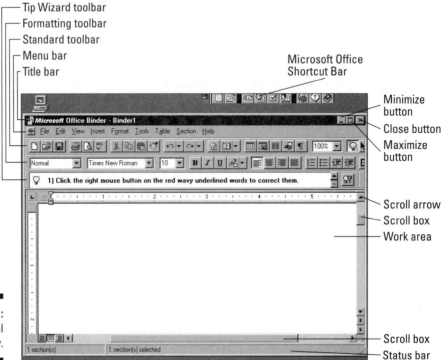

Figure I-1:
A typical window.

Tab

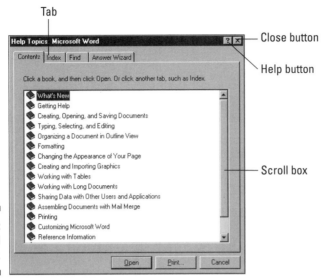

Close button

Help button

Scroll box

Figure I-2:
A typical
dialog box.

Icons used in this book

This icon highlights information that can be helpful (as long as you remember it, of course.)

This icon marks certain steps or procedures that can make your life much easier when using Microsoft Office.

Look out! This icon tells you how to avoid trouble before it starts.

This icon highlights information that's absolutely useless to know for using Microsoft Office but impressive to your trivia buddies.

This icon gives you tips about how to create the most aesthetically pleasing documentation or presentation.

This icon highlights shortcuts that can make you more productive right away — even before you know exactly what you're doing.

Keyboard shortcuts

Microsoft Office gives you two ways to choose commands:

- Clicking the mouse on a button or menu command
- Pressing a keystroke combination, such as Ctrl+S (which means hold down the Ctrl key, tap the S key, and then release both keys at the same time)

Most keyboard shortcuts involve holding down the Ctrl or Alt key (typically located to the left and right of the spacebar on your keyboard) in combination with one of the function keys (the keys labeled F1, F2, F3, and so on) or a letter key (A, B, C, and so on).

You can use whichever method you prefer, just as long as you know what you're doing. Some people swear by the mouse, some swear by the keyboard, and still others just swear at the computer.

Getting Started

By now you're probably anxious to start learning Microsoft Office, so turn on your computer and get ready to jump miles ahead of the competition by having the foresight to use the world's most powerful programs, all of which are bundled in Microsoft Office.

Part I
Getting to Know Microsoft Office

In this part...

Microsoft Office is more than just a collection of applications — it's a collection of applications designed to work together as one coherent unit. With Microsoft Office, you can store separate word processor, spreadsheet, and graphics data in a single file called a *binder*.

Binders let you store related data in one location so you'll never have to hunt around your hard disk again for that missing word processor or spreadsheet file that's absolutely vital to a project that you have to turn in tomorrow. After you get used to using binders to store related data, you may never want to go back to using separate programs again (which will keep Microsoft happy as they continue to enjoy their dominance over the computer industry).

Chapter 1

Getting Help from Microsoft Office

• •

In This Chapter

▶ Calling for help

▶ Using the Answer Wizard

▶ Browsing the Help index

▶ Finding specific words in the Help file

▶ Searching the Help table of contents

• •

Microsoft Office is a big program that probably dwarfs everything else on your hard disk, so don't expect to master it without a fight. Before you start using Microsoft Office, it's helpful to know how to get help before you really need it — sort of like when flight attendants tell you about the emergency exits before your plane takes off from the airport.

Besides using this book, the best way to get help is to use the Microsoft Office Help file. Essentially, this Help file contains everything printed in the Microsoft Office manuals. But unlike the Microsoft Office manuals, which force you to search page by page yourself, the Microsoft Office Help file does the searching for you.

Think of the Help file as an extremely friendly librarian. Just ask the Help file for information on a specific topic, and the Help file diligently digs through its electronic library and retrieves topics that seem relevant. At this point, you can choose the item you think most likely contains the information you need.

Microsoft Office provides four ways for you to get help:

✔ Type your question by using complete or partial sentences, such as "How can I create a form letter?"

✔ Browse through the Help index, which organizes topics alphabetically.

✔ Give the Help file a specific word or phrase (such as *formulas*), and let the Help file find all topics containing that word or phrase.

✔ Browse through the Help table of contents.

Calling for Help

Whenever you need help while using Microsoft Office, you have three choices:

✔ Press F1 to display the Help file.

✔ Click Help and then choose Binder Help or your current program's help, such as Word Help. (This option works only if you're using Word or PowerPoint within a binder.)

✔ Click Help and then choose your current program's help file such as Word Help.

Of the three ways to call for help, it's much easier and faster to press F1.

The Help menu changes depending on the program you're using at the time (Word, Excel, PowerPoint, and so on). If you're using Word, for example, choose Help⇨Word Help⇨Microsoft Word Help Topics.

The moment you call for help, a Help Topics dialog box appears, as shown in Figure 1-1.

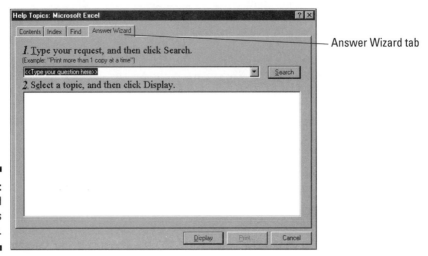

Figure 1-1:
A typical
Help Topics
dialog box.

Using the Answer Wizard

To make the Help file as easy to use as asking another person, Microsoft developed the Answer Wizard, which lets you type complete or partial sentences asking for help, such as "How do I create formulas?"

To use the Answer Wizard, follow these steps:

1. **Press F1 (or choose Help⇨Answer Wizard).**

   The Help Topics dialog box appears.

2. **Click the Answer Wizard tab.**

3. **Type your question in the top text box and press Enter.**

   A list of topics appears in the bottom window (see Figure 1-2).

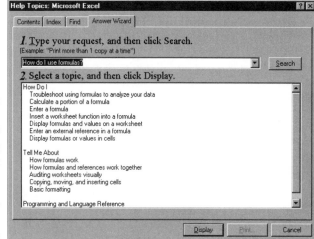

Figure 1-2:
A list of
topics that
Microsoft
Office
hopes will
answer your
question.

4. **Click the topic that you think will answer your question and click Display.**

   A Help window appears.

5. **Click the close box or press Esc to remove the Help window.**

Browsing the Help Index

The most important part of any computer book is usually the index, which lets you jump to the part of the book containing the information you need. If you like looking for information in a book by using the index, browse through the Help file by using the Help index.

To use the Help index, follow these steps:

1. **Press F1. (Or choose Help and the appropriate help topics, such as Microsoft Excel Help Topics.)**

   The Help Topics dialog box appears.

2. **Click the Index tab.**

   A list of index entries appears in the lower window (see Figure 1-3).

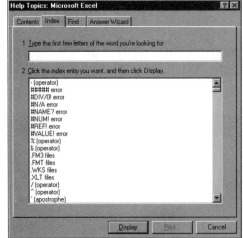

Figure 1-3:
A list of index entries to choose from.

3. **Click the index entry that you want to read and click Display.**

   A Help window appears.

4. **Click the close box or press Esc to remove the Help window.**

Finding Specific Words in the Help File

If you're the impatient type who can't be bothered typing questions or searching the Help file index, call the Help file, click the Find tab, and just type a word or phrase that you want the Help file to find. The Help file will then yank out every topic containing your specified word.

Creating a database of words

Before you can search the Help file for a specific word, you must create a database of all the words in the Help file. To create a database of words, follow these steps:

1. **Press F1. (Or choose Help and the appropriate help topics such as Microsoft Excel Help Topics.)**

   The Help Topics dialog box appears.

2. **Click the Find tab.**

   The Find Setup Wizard dialog box appears (see Figure 1-4).

Figure 1-4:
The Find
Setup
Wizard
dialog box.

3. Select one of the following:

   • <u>M</u>inimize database size (recommended)

   • Ma<u>x</u>imize search capabilities

   • <u>C</u>ustomize search capabilities

4. Click Next.

5. Click Finish.

The Find dialog box appears. Now you're ready to type in a word to search for in the Help file.

Finding a word in the Help file

After you create the database of words in the Help file, you can search for a specific word by following these steps:

1. Press F1. (Or choose Help and the appropriate help topics such as Microsoft Excel Help Topics.)

The Help Topics dialog box appears.

2. Click the Find tab.

The Find dialog box appears (see Figure 1-5).

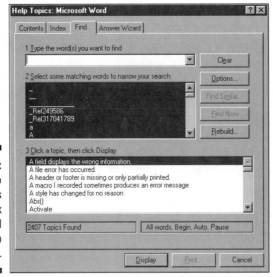

Figure 1-5:
The Help
Topics
dialog box
with the Find
tab
selected.

3. Type the word that you want to search for in the Type the word(s) you want to find text box, located at the top of the dialog box.

4. Click a topic displayed in the Select some matching words to narrow your search list box, located in the middle of the dialog box.

5. **Click a topic displayed in the Click a topic, then click Display list box, located at the bottom of the dialog box.**

6. **Click Display.**

   A Help window appears.

7. **Click the close box or press Esc to remove the Help Topics dialog box.**

Searching the Help Table of Contents

For those of you who just like browsing through the Help file at a leisurely pace to see what you may find, you can also search the Help file using its table of contents. Like all tables of contents, the Help file table of contents is organized by topic.

To search the Help file by its table of contents, follow these steps:

1. **Press F1. (Or choose Help and the appropriate help topics such as Microsoft Excel Help Topics.)**

   The Help Topics dialog box appears.

2. **Click the Contents tab.**

   The table of contents for the Help file appears.

3. **Double-click a topic represented by a closed book icon.**

   The closed book icon representing that topic changes to an open book and displays subtopics underneath, as shown in Figure 1-6.

4. **Double-click a Help screen (represented by a question mark).**

   A Help screen appears (see Figure 1-7).

5. **Click a Help button to display help for a specific item.**

   A pop-up window appears, displaying additional help.

6. **Click the close box or press Esc to remove the Help window.**

Subtopics

Topics

Help screens

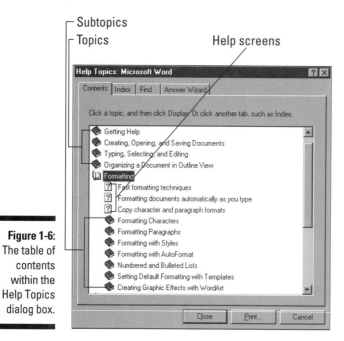

Figure 1-6:
The table of
contents
within the
Help Topics
dialog box.

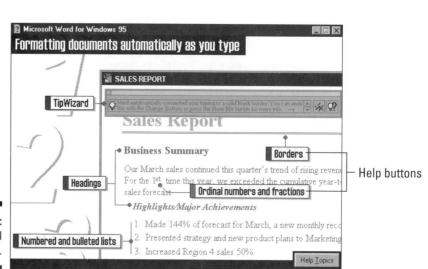

Figure 1-7:
A typical
Help screen.

Help buttons

Chapter 2

Using Microsoft Office

*I*n the old days, personal computers only ran one program at a time and, even then, those programs looked as stark and unappealing as the New York Stock Exchange listing in the *Wall Street Journal.* With the introduction of Microsoft Windows, programs began looking pretty and colorful, offering pull-down menus, overlapping windows, and mouse support — which would have been a revolutionary idea if Macintosh users hadn't already been using a similar interface for the past ten years.

Although Microsoft Windows makes computer programs easier to use, its main benefit is that it allows users to run two or more programs simultaneously. Instead of continually loading and exiting your word processing, spreadsheet, and database programs, you can use Windows to load all three programs and switch among them at the touch of a button.

By making all your programs available to you in an instant, Windows allows you to spend less time loading programs and more time actually getting some work done (or at least creating the illusion that you're getting some work done).

Starting Microsoft Office

Before you can use Microsoft Office, you need to know how to start it; otherwise, it's just going to sit around and take up space — much like a man watching his favorite sports on TV. You can load the separate parts of Microsoft Office individually (Word, Excel, PowerPoint, and so on), but that pretty much destroys the purpose of getting Microsoft Office in the first place.

Basically, you can start Microsoft Office in two ways:

- Run Microsoft Office from the Windows 95 Taskbar
- Run Microsoft Office from the Microsoft Office Shortcut Bar

To run Microsoft Office from the Windows 95 Taskbar, follow these steps:

1. **Click the Start button on the Taskbar.**

   A pop-up menu appears.

2. **Click one of the following:**

   - **New Office Document**
   - **Open Office Document**

Putting the Microsoft Office Shortcut Bar to Work

You can load Microsoft Office as you would any ordinary Windows program, but using the Shortcut Bar instead is a lot easier. If you use the Shortcut Bar, you don't have to wade through globs of program names on your Windows 95 Taskbar. Instead, you can just click on the Shortcut Bar to load Microsoft Office for you.

To load the Microsoft Office Shortcut Bar from the Windows 95 Taskbar, follow these steps:

1. **Click the Start button on the Taskbar and choose Programs.**

   A pop-up menu appears.

2. **Click Microsoft Office Shortcut Bar.**

   The Shortcut Bar appears as a row of icons at the top of your screen (see Figure 2-1).

If you want to have the Microsoft Office Shortcut Bar appear automatically each time you load Windows 95, follow these steps:

1. **Click the Start button, click to Settings, and then click Taskbar.**

   The Taskbar Properties dialog box appears (see Figure 2-2).

2. **Click the Start Menu Programs tab.**

Control menu   Shortcut Bar

Figure 2-1:
The Office
Shortcut
Bar.

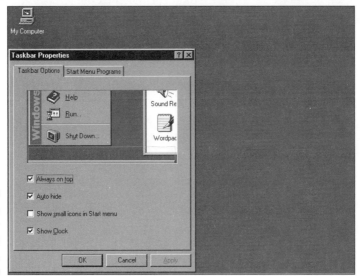

Figure 2-2:
The Taskbar
Properties
dialog box.

3. Click <u>A</u>dd.

The Create Shortcut dialog box appears (see Figure 2-3).

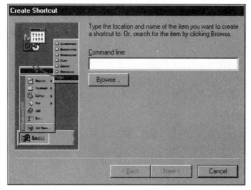

Figure 2-3:
The Create
Shortcut
dialog box.

4. Click <u>B</u>rowse.

The Browse dialog box appears.

5. Double-click the MSoffice folder. Then click the Microsoft Office Shortcut Bar.

6. Click <u>O</u>pen. The Create Shortcut dialog box appears again.

7. Click <u>N</u>ext >.

The Select Program Folder dialog box appears (see Figure 2-4).

Figure 2-4:
The Select
Program
Folder dialog
box.

8. **Click the Startup folder and click Next.**

   The Select a Title for the Program dialog box appears.

9. **Click Finish.**

   The Taskbar Properties dialog box appears again.

10. **Click OK and restart your computer.**

    The Microsoft Office Shortcut Bar now appears each time you load Windows 95.

Customizing the Microsoft Office Shortcut Bar

Because this is your computer, you can adapt the Shortcut Bar in several ways:

- ✔ Changing the size of Shortcut Bar's buttons
- ✔ Changing the position and appearance of the Shortcut Bar
- ✔ Changing the Shortcut Bar's buttons
- ✔ Changing the appearance of the Shortcut Bar's menus

Changing the size of the Shortcut Bar's buttons

Depending on how good your eyesight may be, you can display the Shortcut Bar's buttons as small or large.

To change the size of the Shortcut Bar's buttons, follow these steps:

1. **Point the mouse pointer on the control menu on the Shortcut Bar (the far left edge of the Shortcut Bar, represented by that silly red, blue, green, and yellow square logo).**

2. **Click the right mouse button.**

   The Shortcut Bar menu appears, as shown in Figure 2-5.

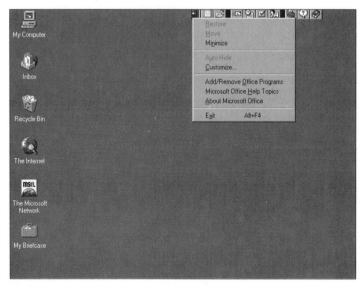

Figure 2-5:
The Shortcut
Bar menu.

3. Click Customize.

The Customize dialog box appears.

4. Click the View tab (see Figure 2-6).

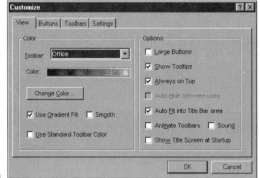

Figure 2-6:
The
Customize
dialog box
with the
View tab
selected.

5. Click in the Large Buttons check box so a check mark appears in the check box. (Or clear the Large Buttons check box to display the Shortcut Bar as smaller buttons.)

6. Click OK.

The Shortcut Bar now appears with large (or small) buttons, as shown in Figure 2-7.

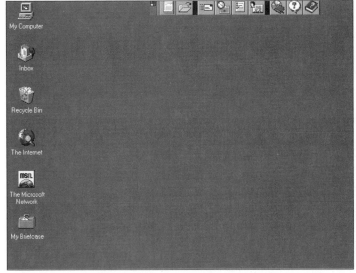

Figure 2-7:
The
Shortcut
Bar
displayed
with large
buttons.

Changing the position and appearance of the Shortcut Bar

Unless you specify otherwise, the Shortcut Bar appears in the upper right corner of your screen, tucked neatly out of the way. You can move the toolbar to another location, however.

If you move the Shortcut Bar to the side, or bottom of your screen, the Shortcut Bar flattens out like a stretched-out Dachshund. If you move the Shortcut Bar to the middle of your screen, the Shortcut Bar appears as a chunky square.

To move the Shortcut Bar's position on your screen, follow these steps:

1. **Point the mouse pointer underneath that weird red, blue, green, and yellow logo on the far left edge of the Shortcut Bar.**

2. **Hold down the left mouse button and move the Shortcut Bar where you want to put it.**

   The Shortcut Bar moves along with the mouse (see Figures 2-8 and 2-9).

3. **Release the mouse button when the Shortcut Bar is where you want it.**

Figure 2-8:
The Shortcut
Bar
smashed
against the
right side of
the screen.

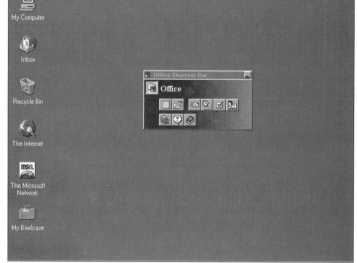

Figure 2-9:
The
Shortcut Bar
hovering in
the middle
of the
screen.

Changing the Shortcut Bar's buttons

By default, the Shortcut Bar only displays icons for Microsoft Office, Microsoft Schedule+, and the Answer Wizard. If you don't like the way these buttons are arranged, or if you want to add or delete buttons, feel free to change them any way you like.

Deleting and adding buttons

For kicks, you can make the Shortcut Bar display buttons that represent Microsoft's biggest competitors (WordPerfect, Lotus 1-2-3, Harvard Graphics, and Paradox). That way it looks like Microsoft is secretly endorsing its competitors' products.

To add or delete buttons representing Microsoft applications from the Shortcut Bar, follow these steps:

1. **Point the mouse pointer underneath the Shortcut Bar control menu (that ugly red, blue, green, and yellow square logo that looks like a Rubik's cube).**

2. **Press the right mouse button.**

   The Shortcut Bar menu appears.

3. **Click Customize.**

   The Customize dialog box appears.

4. **Click the Buttons tab (see Figure 2-10).**

5. **Click the check boxes of the programs you want to appear as buttons on the Shortcut Bar.**

   If you want to add a program that is not already on the Shortcut Bar, click the check box of the program you want to add.

   To remove a program from the Shortcut Bar, click the check box of the program you want to remove from the toolbar. An empty check box means that the button won't appear in the toolbar.

6. **Click OK.**

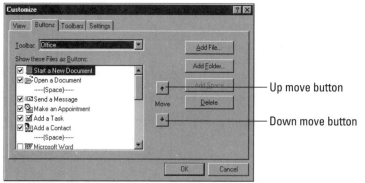

Figure 2-10:
The
Customize
dialog box
with the
Buttons tab
selected.

To add buttons representing non-Microsoft programs to the Shortcut Bar, follow these steps:

1. **Point the mouse pointer on the far left edge of the Shortcut Bar, directly underneath that red, blue, green, and yellow square logo that looks like a puzzle of some sort.**

2. **Press the right mouse button.**

   The Shortcut Bar menu appears.

3. **Choose Customize.**

   The Customize dialog box appears.

4. **Click the Buttons tab.**

5. **Click Add File.**

   The Add File dialog box appears (see Figure 2-11).

6. **Click the program that you want to add to the Shortcut Bar and then click Add.**

   The Customize dialog box appears, displaying your chosen program in the button list.

7. **Click OK.**

   The Shortcut Bar displays your chosen program button.

Figure 2-11:
The Add File
dialog box.

To remove a non-Microsoft program from the Shortcut Bar, follow
these steps:

1. **Point the mouse pointer on the far left edge of the Shortcut Bar, underneath that silly red, blue, green, and yellow square logo that somehow
   represents Microsoft Office.**

2. **Press the right mouse button.**

   The Shortcut menu appears.

3. **Choose Customize.**

   The Customize dialog box appears.

4. **Click the Buttons tab.**

5. **Click the check box of the program that you want to remove so that its
   check box now appears empty.**

6. **Click OK.**

   The Shortcut Bar removes your chosen program button.

If you click the Delete button in step four, the Shortcut Bar not only removes
the program button from the Shortcut Bar, but it also deletes the actual program from your hard disk.

Adding and removing folders on the Shortcut Bar

Besides adding to or deleting individual programs from the Shortcut Bar, you can also add folders containing groups of programs to the Shortcut Bar as well.

To add a folder to or remove a folder from the Shortcut Bar, follow these steps:

1. **Point the mouse pointer on the far left edge of the Shortcut Bar, underneath that silly red, blue, green, and yellow square logo that looks like four tiny squares chasing each other.**

2. **Press the right mouse button.**

   The Shortcut Bar menu appears.

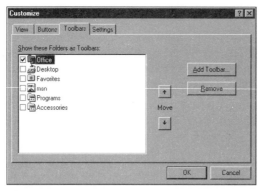

Figure 2-12:
The Customize dialog box with the Toolbars tab selected.

3. **Choose Customize.**

   The Customize dialog box appears.

4. **Click the Toolbars tab (see Figure 2-12).**

5. **Click in the check box of the folder you want to add to the Shortcut Bar. (To remove a folder from the Shortcut Bar, clear the check box of the folder you want to remove.)**

6. **Click OK.**

   The Shortcut Bar displays your newly added folders.

In case you want to get really creative and add your own folders to the Shortcut Bar, follow these steps:

1. **Point the mouse pointer on the far left edge of the Shortcut Bar, underneath that red, blue, green, and yellow square logo.**

2. **Press the right mouse button.**

The Shortcut Bar menu appears.

3. Choose <u>C</u>ustomize.

The Customize dialog box appears.

4. Click the Toolbars tab (refer to Figure 2-12).

5. Click <u>A</u>dd Toolbar.

The Add Toolbar dialog box appears (see Figure 2-13).

Figure 2-13:
The Add
Toolbar
dialog box.

6. Click <u>B</u>rowse.

Another Add Toolbar dialog box appears.

7. Click the folder that you want to add to the Shortcut Bar, click <u>A</u>dd, and then click OK.

8. Click OK.

The Shortcut Bar displays your newly added folders.

Rearranging buttons and folders on the Shortcut Bar

Besides adding buttons to or deleting buttons from the Shortcut Bar, you can rearrange the positions of the buttons. By rearranging buttons, you can truly make your toolbar personal (or just make it look so confusing to others that no one else will bother using your computer).

To rearrange the Shortcut Bar buttons, follow these steps:

1. Point the mouse pointer on the far left edge of the Shortcut Bar, underneath that boring red, blue, green, and yellow square logo.

2. Press the right mouse button.

The Shortcut Bar menu appears.

3. **Choose Customize.**

   The Customize dialog box appears.

4. **Click the Buttons tab (refer to Figure 2-10).**

5. **Click any program that appears with a check in its check box and click the Up or Down Move arrows to the right of the scroll box.**

6. **Click the OK button when you finish moving programs around.**

   The Shortcut Bar displays your newly arranged buttons.

To rearrange the Shortcut Bar folders, follow these steps:

1. **Point the mouse pointer on the far left edge of the Shortcut Bar, underneath that red, blue, green, and yellow square logo.**

2. **Press the right mouse button.**

   The Shortcut Bar menu appears.

3. **Choose Customize.**

   The Customize dialog box appears.

4. **Click the Toolbars tab.**

5. **Click any folder that appears with a check in its check box and click the up or down Move arrows to the right of the scroll box.**

6. **Click OK when you finish moving folders around.**

   The Shortcut Bar shows your newly arranged folders.

Minimizing the Shortcut Bar

Sometimes you might get tired of seeing the Shortcut Bar hovering before your eyes all the time. In those cases when its appearance gets a bit too demanding, you can minimize it and throw it on the Windows 95 Taskbar.

To minimize the Shortcut Bar, follow these steps:

1. **Point the mouse pointer on the far left edge of the Shortcut Bar, underneath that bizarre red, blue, green, and yellow square logo.**

2. **Press the right mouse button.**

   The Shortcut Bar menu appears.

3. **Choose Minimize.**

   The Shortcut Bar immediately appears on the Windows 95 Taskbar.

To maximize the Shortcut Bar after you've minimized it, just click the Microsoft Office Shortcut Bar button on the Windows 95 Taskbar.

Displaying ToolTips

In the old days, programs required you to memorize and type cryptic commands if you wanted the computer to do anything. Then some genius came up with the idea of pull-down menus. Then to continue the spread of illiteracy, other geniuses came up with the idea of displaying icons below the pull-down menus. Each icon represented a specific command, and by clicking the appropriate icon, you could bypass menu commands altogether.

Unfortunately, deciphering the meaning of most icons is like reading Egyptian hieroglyphics. If playing guessing games with icons that are supposed to make programs easier to use isn't your idea of fun, ToolTips can come to the rescue.

Each time you point to an icon on the Shortcut Bar, a little description box appears. This little box, called a ToolTip, explains the function of each icon so that you don't have to guess anymore.

By default, the Shortcut Bar always shows ToolTips. But if you just like being different, you can turn them on or off. To turn ToolTips off or on, follow these steps:

1. **Point the mouse pointer on the far left edge of the Shortcut Bar, underneath that red, blue, green, and yellow square logo that looks like an odd psychedelic pattern of some sort.**

2. **Press the right mouse button.**

   The Shortcut Bar menu appears.

3. **Choose Customize.**

   The Customize dialog box appears.

4. **Click the View tab (refer to Figure 2-6).**

5. **Click the Show ToolTips check box, if appropriate.**

   A check mark in the check box means that the Shortcut Bar will show ToolTips. No check mark, no ToolTips.

6. **Click OK.**

Chapter 3

Binding Your Information Together

● ●

● ●

*Y*ou can use Microsoft Office two ways. You can use the programs separately, just like a normal program from Lotus, Microsoft, or Novell. But the smarter way to use Microsoft Office is to use binders, unique file formats specially designed to hold multiple Word, Excel, or PowerPoint data in a single file. To help you identify binder files, Microsoft Office always names binder files with the OBD file extension, such as PERSONAL.OBD or 1996 TAXES.OBD.

The whole purpose of binder files is to keep all related data together in a single file, whether you created the data in Word, Excel, or PowerPoint. That way, if you want to share that data with others, you just have to copy a single file instead of trying to collect multiple files that may get lost, separated, or damaged. Imagine storing all of your tax papers in one envelope or in multiple envelopes stored in the same drawer. That's the difference between using a binder and storing multiple files in the same directory.

Making a New Binder

You can make and open binders from the Windows 95 Taskbar or from the Shortcut Bar. To create a new binder from the Windows 95 Taskbar or the Shortcut Bar, follow these steps:

1. **Choose one of the following:**

    • **Click the Start button on the Taskbar and choose Open Office Document**

    • **Click on the Open a Document button on the Shortcut Bar**

    The New dialog box appears.

2. **Click the General tab (see Figure 3-1).**

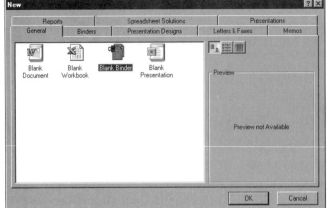

Figure 3-1:
The New
dialog box
with the
General tab
selected.

3. **Click the Blank Binder icon and click OK.**

    A blank binder appears on-screen (see Figure 3-2).

Figure 3-2:
The blank
appearance
of a brand-
new binder.

Opening an Existing Binder

In case you've already created a binder and want to open it so that you can modify, print, or wreck it, follow these steps:

1. **Choose one of the following:**

   - **Click the Start button on the Taskbar and choose Open Office Document**

   - **Click on the Open a Document button on the Shortcut Bar**

   The Open dialog box appears (see Figure 3-3).

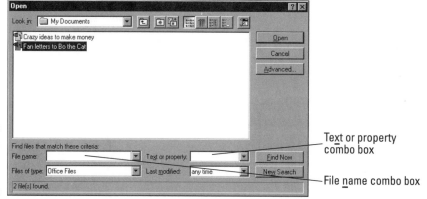

Figure 3-3:
The Open
dialog box.

Text or property combo box

File name combo box

2. **Click on the binder that you want to open and click Open.**

   (Depending on where you've buried your binders, you may have to search through different folders to find the binder you want.)

You can quickly find specific binders if you know the file name or a key word stored in the binder you want. To search for a particular binder by file name, type all or part of the file name you want in the File name box and click Find Now.

To search for a particular binder based on the text it contains, type a key word in the Text or property box and click Find Now.

Stuffing Documents into a Binder

After you create a new binder or open an existing one, you eventually need to stuff a Word, Excel, or PowerPoint document into the binder. Each document in a binder is called a *section* because it forms part of the binder.

The only documents you can stuff into a binder are those created by Microsoft Office compatible programs such as Word, Excel, and PowerPoint. If another company ever makes a Microsoft Office compatible program, you'll be able to stuff files created by that program into a binder, too. But if you try jamming a WordPerfect, Lotus 1-2-3, or Harvard Graphics document into a Microsoft Office binder, it won't work. (This is Microsoft's subtle way of converting the whole world into Microsoft software users.)

You can stuff two types of documents into a binder:

- New documents
- Existing documents

Stuffing a new document (section) into a binder

To stuff a new document into a binder, follow these steps:

1. Choose Section⇨Add from the Binder menu.

The Add Section dialog box appears (see Figure 3-4).

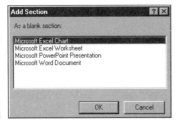

Figure 3-4:
The Add
Section
dialog box.

2. **Choose the type of blank document you want to stuff into your binder (a Word document, Excel chart, PowerPoint presentation, and so on).**

3. **Click OK.**

   You see an icon representing your document in the left pane of the binder along with the program you chose, as shown in Figure 3-5. The type of icon depends on the type of document you add to your binder. If you add a Word document, for example, you see a Word icon in the left pane and the Word menu and screen.

Icon in left pane

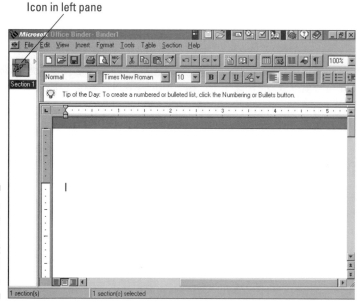

Figure 3-5:
The binder
screen with
a Microsoft
Word
document.

Stuffing an existing file (section) into a binder

You can create a bunch of Word, Excel, PowerPoint, or Access files and then later organize them in a binder before you lose track of them altogether.

To stuff an existing file into a binder, follow these steps:

1. **Choose Section⇨Add from File from the Binder menu.**

   The Add from File dialog box appears (see Figure 3-6).

Files of type list box

Figure 3-6:
The Add
from File
dialog box.

2. **Click in the Files of type list box and choose the type of existing document you want to add to your binder (such as a Word document, Excel workbook, PowerPoint presentation, and so on).**

3. **Click on the file that you want to add to your binder.**

   (You may have to dig through several folders to find the file that you're looking for.)

4. **Click Add.**

   Microsoft Office displays your newly added file to the left pane.

Using the left pane of your binders

The left pane of your binder has two purposes:

 ✔ To let you switch between documents (sections)
 ✔ To show you all the documents (sections) that make up your binder

Switching between sections

A binder only displays one section at a time, such as a Word document or an Excel worksheet. To switch between sections, just click on the section icon that you want to load. Figures 3-7 and 3-8 show a Word document and an Excel document within the same binder.

Microsquirt icon

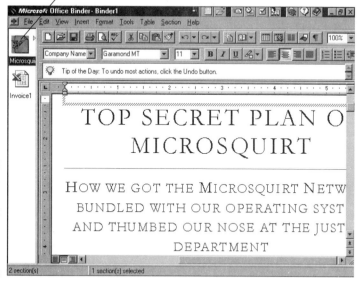

Figure 3-7:
A Word
document
displayed
within a
binder.

Invoice 1 icon

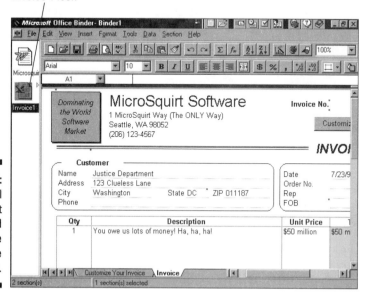

Figure 3-8:
An Excel
worksheet
displayed
within the
same
binder.

Rearranging your section icons

Normally, the binder's left pane shows you the order in which you added
sections. The top icon is the first section you added, and the bottom icon is the
last section you added.

But because this is the world of personal computers where you have the freedom to do anything you want, Microsoft Office lets you rearrange your section icons to suit your personal preferences. For example, you may want the most frequently used sections at the top of the left pane to make them easier to select.

To rearrange your section icons within a binder, follow these steps:

1. Choose Section⇨Rearrange.

The Rearrange Sections dialog box appears (see Figure 3-9).

Figure 3-9:
The
Rearrange
Sections
dialog box.

2. Click on the section that you want to move and then click Move Up or Move Down.

3. Click OK.

Hiding/Unhiding your section icons

The left pane of each binder always displays your section icons so that you can see the contents of your binder. If you have too many section icons (or just want more room to work in), however, you can hide some or all of your section icons from view.

To hide some of your section icons, follow these steps:

1. In the left pane, click the section icon that you want to hide.

2. Choose Section⇨Hide.

Your section icon disappears from view.

To unhide a previously hidden section icon, follow these steps:

1. Choose Section⇨Unhide.

The Unhide Sections dialog box appears (see Figure 3-10).

2. Click the section you want to unhide (is that really a word?) and click OK.

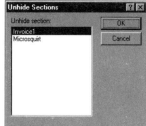

Figure 3-10:
The Unhide
Sections
dialog box.

To hide (or unhide) the entire left pane of a binder, click the Binder
Contents button.

Modifying Binder Documents

After you store documents in a binder, you can copy, rename, or delete them if
you want.

Copying a binder section

Copying a binder is a good idea if you want to use an existing document as a
template for creating a new document. To copy a binder section, follow these
steps:

1. **Click the section icon in the left pane that you want to copy.**

2. **Choose Section⇨Duplicate.**

   The Duplicate Section dialog box appears (see Figure 3-11).

Figure 3-11:
The
Duplicate
Section
dialog box.

3. **Click on the section that you want your newly copied section to appear
   underneath and click OK.**

   Microsoft Office copies your icon and renames it. So if you copied a
   section called Microsquirt, your copy of this section would be named
   Microsquirt (1).

Renaming a binder section

After copying a section icon, it's a good idea to rename it to something more meaningful than "Microsquirt (1)." Or if you get a creative urge to suddenly change the name of a section icon, you can do that, too.

To rename a binder section, follow these steps:

1. **In the left pane, click the section icon that you want to rename.**

2. **Choose Section⇨Rename.**

   The name of your chosen section icon appears highlighted (see Figure 3-12).

3. **Type a new name for the section icon and press Enter.**

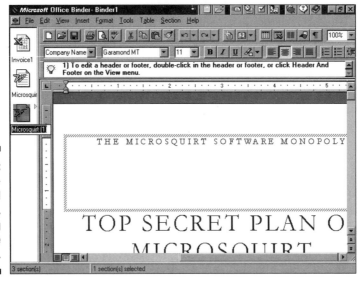

Figure 3-12:
A high-lighted section icon, waiting to be renamed.

Deleting a binder section

Every now and then you realize that you no longer need a section in your binder. Rather than let it sit around and get in the way, delete it from your binder.

To delete a binder section, follow these steps:

1. **Click the section icon in the left pane that you want to delete.**

2. **Choose Section⇨Delete.**

A dialog box appears, asking if you really want to delete the chosen section. This is your last chance to abort this procedure in case you want to save your binder section after all.

3. Click OK.

Creating Binder Templates

Creating binders from scratch can get boring, so Microsoft Office lets you create binder templates. Essentially, a binder template lets you store blank sections (Word, Excel, PowerPoint files) in a binder. That way if you frequently create binders that use one PowerPoint, two Excel, and fifteen Word sections, you don't have to create a blank binder and then add all eighteen sections manually.

For example, you might have a binder section containing a form letter (stored in a Word document), a business expense spreadsheet (stored in an Excel worksheet), and a sales presentation (stored in a PowerPoint presentation). That way if a clueless coworker begs you for help in using a computer, you can just hand them a copy of your binder template and tell them to modify it themselves.

To create your very own binder template for posterity, follow these steps:

1. Choose one of the following:

- **Click the Start button on the Taskbar and choose Open Office Document**
- **Click the Open a Document button on the Shortcut Bar**

The Open dialog box appears.

2. Click the binder that you want to use to create your binder template and click Open.

(Depending on where you've buried your binders, you may have to search through different folders to find the binder you want.)

3. Choose File➪Save Binder As.

The Save Binder As dialog box appears (see Figure 3-13).

4. Click in the Save as type list box and choose Binder Templates.

5. Type a name for your binder template in the File name combo box.

6. Click a folder (such as the Binders folder) where you want to store your binder template and click Save.

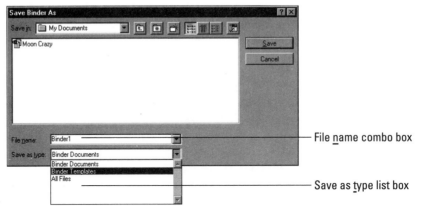

Figure 3-13:
The Save
Binder As
dialog box.

Save as type list box

To use a binder template, follow these steps:

1. **Choose one of the following:**

    • **Click the Start button on the Taskbar and choose New Office Document**

    • **Click the Start a New Document button on the Shortcut Bar**

    The New dialog box appears (refer to Figure 3-1).

2. **Click the Binders tab.**

    A list of all binder templates appears (see Figure 3-14). If you stored your binder template in a folder other than the Binders folder, it won't appear here.

3. **Click the binder template that you want to use and click OK.**

Binder template

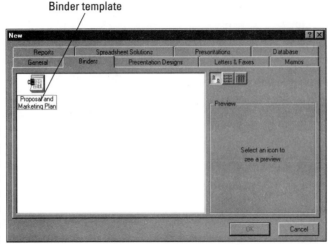

Figure 3-14:
The New
dialog box
with the
Binders tab
displayed.

Part II
Working with Words

"A CONSULTANT TOLD US THAT POLYESTER CAN CAUSE SHORTS IN THE SYSTEM, SO WE'RE TRYING AN ALL LEATHER AND LATEX DATA ENTRY DEPARTMENT."

In this part...

Word for Windows lets you convert ordinary words into fancy newsletters, pamphlets, reports, or form letters that you can send to people you don't feel like calling or seeing in person. Word processing continues to be the most popular use for personal computers today, and Word for Windows is one of the most powerful word processors you can use.

Whether you want to write a novel, a business report, or a simple letter, Word for Windows can help you complete the task faster and easier than you ever thought possible. After using Word for Windows, you may never want to use a pencil and paper again.

Chapter 4

Getting Ready to Write the Great American Novel

As the name implies, Microsoft Word lets you write letters, reports, proposals, brochures, newsletters, pink slips, and practically anything else that requires a rudimentary command of the written language. Depending on whether you want to write a quick note or a fancy report related to separate Excel, PowerPoint, or Access files, you can use Word as a separate program or as part of a binder (see Chapter 3 for an explanation of how to create and use binders).

Starting Word for Windows

You can start Word as a separate program or as part of a binder. If you decide to start Word as a separate program, you have two choices, which is the same number of choices realistically available to American voters:

✔ Start Word from the Windows 95 Taskbar.

✔ Start Word from the Shortcut Bar.

Starting Word from the Windows 95 Taskbar

Starting Word from the Windows 95 Taskbar is a good idea if you want to load a blank document in a hurry. To start Word from the Windows 95 Taskbar, follow these steps:

1. **Click the Start button in the Windows 95 Taskbar.**

   A pop-up menu appears.

2. **Choose Programs⇨Microsoft Word.**

   Word obediently displays a blank document.

Starting Word from the Shortcut Bar

When you start Word from the Shortcut Bar, you can choose whether to start with a blank document or use a document template. Use a blank document if you want to create something from scratch or if no document template exists for what you want to do (such as writing a screenplay). Use a document template when you want to save time and modify an existing document (otherwise known as *plagiarism*).

A document template contains one or more styles, where each style acts like a cookie cutter that automatically formats text a certain way. For example, one style might center text and underline it while another style might display text in boldface using the Times Roman font.

If you need to create documents formatted in a certain, predictable way, create a document template containing all the styles you need. Then the next time you need to format text, use a document template.

To start Word from the Shortcut Bar, follow these steps:

1. **Click the Start a New Document icon in the Shortcut Bar.**

   The New dialog box appears, as shown in Figure 4-1.

2. **Click the General tab and click Blank Document if you want to start with a blank document; otherwise, click one of the following tabs and choose the document template that you want to use:**

   - **Reports tab**

   - **Memos tab**

   - **Letters & Faxes tab**

3. **Click OK.**

   Word displays your selected document template (blank or otherwise) on-screen.

General tab   Reports tab   Letters & Faxes tab

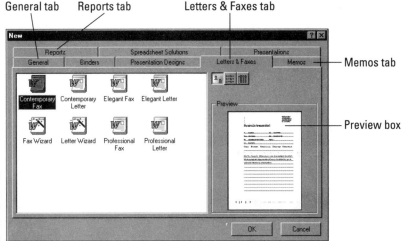

Memos tab

Preview box

Figure 4-1:
The New
dialog box

Starting Word from within a binder

Because the whole purpose of Microsoft Office is to integrate your program data, you might as well shed your old work habits and get used to using binders to hold related documents together. Once you start using binders, you'll soon forget about using the separate programs in Microsoft Office by themselves. (See Chapter 3 for more information about using binders.)

To start Word from within a binder, follow these steps:

1. **Choose S̲ection⇨A̲dd.**

   The Add Section dialog box appears.

2. **Click Microsoft Word Document and click OK.**

   Word obediently displays a blank document.

Getting to Know Microsoft Word

At first glance, Microsoft Word may look like an ungainly mess of icons, menu commands, and buttons that look almost as complicated as the cockpit of a Boeing 747. Fortunately, if you don't like the way Microsoft Word looks, you can change its appearance to something more aesthetically pleasing.

Choosing a different view of a document

Word lets you see your document from a variety of perspectives, which alter the appearance and amount of text and graphics displayed on-screen. Word has four ways to view your document. To switch the view of your document, choose <u>V</u>iew from the menu bar and then one of the following:

- ✔ <u>N</u>ormal
- ✔ <u>O</u>utline
- ✔ <u>P</u>age Layout
- ✔ <u>M</u>aster Document

 As a quick way to switch document views, just click the Normal, Page Layout, or Master Document button that can barely be seen on the far left of the horizontal scroll bar at the bottom of the screen. The scroll bar and the buttons are shown in Figure 4-2.

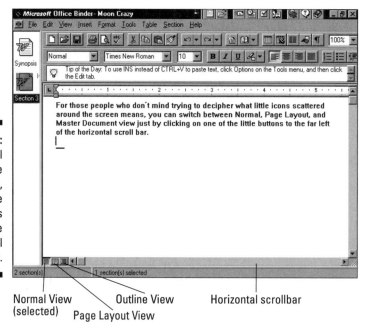

Figure 4-2:
The Normal
View, Page
Layout View,
and Outline
View buttons
on the
horizontal
scroll bar.

Normal View
(selected)   Outline View   Horizontal scrollbar
          Page Layout View

Normal view is great when you want a clean screen to write without headers, footers, or page numbers getting in your way.

Outline view comes in handy when you don't have the slightest idea what to write, but you want to create an outline to help organize your thoughts.

Page Layout view shows you exactly how your document will look when printed, including headers and footers.

In case Word displays text way too small for you to see comfortably, here's a quick tip for displaying text in a large, easy-to-read draft font, which is a font designed to be easy to read:

1. **Choose <u>V</u>iew⇨<u>N</u>ormal (unless you're already in Normal view).**

2. **Choose <u>T</u>ools⇨<u>O</u>ptions.**

   The Options dialog box appears.

3. **Click the View tab (see Figure 4-3).**

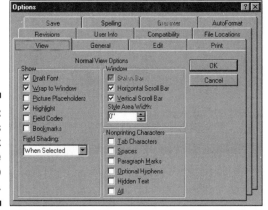

Figure 4-3:
The Options
dialog box
with the
View tab
selected.

4. **Click the check boxes next to <u>D</u>raft Font and <u>W</u>rap to Window. (A check mark should appear in each check box.)**

5. **Click OK.**

   Word now displays your text in easy-to-read, bold letters.

Hiding the scroll bars

To give you a little bit more room on-screen so you can see your text (instead of Word's scroll bars), you can hide both the horizontal and the vertical scroll bar. To hide the scroll bars, follow these steps:

1. **Choose Tools⇨Options.**

   The Options dialog box appears.

2. **Click the View tab.**

3. **Click the check boxes next to Horizontal Scroll Bar and Vertical Scroll Bar. (Both check boxes should appear empty.)**

4. **Click OK.**

   Voilà! Word hides both scroll bars, giving you another few millimeters to work with. When you want to display your scroll bars, just repeat Steps 1 and 2 and put check marks in the check boxes for Step 3.

 If you're using Word within a binder, you can save even more room by clicking the Binder Contents button to hide the left pane (containing the section icons) from view. The Binder Contents button appears to the left of the File menu and looks like two parallel lines with arrows pointing in opposite directions.

Changing screen magnification

If you're using Draft Font, your document won't look any different if you change screen magnification.

Sometimes you might get tired of seeing just a portion of your letter and may want to see how the whole letter looks. To change your screen's magnification, follow these steps:

1. **Choose View⇨Zoom.**

   The Zoom dialog box appears, as shown in Figure 4-4.

2. **Click one of the following radio buttons in the Zoom To group:**

   - **200%** (displays your document in twice its size)

   - **100%**

   - **75%**

   - **Page Width** (scales your text to the width of your screen)

3. **Click OK.**

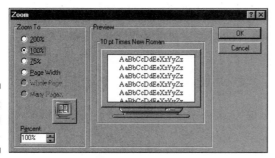

Figure 4-4:
The Zoom
dialog box.

For those individualists who absolutely must be different, you can also specify a percent magnification to display your document by using the P̲ercent list box. This list box lets you display your document in odd percentages, such as 57% or 93%.

When you change the magnification, you're changing your view of the document — not the actual size of the document itself.

Rather than force you to memorize obscure keystroke combinations or wade through multiple layers of pull-down menus, Word lets you choose commands by clicking obscure buttons organized in groups called *toolbars*.

Each toolbar displays a different category of command buttons. The two most common are the Standard and Formatting toolbars. These two toolbars automatically appear when you first install and start Word, although you can hide them to make your screen look less cluttered.

Hiding/displaying toolbars

To hide or display a toolbar, follow these steps:

1. **Choose V̲iew⇨T̲oolbars.**

   The Toolbars dialog box appears, as shown in Figure 4-5.

2. **Click the check box of the toolbar that you want to display. (Or clear the check box of the toolbar you want to hide.)**

3. **Make sure that a check mark appears in the C̲olor Buttons check box if you want to display your toolbars in color.**

4. **Make sure that a check mark appears in the S̲how ToolTips check box if you want to display ToolTips when you point at an icon on the toolbar. (ToolTips displays a brief description of a toolbar button when you move the mouse over it.)**

5. Click OK.

Since the two most common toolbars are the Standard and Formatting toolbars, it's a good idea to know how to use each one.

Exploring the Standard toolbar

The Standard toolbar offers access to Word's most frequently used commands, arranged from left to right in roughly the order of their frequency of use (see Figure 4-6):

- **New:** Creates a new document

- **Open:** Opens an existing document

- **Save:** Saves your current document

- **Print:** Prints your current document

- **Print Preview:** Shows you what your document will look like when printed (not available when using Word within a binder)

- **Spelling:** Spell checks your document

- **Cut:** Cuts the currently selected text

- **Copy:** Copies the currently selected text

- **Paste:** Pastes text previously cut or copied

- **Format Painter:** Copies the format from selected text and applies it to new text

- **Undo:** Undoes your last command

- **Redo:** The opposite of Undo — restores what the Undo command last did

- **AutoFormat:** Formats text based on a previously defined format

✔ **Insert Address:** Inserts an address from your personal address book that's stored in Microsoft Schedule+ (see Chapter 13)

✔ **Insert Table:** Inserts a table into your document

✔ **Insert Microsoft Excel Worksheet:** Just like it says — inserts a Microsoft Excel worksheet into your document

✔ **Columns:** Lets you create multiple-column documents

✔ **Drawing:** Lets you get creative and draw objects in your document

✔ **Show/Hide Paragraph Marks:** Shows or hides the symbols that represent spaces and carriage returns in your document

✔ **Zoom Control:** Adjusts the magnification of your document

✔ **TipWizard:** Displays a tip that Microsoft thinks you'll find helpful

✔ **Help:** Lets you point to a toolbar button or menu command and display a brief description on what that button or command will do

If you're using Word within a binder, close the binder left pane by clicking the Binder Contents button. This brings the TipWizard and Help buttons into view.

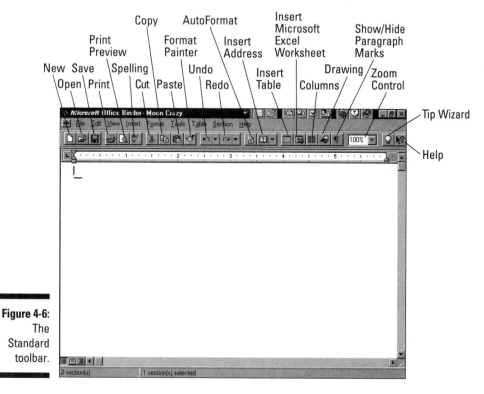

Figure 4-6:
The Standard toolbar.

To quickly learn what each button on the Standard toolbar does, point the mouse over each icon until the ToolTip appears. (If nothing appears when you place the arrow over a button, open the <u>V</u>iew menu, choose <u>T</u>oolbars, and make sure that the check box next to <u>S</u>how ToolTips is checked.)

Sometimes you may think your document is aligned, spaced, or formatted correctly, but for some odd reason, paragraphs or sentences still seem crooked. To see how Word is displaying text, click the Show/Hide Paragraph Marks button in the Standard toolbar, as shown in Figure 4-7.

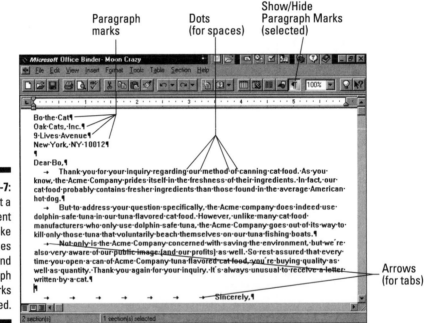

Figure 4-7:
What a document looks like with spaces and paragraph marks displayed.

When you click this button for the first time, Word displays dots (to show each space between words), arrows (to show where you pressed the Tab key), and a paragraph mark (insert mark, which looks like a backwards capital P) wherever you pressed the Enter key.

(If you click the Show/Hide Paragraph Marks button a second time, Word hides all of these odd little symbols from view.)

The Paragraph button is valuable for three reasons:

✔ If your document ever exhibits strange word or paragraph spacing, the Paragraph button helps you discover whether you've inadvertently entered two spaces between words (or none at all) or pressed the Enter key twice after paragraphs.

✔ Word stores character and paragraph formatting in the paragraph mark at the end of each paragraph. If, while editing your document, you inadvertently erase a paragraph mark along with text, the paragraph joins the next paragraph and — equally important — adopts the formatting of the next paragraph. This can lead to some strange surprises!

✔ If you insert nonprinting, or hidden, text into your document — such as secret messages revealing atom bomb secrets — these hidden words are revealed when you click the Paragraph button.

If you want to be more selective in what you reveal when you click the Show/Hide Paragraph Marks button, follow these steps:

1. **Choose Tools➪Options.**

   The Options dialog box appears.

2. **Click the View tab.**

   The View dialog box appears, as shown in Figure 4-8.

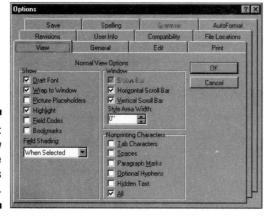

Figure 4-8:
The View
tab in the
Options
dialog box.

3. **In the Nonprinting Characters group, located in the lower right, choose one or more of the following:**

- **T**ab Characters
- **S**paces
- Paragraph **M**arks
- **O**ptional Hyphens
- H**i**dden Text
- **A**ll

Remember, a checked box displays the selected characters, and an unchecked box means those selected characters will be hidden.

4. **Click OK.**

Exploring the Formatting toolbar (where people go to look good)

The Formatting toolbar contains commands to make your text look pretty with different fonts, type sizes, or typefaces, such as bold, italic, and underline (see Figure 4-9).

- ✔ **Style:** Lets you choose a style, based on the current document template you're using
- ✔ **Font:** Lets you choose a different font
- ✔ **Font Size:** Lets you choose a different type size
- ✔ **Bold:** Displays selected text in bold
- ✔ **Italic:** Displays selected text in italic
- ✔ **Underline:** Displays selected text in underline
- ✔ **Highlight:** Displays selected text in yellow highlight
- ✔ **Align Left:** Aligns selected text to the left
- ✔ **Center:** Centers selected text
- ✔ **Align Right:** Aligns selected text to the right
- ✔ **Justify:** Displays selected text with the left and right margins perfectly straight
- ✔ **Numbering:** Adds (or removes) numbers from selected paragraphs

✔ **Bullets:** Adds (or removes) bullets from selected paragraphs

✔ **Decrease Indent:** Moves the selected paragraph to the previous tab stop

✔ **Increase Indent:** Moves the selected paragraph to the next tab stop

✔ **Borders:** Lets you draw borders around selected paragraphs and tables

You can choose a format (such as bullets or bold) and then type new text. Your newly typed text will then appear in your chosen format (bullets or bold).

Clicking the Bold, Italic, and Underline buttons toggles this feature on and off. If text is bold, the Bold button appears pressed. Clicking the Bold button turns off boldface.

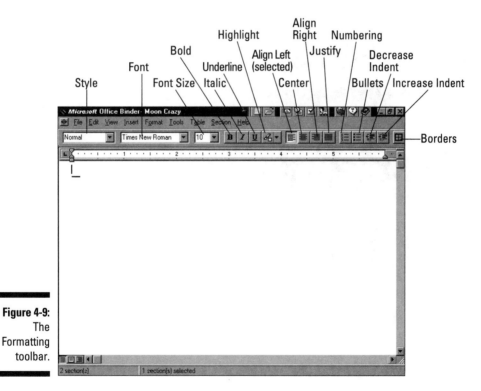

Figure 4-9:
The
Formatting
toolbar.

To use any of the commands in the Formatting toolbar, just select the text that you want to format and then click a button in the Formatting toolbar, such as the Font or Bold button.

Exploring Word's ruler

The ruler shows the margins and tabs of your document and, if you're creating a multicolumn document, the column placement and the distance between the columns.

Hiding/displaying the ruler

Just in case you don't want to see the ruler on-screen (or if you want to display the ruler after you've hidden it), you can hide it (or display it) by choosing View➪Ruler.

Setting tabs on the ruler

Word provides three types of tabs that you can set on the ruler (shown in Figure 4-10):

- ✔ **Left Alignment (looks like an L):** Moves text towards the right edge of the page as you type

- ✔ **Center Alignment (looks like an upside-down T):** Centers text around the tab

- ✔ **Right Alignment (looks like a backwards L):** Moves text away from the right edge of the page as you type

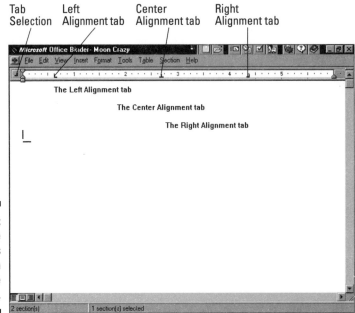

Figure 4-10:
The three types of tabs that you can place on the ruler.

To place a tab on the ruler, follow these steps:

1. **Click the Tab Selection button until it displays the tab that you want to use.**

2. **Click the spot on the bottom of the ruler where you want to place the tab.**

To move an existing tab on the ruler, follow these steps:

1. **Point the mouse on the tab that you want to move.**

2. **Hold down the left mouse button until you see a dotted line appear directly beneath the tab (see Figure 4-11).**

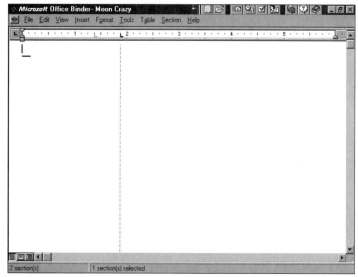

Figure 4-11:
Moving a
tab on the
ruler.

3. **Move the mouse where you want to move the tab.**

4. **Release the left mouse button.**

To remove a tab from the ruler, follow these steps:

1. **Point the mouse on the tab that you want to remove.**

2. **Hold down the left mouse button until you see a dotted line appear directly beneath the tab.**

3. **Move the mouse down below the ruler.**

4. **Release the left mouse button.**

Indents on your ruler

To help you indent paragraphs, the ruler also has four silly little icons that you can adjust to indent entire paragraphs, indent just the first line of each paragraph, or create hanging indents (see Figure 4-12).

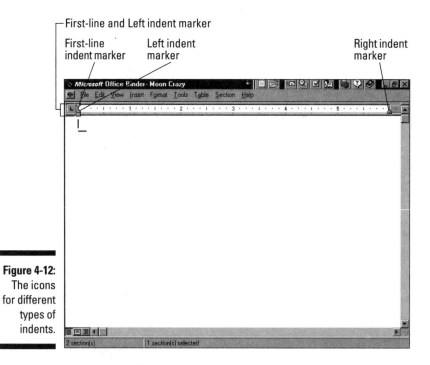

Figure 4-12:
The icons
for different
types of
indents.

To indent entire paragraphs, follow these steps:

1. **Select the paragraphs that you want to indent. (Skip this step if you haven't written any paragraphs to indent yet.)**

2. **Point the mouse on the First-Line and Left Indent marker and hold down the left mouse button.**

   Word displays a dotted line directly under the marker.

3. **Move the mouse where you want to indent the paragraph and release the mouse button (see Figure 4-13).**

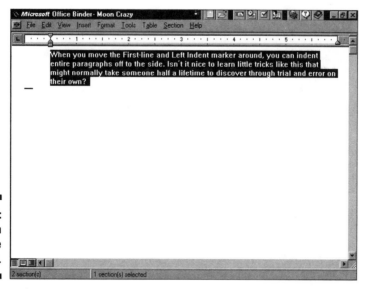

When you move the First-line and Left Indent marker around, you can indent entire paragraphs off to the side. Isn't it nice to learn little tricks like this that might normally take someone half a lifetime to discover through trial and error on their own?

Figure 4-13:
Indenting an
entire
paragraph.

To indent just the first line of each paragraph, follow these steps:

1. **Select the paragraphs that you want to indent. (Skip this step if you haven't written any paragraphs to indent yet.)**

2. **Point the mouse on the First-line Indent marker and hold down the left mouse button.**

   Word displays a dotted line directly under the marker.

3. **Move the mouse where you want to indent the paragraph and release the mouse button (see Figure 4-14).**

To create a hanging indent, follow these steps:

1. **Select the paragraphs that you want to indent. (Skip this step if you haven't written any paragraphs to indent yet.)**

2. **Point the mouse on the Left Indent marker and hold down the left mouse button.**

   Word displays a dotted line directly under the marker.

3. **Move the mouse where you want to indent the paragraph and release the mouse button (see Figure 4-15).**

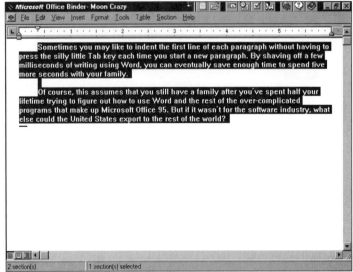

Figure 4-14:
Indenting
the first line
of every
paragraph.

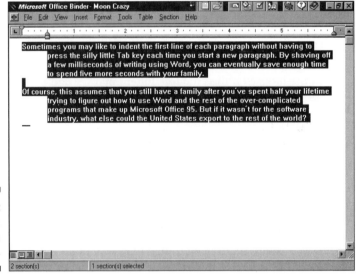

Figure 4-15:
Creating
hanging
indents.

Saving Your Stuff

Obviously, if you're going to take the time and trouble to write something in Word, you'll want to save it eventually. Word provides three ways to save your stuff.

Always save your work periodically in case your computer crashes, the power goes out, or some jerk comes along and starts erasing everything you've done.

Saving your file

It's always a good idea to save your file as you're working on it (every 10 minutes or so), just in case something terrible happens to your computer. To save your file, choose one of the following methods:

- ✔ Press Ctrl+S.
- ✔ Click the Save icon on the Standard toolbar (the icon that looks like a floppy disk).
- ✔ Choose File⇨Save Binder (if you're using Word within a binder).
- ✔ Choose File⇨Save (if you're using Word as a separate program).

If you're saving a file for the first time, Word asks you to choose a name. Ideally, you want to make your filename as descriptive as possible, such as LETTER TO DAD or HATE MAIL TO EX-SPOUSE.

Saving your file under a new name

To save your file under a different name, choose one of the following methods:

- ✔ Choose Section⇨Save as File (if you're using Word within a binder).
- ✔ Choose File⇨Save As (if you're using Word as a separate program).

If you're using Word within a binder and you choose File⇨Save Binder As, you'll create a new binder, not just a new Word document.

Saving automatically with Autosave

Since few people ever listen to the advice to save your work periodically, Word can do it for you with a feature known as *Autosave*. Essentially, turning this feature on means that every few minutes, Word saves your document, whether you want it to or not.

If you're furiously typing away, Word may suddenly stop everything you're doing to save your document, which can get annoying once in a while. But in general, it's a good idea to use the Autosave feature to keep from losing valuable documents because of a power outage.

To modify the Autosave feature, follow these steps:

1. **Choose Tools⇨Options.**

   An Options dialog box appears.

2. **Click the Save tab (see Figure 4-16).**

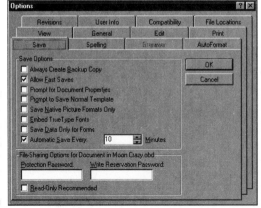

Figure 4-16: The Options dialog box with the Save tab selected.

3. **Make sure that a check mark appears in the Automatic Save Every check box.**

4. **Click the Minutes scroll box to define how many minutes you want Word to wait before saving your document automatically (such as 10 minutes).**

5. **Click OK.**

Previewing and Printing Your Stuff

To help contribute to global deforestation of the rain forests around the world, feel free to print every chance you get, just to see if your documents are properly aligned. But if you're one of the growing crowd who cringes at the thought of wasting precious resources for the sake of printing out your stuff, use Word's print preview feature.

Putting print preview to work

Print preview lets you see how your document will look before you print it out on paper. That way, you can see if your margins are aligned properly and your page numbers appear in the right place. Figure 4-17 shows a document in print preview.

To use print preview, follow these steps:

1. **Choose Section⇨View Outside. (Skip this step if you're using Word as a separate program.)**

2. **Choose File⇨Print Preview.**

Magnifier (selected)   View   Full
Multiple Pages   Ruler   Screen
One   Zoom   Shrink   Help
Print Page Control to Fit Close

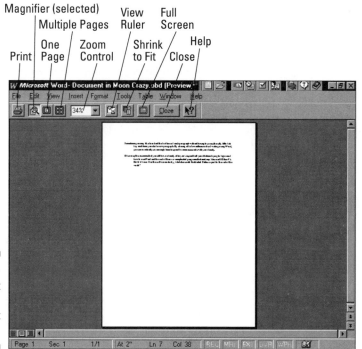

Figure 4-17:
A document
displayed in
print
preview.

Word displays your document in minuscule print and displays the cursor as a magnifying glass.

3. **Move the mouse cursor (the magnifying glass) over the document and click to view your document in its full size.**

4. **Click Close to exit print preview.**

5. **Choose File⇨Close and Return to. (Skip this step if you're using Word as a separate program.)**

When displaying a document in print preview, Word displays a Print Preview toolbar, which contains the following buttons from left to right:

✔ **Print:** Lets you print right away (for you impatient types)

✔ **Magnifier:** Toggles the cursor from a magnifying glass icon to an insertion point icon; when the cursor appears as an insertion point, you can edit your document (provided, of course, that you can see what you're doing)

✔ **One Page:** Displays a single page

✔ **Multiple Pages:** Displays more than one page at a time

✔ **Zoom Control:** Changes the degree of print preview magnification from 10 percent (which means you won't see a thing) to 200 percent (which displays your pages in full size), plus Page Width, Whole Page, and Two Pages

✔ **View Ruler:** Hides or reveals the Print Preview ruler

✔ **Shrink to Fit:** Reduces the number of pages in a document by one to prevent small amounts of text from getting stranded on the last page

✔ **Full Screen:** Toggles the appearance of your document from a full screen (by hiding your menus) to its normal screen (which displays the menus)

✔ **Close:** Exits print preview

✔ **Help:** Lets you click on the Help button and then click on any icons or menu command to get help on them so you don't have to look at this page again

Printing your work

Eventually, you'll need to print something you've written in Word. You have four ways to print your Word document:

✔ Press Ctrl+P

✔ Choose File⇨Print Binder (if you're using Word within a binder)

✔ Choose File⇨Print (if you're using Word as a separate program)

✔ Click the Print button in the Standard toolbar (the button that looks like a printer)

When you click the Print button, Word immediately starts printing your entire document, bypassing the Print dialog box. If you want to print specific pages or a certain number of copies, don't click the Print button.

When you're printing within a binder, make sure that you click the Selected section(s) radio button that appears in the Print Binder dialog box. If you don't choose this option, Word prints the contents of your entire binder.

Exiting Word

No matter how much you may like writing with Word, eventually you'll have to stop. To make matters more confusing, Word provides different ways to exit if you're using it as a separate program or within a binder.

If you're using Word as a separate program, here are the two ways to exit Word:

✔ If you want to close the current document but still keep Word running, choose File⇨Close.

✔ If you want to exit Word completely, choose File⇨Exit.

If you're using Word within a binder, here are the two ways to exit Word:

✔ If you want to switch to a different section in your binder, click a section icon that appears in the binder left pane.

✔ If you want to exit your binder completely, choose File⇨Close.

If you've made any changes since the last save and you try to exit, Word asks if you want to save the changes and offers you the following options: Yes, No, and Cancel.

✔ Click Yes to save your document.

✔ Click No if you don't want to save any recent changes.

✔ Click Cancel (or press the Esc key on your keyboard) if you suddenly don't want to exit after all.

Chapter 5
Choosing the Right Words

● ●

In This Chapter

▶ Opening an existing Word document

▶ Moving through a Word document

▶ Selecting text

▶ Editing text

▶ Using find and replace

▶ Checking your spelling

▶ Counting your words

● ●

*E*ven the best writers in the world need to edit their writing once in a while to delete or rearrange paragraphs or check their spelling and grammar. Fortunately, Word can simplify (or even automate) most of these tasks for you. That way, you can concentrate on getting your ideas in print and then worry about the trivial tasks of spelling and grammar afterward.

Opening a Previously Saved File

If you're using Word within a binder, you can open an existing Word document by clicking the section icon in the left pane of the binder. (See Chapter 3 for more information about binders.)

If you're using Word as a separate program, you have four ways to open a previously saved file:

　✔ Press Ctrl+O.

　✔ Click the Open icon in the Standard toolbar.

　✔ Choose File➪Open.

　✔ Choose one of the last four files you saved, which appear at the bottom of the File menu, as shown in Figure 5-1.

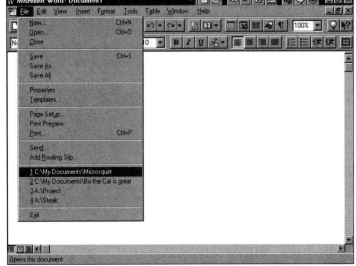

Figure 5-1:
At the
bottom of
the File
menu, Word
displays the
last four files
saved.

To increase the number of files displayed at the bottom of the File menu, choose Tools⇨Options and click the General tab. (If you don't see the Tools menu, open or create a new document first.) Next to the Recently Used File List check box, type the number of files (between 0 and 9) you want Word to display on its File menu.

Moving through a Word Document

You can navigate through a Word document by using the mouse or the keyboard. Although the mouse is easier to master, the keyboard can be more convenient to use because you don't have to keep reaching for the mouse every now and then.

Using the mouse to jump around a document

To jump around a document with the mouse, you must have the vertical scroll bar displayed (otherwise, there's nothing for the mouse to click on). The vertical scroll bar appears to the far right side of the window.

✔ Click the down arrow to scroll down one line at a time.

✔ Drag the scroll box in the vertical scroll bar in the desired direction to jump to an approximate location in your document.

✔ Click the scroll bar below the scroll box to page down one window at a time.

✔ Click the scroll bar above the scroll box to page up one window at a time.

✔ Click the twin down arrows at the bottom of the scroll bar to jump up to the top of the next page.

✔ Click the twin up arrows in the scroll bar to jump down to the top of the preceding page. (*Note:* These double arrow buttons only appear in Page Layout view.)

Using the keyboard to jump around a document

For those who hate the mouse or just like using the keyboard, here are the different ways to jump around your document by pressing keys:

✔ Press the down-arrow key to move one line down in your document.

✔ Press the up-arrow key to move one line up in your document.

✔ Hold down Ctrl and press the up- or down-arrow key to jump up or down a paragraph at a time.

✔ Press PgDn (or Page Down, on some keyboards) to move down the document one window at a time.

✔ Press PgUp (or Page Up, on some keyboards) to move up the document one window at a time.

✔ Hold down Ctrl and press Home to jump to the beginning of your document.

✔ Hold down Ctrl and press End to jump to the end of your document.

Using the Go To command

When you want to jump to a specific part of your document, the Go To command is a lot easier and faster than either the mouse or the keyboard.

To use the Go To command, follow these steps:

1. Choose Edit⇨Go To (or press Ctrl+G).

The Go To dialog box appears, as shown in Figure 5-2.

Figure 5-2:
The Go To
dialog box.

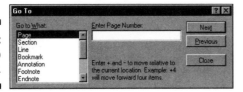

2. Choose one of the following:

- **Press Alt+T to advance to the top of the Next page.**

- **Press Alt+P to return to the top of the Previous page.**

- **Type a page number and press Enter.**

Instead of typing a specific page number, you can type a plus or minus sign, followed by a desired number of pages. For example, **+2** advances two pages, and **–5** moves back five pages.

Selecting Text

Before you can delete, move, copy, or format text, you must select it. Selecting it tells Word, "See this text? That's what I want you to change."

You have two ways to select text:

  ✔ Drag or click the mouse.
  ✔ Use the keyboard.

Dragging and clicking the mouse to select text

Dragging the mouse is the easiest and most intuitive way to select text. To select text with the mouse, follow these steps:

1. **Move the mouse pointer to the uppermost part of the text that you want to select. (For example, if you wanted to select this entire paragraph, you would move the mouse pointer in front of the word "Move" in the first sentence.)**

2. **Hold down the left mouse button and move the mouse, highlighting all the text that you want to select.**

3. **Release the left mouse button when you come to the end of the text that you want to select.**

If you're daring enough to trust your mouse clicking, try these other ways to select text:

✔ Double-click a word. This selects the word as well as the space that follows it. (This feature eliminates an unwanted space before the next word or a punctuation mark if you delete it.)

✔ Hold down the Ctrl key and click inside a sentence to select the entire sentence.

✔ Triple-click inside a paragraph to select the entire paragraph.

✔ Click to the left of the first word in a line to select the entire line.

✔ Double-click to the left of a paragraph to select the entire paragraph.

✔ Vertically dragging the mouse to the left of text selects multiple lines, whether those lines are contained in the same paragraph or in different paragraphs (see Figure 5-3).

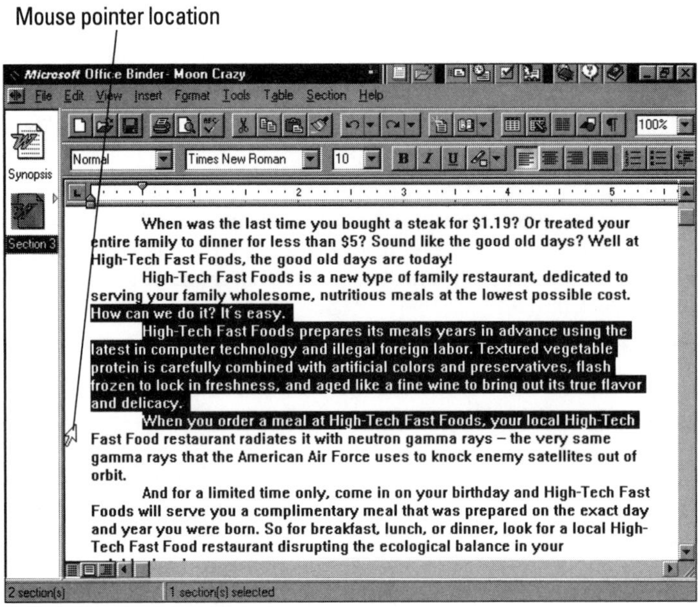

Mouse pointer location

Figure 5-3:
Vertically
dragging the
mouse.

Using the keyboard to select text

Instead of reaching for the mouse, you may find it easier to select text by using one of the following keyboard shortcuts:

- ✔ Press Shift with an arrow key.

- ✔ Press the F8 key, followed by an arrow key.

- ✔ Press Ctrl+Shift+right-arrow key to select words to the right of the insertion point.

- ✔ Press Ctrl+Shift+left-arrow key to select words to the left of the insertion point.

- ✔ Press Ctrl+Shift+up-arrow key to select the text before the insertion point in the current paragraph. Each time that you hold down Ctrl+Shift and press the up-arrow key again, you select the entire preceding paragraph.

- ✔ Press Ctrl+Shift+down-arrow key to select the text after the insertion point in the current paragraph. Each time that you hold down Ctrl+Shift and press the down-arrow key again, you select the entire following paragraph.

- ✔ Press Ctrl+A to select an entire document — highlighting all text, including footnotes (but excluding headers and footers). This shortcut makes it easy to change the typeface or type size throughout an informal letter or manuscript set in a single typeface and type size.

Editing Text

Editing involves deleting words, replacing old words with new words, and moving words to new locations. You can edit text in several ways:

- ✔ Deleting text
- ✔ Copying and moving text
- ✔ Using drag-and-drop editing
- ✔ Spiking

Deleting text

Two keys can delete individual characters and selected text:

- ✔ The Backspace key (typically gray, with an arrow pointing to the left), at the top of your keyboard
- ✔ The Delete key, which often is located in more than one place. On many keyboards, the Delete key appears below the Insert key to the left of the arrow keys and below the 3 key in the numeric keypad

Instead of pressing the Delete key, you can also choose Edit⇨Clear.

Although the Backspace and Delete keys can delete unwanted characters and text, they differ in the following ways:

- ✔ Backspace eliminates characters to the *left* of the insertion point.
- ✔ Delete eliminates characters to the *right* of the insertion point.

You can also delete entire blocks of text (or graphics) by selecting the text (or graphics) first and then pressing either Backspace or Delete.

Rather than deleting text and then typing something new, you can delete and replace text at the same time by selecting the text and then typing your new text.

Everyone changes his or her mind (some more than others, especially politicians). In case you delete text and suddenly decide you really need it after all, you have three options to restore that deleted text:

    ✔ Press Ctrl+Z.

    ✔ Choose Edit⇨Undo.

    ✔ Click the Undo button in the Standard toolbar.

Avoid pressing the Insert key (or Ins, on some keyboards). Word's default mode is Insert mode, which means that when you type, your newly typed words push any existing words to the side. If you accidentally press the Insert key, you enter Overtype mode. When you're in Overtype mode, typing new text simply wipes out any existing text that gets in the way.

Copying and moving text

Copying and moving text requires two steps. First, you have to tell Word what you want to copy or move. Then you have to tell Word where to "paste" the text that you wanted to copy or move.

The terms *copy, cut,* and *paste* all derive from the old days when people would literally cut out words or paragraphs with scissors and paste them in a new location. With the invention of the word processor, this antiquated method of rearranging text has gone away, except in those corporations too cheap to buy word processors.

If you want to copy text, follow these steps:

1. **Select the text that you want to copy by using the mouse or one of the keyboard shortcuts.**

2. **Choose the Copy command in one of the following ways:**

    • **Choose Edit⇨Copy.**

    • **Press Ctrl+C.**

    • **Click the Copy button in the Standard toolbar.**

    • **Press the right mouse button and choose Copy from the pop-up menu.**

3. **Move the cursor where you want to place the copied text.**

4. **Choose the Paste command in one of the following ways:**

- **Choose Edit⇨Paste.**
- **Press Ctrl+V.**
- **Click the Paste button in the Standard toolbar.**
- **Press the right mouse button and choose Paste from the pop-up menu.**

If you want to move text, follow these steps:

1. **Select the text that you want to move by using the mouse or one of the keyboard shortcuts.**

2. **Choose the Cut command in one of the following ways:**

- **Choose Edit⇨Cut.**
- **Press Ctrl+X.**
- **Click the Cut button in the Standard toolbar.**
- **Press the right mouse button and choose Cut from the pop-up menu.**

3. **Move the cursor where you want to place the moved text.**

4. **Choose the Paste command in one of the following ways:**

- **Choose Edit⇨Paste.**
- **Press Ctrl+V.**
- **Click the Paste button in the Standard toolbar.**
- **Press the right mouse button and choose Paste from the pop-up menu.**

Each time you copy or cut text, Windows stores this text on the Clipboard, which is a temporary storage place for copied or cut objects. Since Windows is fairly stupid, the Clipboard can only hold the last copied or cut object at a time. So if you cut or copy text and then cut or copy different text before you paste the first text, the second text overwrites the first text on the Clipboard.

Drag-and-drop editing

While drag and drop sounds like something you might do when shopping at the last minute during Christmas, it's actually a shortcut for cutting and pasting. Instead of cutting text and pasting it somewhere else, drag-and-drop editing lets you drag text to a new location. Then you can drop the text by releasing the mouse button.

Drag-and-drop editing works within a document as well as between documents. If you have two documents open, you can simply drag and drop text between the two documents.

To drag and drop a paragraph into a new location, follow these steps:

1. **Select the paragraph by using the mouse or one of the keyboard shortcuts.**

2. **Place the mouse pointer on the selected paragraph and hold down the left mouse button.**

3. **Drag the paragraph to the new location.**

4. **Release the mouse button.**

When you drag text, the selected text remains in its original location, and a rectangle appears below the mouse pointer to show that the pointer contains text. As you move through the document, a vertical line indicates where the text will be dropped when you release the mouse button (see Figure 5-4).

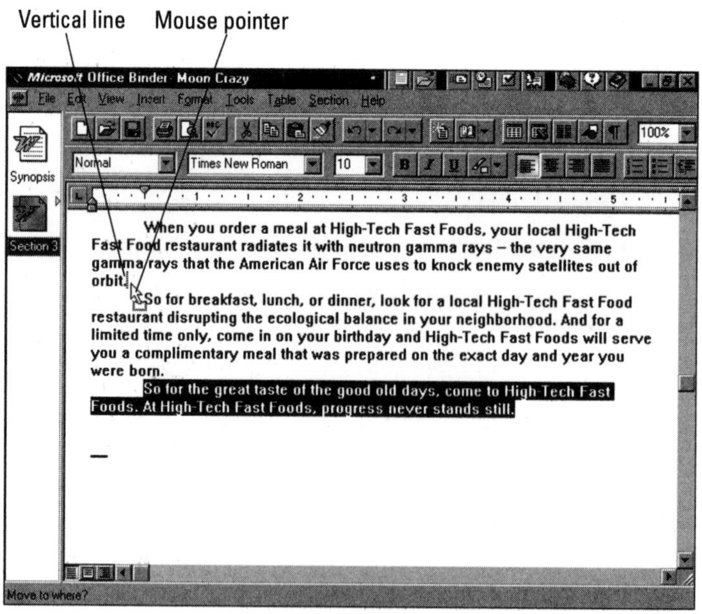

Vertical line   Mouse pointer

Figure 5-4:
Vertically
dragging the
mouse.

If you want to copy text rather than move it, follow these steps:

1. **Select the paragraph by using the mouse or one of the keyboard shortcuts.**

2. **Hold down the Ctrl key.**

3. **Place the mouse pointer on the selected paragraph and hold down the left mouse button.**

4. **Drag the paragraph to the new location.**

5. **Release the mouse button and the Ctrl key.**

Spike (the new kid on the block)

The Clipboard can hold only one item at a time. If you want to move several items, you have to cut and paste them one at a time. Rather than do that, move items to the Spike. The Spike acts like a super Clipboard that can contain multiple items at once.

(Think of the Spike like those paper spikes on your desk, where you can stab loose pieces of paper and hold them in place.)

To put items in the Spike, follow these steps:

1. **Select the text that you want to move by using the mouse or one of the keyboard shortcuts.**

2. **Press Ctrl+F3.**

Repeat these steps as many times as desired.

To insert items from the Spike into a document, follow these steps:

1. **Move the insertion point in your document where you want the Spike's contents to appear.**

2. **Press Ctrl+Shift+F3.**

   All the items appear in the document, in the order in which they were placed in the Spike — just like pieces of paper speared by a spike on your desk. (Quiz: How did Microsoft come up with "Spike" as the name of this feature?)

Checking Your Spelling

Some of the best writers in the world can't spell correctly (just look at all the weird spellings in Shakespeare's original plays). To make sure that you don't wreck your writing by spelling words wrong and making your high-powered business presentation look like the scribblings of a five-year-old, let Word check your spelling for you.

The moment you type a word that Word thinks is misspelled, it underlines the suspected word with a red, wavy line. If you press the right mouse button, a pop-up menu appears (as shown in Figure 5-5), listing a few of the words that Word thinks you really meant to type.

At this point, you can click one of the suggested words, click Ignore, add the word to your dictionary, or spell check the rest of your document.

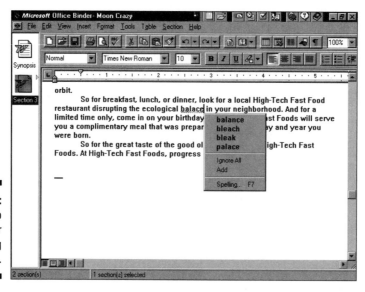

Figure 5-5:
The pop-up menu for checking spelling.

Spell checking your work

No matter how clearly organized your ideas may be, poor spelling can destroy the credibility of your words. To check the spelling of your entire document, use one of the following methods:

✔ Choose <u>T</u>ools⇨<u>S</u>pelling.

✔ Press F7.

✔ Click the Spelling button in the Standard toolbar (the one with the check mark and the letters *ABC*).

The moment Word finds a misspelled word, it stops and offers several alternative spellings (see Figure 5-6). In most cases, the first alternative word is the correct one; you can accept it by clicking the <u>C</u>hange button. If you don't like the first alternative word, scroll through the list of words and highlight the word you want. Then click <u>C</u>hange.

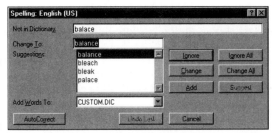

Figure 5-6:
The Spelling
dialog box.

In case the spell checker doesn't offer any alternatives that you want to use, you can type the correct spelling in the Change <u>T</u>o box and then click <u>C</u>hange.

Rather than highlighting an alternative and clicking <u>C</u>hange, you can accept a spelling checker alternative by double-clicking the word displayed within the Spelling dialog box.

Word's Spelling dialog box offers several other important options:

✔ Click the <u>I</u>gnore button if the highlighted word in the document is correctly spelled — if the word is a proper noun, technical term, or four-letter word that you know is spelled correctly.

✔ Click Ignore All if you use the word in the document more than once. Thereafter, Word ignores that same word throughout the current document.

✔ Click Change All if you think that you misspelled the word in the document more than once.

✔ Click <u>A</u>dd if you're going to use that word in other documents. Word adds the word to the dictionary. (For power users, you can create additional dictionary files to hold the correct spellings of words used in specialized documents, such as medical or legal documents.)

✔ Click the AutoCorrect button to add the word to the AutoCorrect dictionary. Thereafter, the word is corrected automatically as you type it. This procedure can save you a lot of time if you continually misspell the same words (such as "hte" instead of "the") and haven't taken the time to enter them in the AutoCorrect dictionary.

✔ Click Cancel when you're tired of using the spell checker.

When Word finishes spell checking your document, it displays the message `The spelling check is complete.` Click OK to return to your document.

Saving time with AutoCorrect

AutoCorrect contains a list of common typographical errors along with their corrections. The moment you type a word that matches AutoCorrect's list of typographical errors (such as *teh* instead of *the* or *adn* instead of *and*), AutoCorrect springs into action and corrects the misspelling right away (giving you the illusion that you actually spelled everything correctly).

✔ You can add your own common spelling mistakes to the AutoCorrect dictionary so it corrects them automatically.

✔ If you use a lot of bizarre technical terms or proper names, you can store shorthand references in AutoCorrect. For example, instead of typing **Massachusetts Institute of Technology** each time, just store the phrase **mit** in AutoCorrect. Each time AutoCorrect sees *mit,* it will automatically replace it with *Massachusetts Institute of Technology.*

To modify AutoCorrect, follow these steps:

1. **Choose Tools⇨AutoCorrect.**

   The AutoCorrect dialog box appears, as shown in Figure 5-7.

2. **Type in the Replace box a word that you frequently misspell. (Or type a shorthand word that you want to represent a longer word or phrase, such as** mit **for** Massachusetts Institute of Technology.**)**

3. **Type the correct spelling of the word in the With box. (Or type the longer word or phrase that you want AutoCorrect to use, such as** Massachusetts Institute of Technology.**)**

4. **Click Add.**

5. **Click OK.**

As a faster way to use AutoCorrect, click on the AutoCorrect button in the Spelling dialog box each time Word finds a misspelled word.

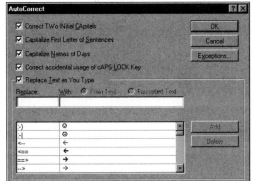

Figure 5-7:
The
AutoCorrect
dialog box.

If you enter a misspelled word in the <u>W</u>ith box, AutoCorrect will misspell the word consistently (which goes to show you that computers aren't that smart after all).

To remove a word from AutoCorrect, follow these steps:

1. **Choose <u>T</u>ools⇨<u>A</u>utoCorrect.**

   The AutoCorrect dialog box appears.

2. **Highlight the word that you want to remove from AutoCorrect.**

3. **Click <u>D</u>elete.**

4. **Click OK.**

If you make a mistake in entering a word in the AutoCorrect dialog box, select the misspelled word, click the Delete button, and repeat the process, trying to type a little more carefully this time.

Working with AutoText

AutoText lets you store and retrieve previously stored formatted text and graphics. Think of AutoText as being a permanent hard disk-based Clipboard. You can save all sorts of items with AutoText, including formatted tables.

AutoText differs from AutoCorrect in two ways:

  ✔ AutoText can save both text and graphics.

  ✔ You must select AutoText and scroll through the list of available choices before it will insert the text or graphic into your document.

Use AutoCorrect to insert frequently used abbreviations that you want Word to spell out automatically. Use AutoText to insert infrequently used text and graphics.

For example, you may have to type the following in documents periodically:

> **All proposed fees are nonnegotiable. Terms include a 40 percent deposit and signed purchase order by a company officer at the start of the project and a 30 percent progress fee upon the approval of first drafts. The remaining 30 percent is due within 10 days of project completion. A 1 ¹/₂ percent service charge will be applied for all accounts more than 15 days overdue. Client agrees to assume any and all collection and legal fees caused by late payment.**

Unless you love typing, you probably don't want to type this paragraph more than once, which makes it an ideal AutoText candidate.

To add text (or graphics) to AutoText, follow these steps:

1. **Select the text or graphics that you want to add.**

2. **Choose Edit➪AutoText.**

    The AutoText dialog box appears (see Figure 5-8). The selected text appears in the Selection window, while the Name box contains a portion of the selected text.

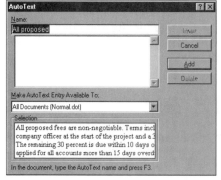

Figure 5-8:
The
AutoText
dialog box.

3. **Type a name to represent your text (such as** Terms **or** Legal Junk**).**

4. **Click Add.**

    The AutoText dialog box closes, and you return to your document.

After you store text or graphics in AutoText, you have two ways to insert AutoText text (or graphics) into a document.

To insert text or graphics from AutoText the hard way (in case you don't want to type the name you used to represent your text), follow these steps:

1. **Move the cursor where you want to insert the AutoText items.**

2. **Choose Edit⬚AutoText.**

   The AutoText dialog box appears.

3. **Click the name of the AutoText item that you want to use and click Insert. (If numerous AutoText objects appear in the dialog box, you may have to scroll through the list.)**

Two radio buttons appear in the AutoText box under the Insert As group. Choosing Formatted Text inserts text in the typeface and type size in which it originally was formatted. If you click the Plain Text radio button, the text will be formatted the same as adjacent text in the document.

To insert text or graphics from AutoText the easy way, follow these steps:

1. **Move the cursor where you want to insert the AutoText items.**

2. **Type the name of the AutoText selection that you want to insert (such as** Terms **or** Legal Junk**).**

3. **Press F3.**

If you find that you aren't using some of the AutoText selections, choose Edit⬚AutoText to display the AutoText dialog box, highlight the unwanted selection, and click the Delete button.

Using Find and Replace

When you want to find a certain word or phrase in your document, you can either scroll through and examine it line by line yourself, or you can do it the easy way and let Word find the word or phrase for you.

Word's find feature can also come in handy when you want to find and replace certain words or phrases but don't feel like doing it yourself. For example, you may have a prenuptial agreement with the name *Frank* or *Cindy* written everywhere. If you want to replace all references to *Frank* with *Bob,* Word's find and replace feature can do it for you faster and more accurately than even a high-priced lawyer.

Using the find feature

To find a word or phrase, follow these steps:

1. Choose Edit⇨Find (or press Ctrl+F).

The Find dialog box appears, as shown in Figure 5-9.

Figure 5-9:
The Find
dialog box.

2. Type in the Find What box the word or phrase that you want to find within your document.

If you're repeating a previous search, click the down arrow next to the Find What box to display a list of your last four searches.

3. Click the Search list box and choose one of the following:

- **All:** Searches the entire document

- **Down:** Searches from the current insertion point to the end of the document

- **Up:** Searches from the current insertion point to the beginning of the document

4. Click the appropriate check boxes to limit your search to specific criteria:

- **Match Case:** Searches for the exact upper- and lowercase word or phrase that you type in the Find What box. (For example, searching for "FoxPro" would never find the words "foxpro" or "Foxpro.")

- **Find Whole Words Only:** Searches for complete words. (For example, searching for "Tea" would never find "Teamster" or "Teak.")

- **Sounds Like:** Searches words phonetically. (For example, searching for "Kat" would find "cat.")

- **Use Pattern Matching:** Searches words based on patterns. (For example, searching for "c?t" would find all three-letter words that begin with *c* and end with *t*.)

- **Find All Word Forms:** Searches for all different variations of a word such as past tense or plural. (For example, searching for "House" would find "Houses.")

5. **Click Format if you want to search for words in a specified Font, Paragraph, Language, or Style. (For example, you can search for only those words in Dutch, displayed in Times New Roman font, indented two inches from the left margin.)**

6. **Click Special if you want to search for particular punctuation marks such as tab characters, caret characters, or page breaks.**

7. **Start the search by clicking Find Next.**

8. **After reaching the first selection, click the Cancel button if you want to close the Find dialog box and work on your document. (Or click Find Next again if you want to search for the next occurrence.)**

Using the find and replace feature

To find a word or phrase and replace it with another word or phrase, follow these steps:

1. **Choose Edit⇨Replace (or press Ctrl+H).**

   The Replace dialog box appears, as shown in Figure 5-10.

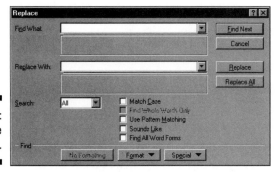

Figure 5-10:
The Replace
dialog box.

2. **Type in the Find What box the word or phrase that you want to find within your document.**

3. **Type in the Replace With box the word or phrase that you want to use for replacing text.**

4. Click the Search list box and choose one of the following:

- **All:** Searches the entire document

- **Down:** Searches from the current insertion point to the end of the document

- **Up:** Searches from the current insertion point to the beginning of the document

5. Click the appropriate check boxes to limit your search to specific criteria:

- **Match Case:** Searches for the exact upper- and lowercase word or phrase that you type in the Find What box. (For example, searching for "Microsoft" would never find "MicroSoft.")

- **Find Whole Words Only:** Searches for complete words. (For example, searching for "do" would never find "doughnuts," "dog," or "doodle.")

- **Sounds Like:** Searches words phonetically. (For example, searching for "fantom" would find "phantom.")

- **Use Pattern Matching:** Searches words based on patterns. (For example, searching for "h??l" would find all four-letter words that begin with *h* and end with *l*.)

- **Find All Word Forms:** Searches for all different variations of a word such as past tense or plural. (For example, searching for "Home" would also find "Homeless.")

6. Click Format if you want to search and replace words in a specified Font, Paragraph, Language, or Style.

7. Click Special if you want to search and replace particular punctuation marks or section breaks.

8. Start the search and replace by clicking Find Next.

9. When Word locates the desired word or phrase, choose one of the following:

- **If you want to do nothing and continue searching, click Find Next.**

- **If you want to quit the search, click Close.**

- **Click Replace if you want to use replacement text in place of the text that Word just located.**

- **Click Replace All if you want to replace every occurrence of the selected text with the replacement text. (This is known as *trust.*)**

Using the Thesaurus

Sometimes you know what you want to say but don't know the exact word to use. Rather than stop writing, go ahead and write the closest word that says what you want. Then use Word's thesaurus to help you find a better choice of words.

To use the thesaurus, follow these steps:

1. Move the cursor on the word that you want to look up in the thesaurus.

2. Choose Tools⇨Thesaurus. (Or press Shift+F7).

The Thesaurus dialog box appears, as shown in Figure 5-11.

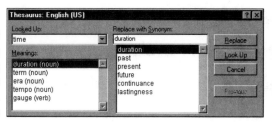

Figure 5-11:
The
Thesaurus
dialog box.

3. Click the closest meaning of your word in the Meanings list box.

4. Choose one of the following:

- **Click the word that you want to use in the Replace with Synonym box and click Replace.**

- **To continue searching for a word with precisely the right nuance, select the closest synonym and click Look Up. A new set of words appears.**

- **Click one of the words in the Meanings list box and choose the nouns, adjectives, or verbs that have definitions similar to your selected word.**

- **If you want to view the last word that you looked up — and the synonyms for that word appeared in the dialog box — click Previous.**

- **Press Esc or click the Cancel button of the Thesaurus dialog box if you despair of writing and want to become a firefighter instead.**

Counting Your Words

Because many writers get paid by the word (Charles Dickens used to get paid a penny per word, which is why his novels are so long), you may need to count your words to see if you have enough of them.

To count your words, follow these steps:

1. **Choose Tools⇨Word Count.**

   A Word Count dialog box (shown in Figure 5-12) appears, listing the total number of pages, words, characters, paragraphs, and lines in your document (in case you really need to know all this).

2. **Click Close.**

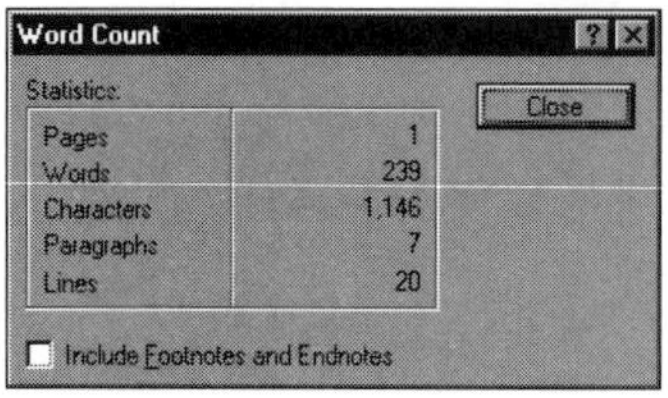

Figure 5-12:
The Word
Count dialog
box.

Word Count	? X
Statistics:	Close

Pages	1
Words	239
Characters	1,146
Paragraphs	7
Lines	20

☐ Include Footnotes and Endnotes

Chapter 6

Expanding Your Horizons with Advanced Tools

In This Chapter

▶ Formatting your document the easy way

▶ Working with tables

▶ Saving time by working efficiently

▶ Automating your work with macros

Words alone won't sway an audience. Not only do you have to write clearly, but you have to present your writing in an aesthetically pleasing way as well. The better-looking your document, the more likely someone will actually pick it up and read it.

Formatting Your Document the Easy Way

If you really love using Word, you could format your text by using all of Word's arcane commands each time. However, Word has already formatted several documents (in the form of faxes, reports, proposals, and memos) that you can use for your own documents. These preformatted documents are called *style templates*.

Using style templates yourself

Each style template consists of one or more individual styles, each of which formats text using different margins, fonts, typefaces, and type sizes.

A *style* is a specific way to format text, such as displaying text in italic and indented two inches from the left margin. A *template* is a blank document that contains one or more styles. If you need to format text the same way over and over again, such as formatting a screenplay or a legal form, using styles stored in a template is generally faster than formatting text yourself. To choose one of Word's predefined formats, follow these steps:

1. Choose Format➪Style Gallery.

The Style Gallery dialog box appears, as shown in Figure 6-1.

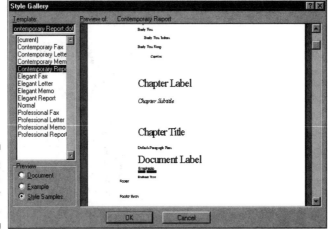

Figure 6-1:
The Style
Gallery
dialog box.

2. Click one of the style templates, such as Elegant Fax or Professional Letter.

3. Click one of the following radio buttons in the Preview group:

- **Document:** Shows you what your current document will look like if you switch to a different style template

- **Example:** Shows how a typical letter looks using a particular style template

- **Style Sample:** Shows the different styles that make up the style template

4. Click OK when you've found a style template that you want to use.

Once you've chosen a style template, it's time to use its styles to make your text look pretty. To use a style, follow these steps:

1. **Move the cursor to the part of your document that you want to format using a particular style.**

2. **Click the Style list box (which appears to the left of the Formatting toolbar) to choose a style.**

   A list of different styles appears, as shown in Figure 6-2.

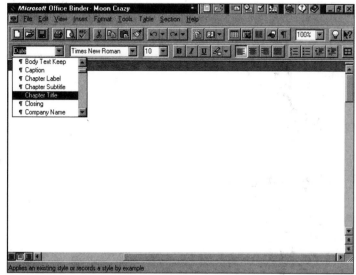

Figure 6-2:
The list of
choices
displayed in
the Style list
box.

3. **Type your text and watch Word format it before your eyes. (If you moved the cursor to an existing block of text in Step 1, Word formats your text right away.)**

Figure 6-3 shows a document using some different styles.

Applying AutoFormatting

If you're in a hurry, you can use Word's AutoFormatting feature, which essentially tells Word, "Go ahead and reformat my entire document automatically."

The main advantage is that AutoFormat can save you time by formatting your entire document in one quick step. The disadvantage is that AutoFormat blindly formats everything in your document, and it may format text using a style that you didn't want to use. To make sure that this doesn't happen, you'll have to browse through your entire document to verify that everything is formatted correctly.

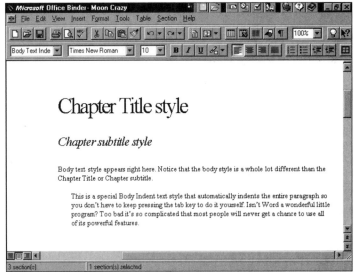

To use AutoFormatting, follow these steps:

1. Choose Format⇨AutoFormat.

The AutoFormat dialog box appears, as shown in Figure 6-4.

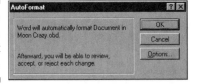

Figure 6-4:
The
AutoFormat
dialog box.

2. Click Options.

The Options dialog box (shown in Figure 6-5) appears, explaining the changes Word will make to your document.

3. Choose the options that you want (or don't want) Word to use and click OK. (A check mark means that option is chosen. An empty check box means that the option will not be used. Click in a check box to place or remove its check mark inside.)

The AutoFormat dialog box appears again.

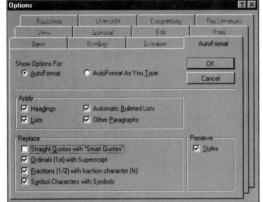

Figure 6-5:
The
Options
dialog box.

4. **Click OK.**

Word automatically reformats your text and displays a new AutoFormat dialog box, shown in Figure 6-6.

Figure 6-6:
Another
AutoFormat
dialog box.

5. **Click Style Gallery.**

A Style Gallery dialog box appears, displaying your current document in the preview window (see the previous section, "Using style templates yourself," for more information about the Style Gallery dialog box).

6. **Click different templates to see how each one formats your document.**

7. **Click OK when you've chosen a specific style template to use.**

The obnoxious AutoFormat dialog box appears again.

8. **Click Accept to have Word automatically format your entire document.**

Instead of choosing Format⇨AutoFormat, you can click the AutoFormat button in the Standard toolbar. However, your options will be entirely different. When you click the AutoFormat button, here's what happens:

  ✔ Word applies formatting automatically, without giving you a chance to decide which formatting options you want to change and which you want to preserve.

  ✔ You do not get a chance to review (and reject, if desired) each formatting change.

  ✔ You do not get a chance to choose a different style from the Style Gallery.

Allow Me to Show You to Your Table

Tables let you organize information in rows and columns, which can be useful to display data in an easy-to-read format.

  ✔ A *row* displays information horizontally.

  ✔ A *column* displays information vertically.

  ✔ A *cell* is a single box formed by the intersection of a row and a column.

For example, consider the following data:

> The LX series comes complete with plastic steering wheel, AM radio, two-way adjustable seats, and front-wheel hydraulic braking. The LX-2 package includes the Semi-Luxury Module, which includes a wood-spoked steering wheel; AM/FM radio; precision eight-day, spring-wound analog clock; four-way adjustable seats; and hydraulic braking. The LX-3 includes eight-way adjustable, heated power seats; a hand-tooled-leather steering wheel; AM/FM cassette stereo; digital clock; and computer-controlled Anchor-Lok braking.

Rather than bombard readers with globs of information, it's a whole lot easier to present it in a table, as shown in Figure 6-7.

You can display tables with the grid lines displayed or hidden. By hiding the grid lines, you can format text quickly and easily without the ugly grid lines getting in the way. To hide grid lines, choose Table➪Gridlines, which removes the check mark next to Gridlines and gives you a table like the one shown in Figure 6-8.

Grid lines   Cell   Column

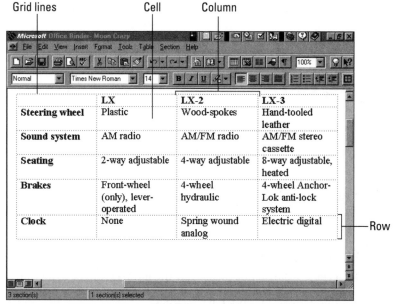

Figure 6-7:
An easy-to-
understand
table.

	LX	LX-2	LX-3
Steering wheel	Plastic	Wood-spokes	Hand-tooled leather
Sound system	AM radio	AM/FM radio	AM/FM stereo cassette
Seating	2-way adjustable	4-way adjustable	8-way adjustable, heated
Brakes	Front-wheel (only), lever-operated	4-wheel hydraulic	4-wheel Anchor-Lok anti-lock system
Clock	None	Spring wound analog	Electric digital

Row

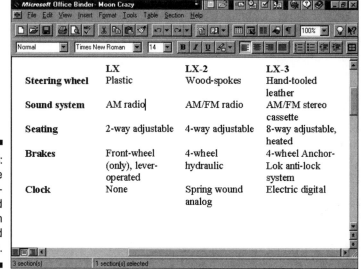

Figure 6-8:
The same
easy-to-
understand
table with
the grid
lines hidden.

	LX	LX-2	LX-3
Steering wheel	Plastic	Wood-spokes	Hand-tooled leather
Sound system	AM radio	AM/FM radio	AM/FM stereo cassette
Seating	2-way adjustable	4-way adjustable	8-way adjustable, heated
Brakes	Front-wheel (only), lever-operated	4-wheel hydraulic	4-wheel Anchor-Lok anti-lock system
Clock	None	Spring wound analog	Electric digital

Adding a table

To add a table by using Word's pull-down menus, follow these steps:

1. Choose Table⇨Insert Table.

An Insert Table dialog box appears, as shown in Figure 6-9.

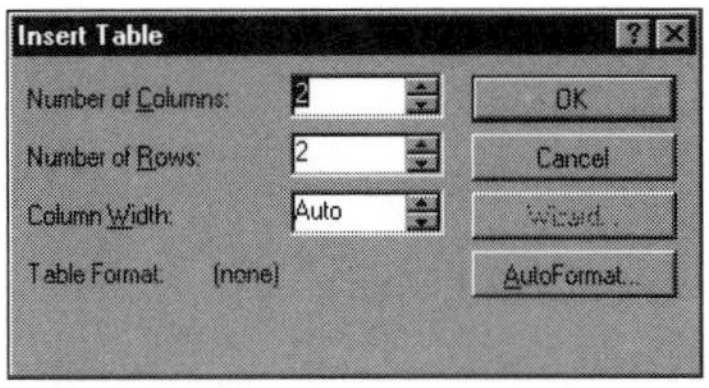

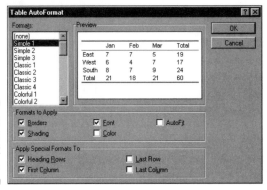

Figure 6-9:
The Insert
Table dialog
box.

2. In the Number of Columns box, type the number of columns you want.

3. In the Number of Rows box, type the number of rows you want.

4. Click the up or down arrow in the Column Width box to choose a column width.

The default is Auto, which tells Word to adjust the column widths depending on the amount of text you jam into each column.

5. Click AutoFormat.

The Table AutoFormat dialog box appears, as shown in Figure 6-10.

Figure 6-10:
The Table
AutoFormat
dialog box.

6. Click a different table format (such as Classic 3 or Simple 1).

7. **Click any check boxes under the Formats to Apply group to modify your table.**

   If you want borders around your table, for example, make sure that a check mark appears in the Borders check box. Word displays any changes you make in the Preview window.

8. **Click any check boxes under the Apply Special Formats To group to modify your table.**

   Word displays any changes you make in the Preview window.

9. **Click OK.**

   The Insert Table dialog box appears again.

10. **Click OK.**

In the name of freedom (and confusion), you can insert tables by clicking the Insert Table icon in the Standard toolbar by following these steps:

1. **Click the Insert Table icon in the Standard toolbar.**

   A table appears underneath, as shown in Figure 6-11.

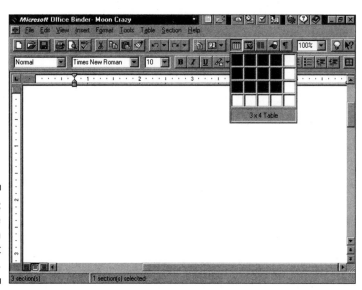

Figure 6-11:
The table underneath the Insert Table icon.

2. **Hold down the left mouse button and drag the mouse to highlight the number of rows and columns you want.**

3. **Release the mouse button.**

   Word displays the table in your document.

Modifying the size of your table

After you create a table, you may want to make it bigger or smaller by adding or deleting rows and columns.

To delete a row or column, follow these steps:

1. **Move the cursor in the row or column that you want to delete.**

2. **Choose Table⇨Select Row (or Select Column).**

   Word highlights your chosen row or column.

3. **Choose Table⇨Delete Rows (or Delete Columns).**

To add a row or column, follow these steps:

1. **Move the cursor in a row or column. (When you add a row, it appears directly above the row that you've chosen. When you add a column, it appears to the left of the column you've chosen.)**

2. **Choose Table⇨Select Row (or Select Column).**

   Word highlights your chosen row or column.

3. **Choose Table⇨Insert Rows (or Insert Columns).**

Entering and editing table data

You can enter and edit table data in two ways:

✔ Click the desired cell and start typing.

✔ Click in the table and press the Tab key to move the cursor to the next cell to the right in the same row. Press Shift+Tab to move backward (to the left) in the row. Then type your data.

✔ Click in the table and press the up- or down-arrow key and then type your data.

Changing the column width and row height in your table

Normally, Word makes all the rows and columns in a table uniform in width and height. However, if you want some rows or columns to be a different size, Word gives you the option of changing them.

To change the column width, follow these steps:

1. **Click in the column that you want to modify.**

2. **Choose Table⇨Cell Height and Width.**

   A Cell Height and Width dialog box appears.

3. **Click the Column tab (see Figure 6-12).**

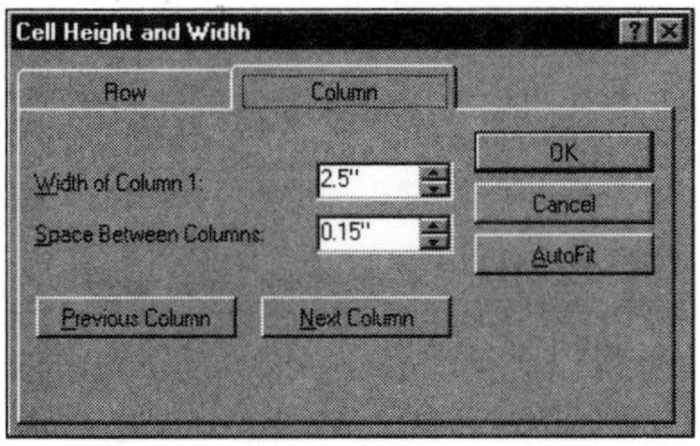

Figure 6-12:
The Cell Height and Width dialog box with the Column tab selected.

4. **Click the up/down arrows in the Width of Column box to change the column width.**

5. **Click the up/down arrows in the Space Between Columns box to change the spacing between columns. (If the spacing between columns is too small, text and numbers in your table may appear too close together.)**

6. **Click OK.**

To change the row height, follow these steps:

1. **Click in the row that you want to modify.**

2. **Choose Table⇨Cell Height and Width.**

   A Cell Height and Width dialog box appears.

3. **Click the Row tab (see Figure 6-13).**

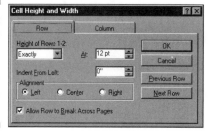

Figure 6-13:
The Cell
Height and
Width dialog
box with the
Row tab
selected.

4. Click the Height of Rows list box and choose one of the following:

- **Auto:** Automatically adjusts the height of rows

- **At Least:** Lets you define the minimum point size of the row (such as 16 pt). This means that all text and numbers in a row must be a certain point size or larger, such as 16 point size.

- **Exactly:** Lets you define the exact size of the row (such as 16 pt). This means all text and numbers in that row appears in a specific point size, such as 16 point size.

5. Click OK.

Saving a table as an AutoText entry

After you create the perfect table, you may want to copy it to the AutoText dialog box so that you can reuse your formatting.

To make a formatted table available as an AutoText entry, follow these steps:

1. Click anywhere inside the table and choose Table⇨Select Table.

2. Click the right mouse button inside the table.

A pop-up menu appears.

3. Choose Copy.

4. Choose Edit⇨AutoText.

The AutoText dialog box appears.

5. Type a name for your table in the Name box.

6. Click Add.

Deleting a table

Word gives you two ways to delete a table:

✔ Delete the entire table, including the contents of the table

✔ Delete just the contents of the table

To delete the entire table, including the contents of the table, follow these steps:

1. **Click the mouse one line above or below the table that you want to delete.**

2. **Hold down the left mouse button and drag the mouse to highlight the entire table.**

3. **Press Delete.**

To delete just the contents of the table, follow these steps:

1. **Click the mouse anywhere in the table.**

2. **Choose Table⇨Select Table.**

   Word highlights your chosen table.

3. **Press Delete.**

Saving Time by Working Efficiently

To save a little bit of time while you use Word, try one or more of the following features that are buried inside Word's electronic brain.

Using bookmarks to find specific locations

If you're in the middle of a long document and suddenly have to return to page 4 for a second, you can jump to page 4, but then you have to remember what page you just left.

Just as you can insert bookmarks in books to help you find your place, you can also add invisible, electronic bookmarks to Word documents to help you jump from one part of your document to another.

To place a bookmark in your document, follow these steps:

1. **Move the cursor to the place in your document where you want to place the bookmark.**

2. **Choose Edit⇨Bookmark.**

   The Bookmark dialog box appears, as shown in Figure 6-14.

Figure 6-14:
The
Bookmark
dialog box.

3. **Type a name for your bookmark in the Bookmark Name box.**

   It's a good idea to make the bookmark name descriptive, such as **Page1** or **Chapter4**. Remember, you're limited to a single word with no spaces and just 40 characters in length.

4. **Click Add.**

To jump to a bookmark, follow these steps:

1. **Choose Edit⇨Bookmark.**

   The Bookmark dialog box appears.

2. **Click the bookmark name that you want to jump to.**

3. **Click Go To.**

   Word jumps to your bookmark.

4. **Click Close (or press Esc) to get the annoying Bookmark dialog box out of the way.**

To move an existing bookmark, follow these steps:

1. **Move the cursor to the new location where you want to move an existing bookmark.**

2. **Choose Edit⇨Bookmark.**

   The Bookmark dialog box appears.

3. **Click the bookmark name that you want to move.**

4. **Click Add.**

Numbering pages

For long documents, it's a good idea to number your pages so that when you print them out, you'll know how to arrange them.

To add page numbers to your document, follow these steps:

1. **Choose Insert⇨Page Numbers.**

   The Page Numbers dialog box appears, as shown in Figure 6-15.

Figure 6-15:
The Page
Numbers
dialog box.

2. **Click the Position list box to choose whether to display page numbers at the Top of Page (Header) or the Bottom of Page (Footer).**

3. **Click the Alignment list box to choose how to align your page numbers (Left, Center, Right, Inside, or Outside).**

4. **Click Format.**

   A Page Number Format dialog box appears, as shown in Figure 6-16.

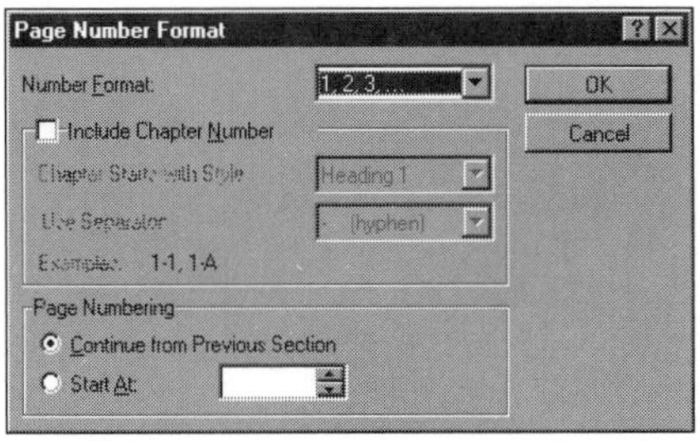

Figure 6-16:
The Page
Number
Format
dialog box.

5. **Click the Number Format list box to choose the type of numbers to use (Roman numerals, ordinary numbers, letters, and so on).**

6. **Click OK.**

   The Page Numbers dialog box reappears.

7. **Click OK.**

If you don't want to number the first page of your document (for example, you don't want a page number on your title page), clear the <u>S</u>how Number on First Page check box.

Dating your documents

When you need to type a date or time in your document, you could do it yourself. However, with the aid of your computer's internal clock, Word can insert the date and time for you so you don't have to look at a clock or calendar.

You have two ways to add the current date and time to your documents:

✔ Insert the date or time as text

✔ Insert the date or time as a field

If you insert the date or time as *text,* the date and time always remain the same, even if you open or print the document months later.

If you insert the date or time as a *field,* Word automatically updates the date or time whenever you open the file or print the document.

To insert the date or time as either text or a field, follow these steps:

1. Choose <u>I</u>nsert⇨Date and <u>T</u>ime.

The Date and Time dialog box appears, as shown in Figure 6-17.

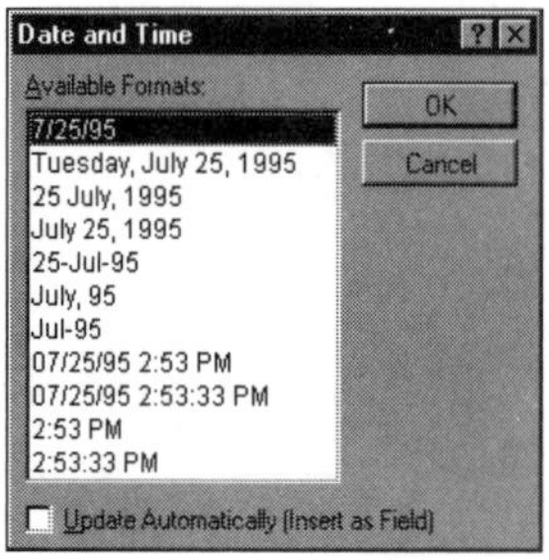

Figure 6-17:
The Date
and Time
dialog box.

2. Choose the date and time format that you want to use.

If you're inserting the date and time as text, just click OK. To insert the date and time as a field, click the <u>U</u>pdate Automatically check box before you click OK.

Sorting lists

Just like Santa Claus, Word can create a list and sort it for you. When you create a list, you must press Enter after each item that makes up your list, such as

Bob (press Enter)

John (press Enter)

Mary (press Enter)

To sort a list, follow these steps:

1. **Type your list that you want to sort. (Skip this step if you've already typed your list.)**

2. **Highlight the entire list.**

3. **Choose Table⇨Sort Text.**

   A Sort Text dialog box appears, as shown in Figure 6-18.

Figure 6-18:
The Sort
Text dialog
box.

4. **Click the Ascending or Descending radio button.**

5. **Click OK.**

   Word sorts your list alphabetically in either ascending or descending order.

Numbering and bulleting lists

In case you want Word to number or bullet your lists as you create them, follow these steps:

1. **Type your list that you want to number or bullet. (Skip this step if you've already typed your list.)**

2. **Highlight the entire list.**

3. **Choose F_ormat⇨Bullets and _Numbering.**

   A Bullets and Numbering dialog box appears, as shown in Figure 6-19.

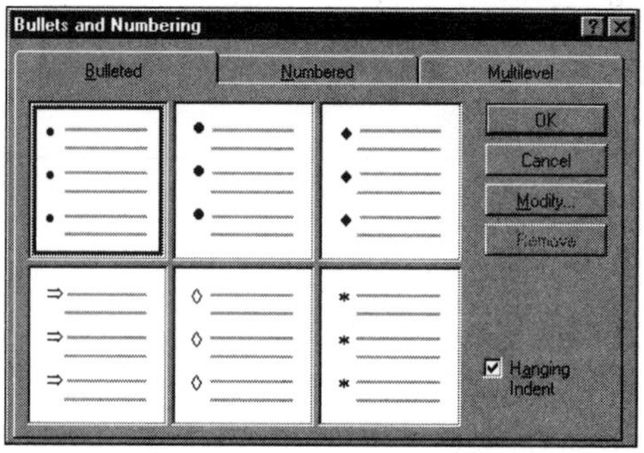

Figure 6-19:
The Bullets
and
Numbering
dialog box.

4. **Click the _Bulleted tab, the _Numbered tab, or the M_ultilevel tab. Multilevel lists appear with one or more items indented. Bulleted and Numbered lists appear with no items indented.**

5. **Click the type of bullet or number style that you want to use and click OK.**

If you want Word to automatically bullet or number your list as you type it, start with step 3 and then type your list.

Automating your work with macros

If you get tired of typing the same stuff over and over again (such as "The United States Department of Censorship and Other Unconstitutional Acts"), make sure that you know how to use macros.

If you get tired of pressing the same keys over and over again, such as running the spell checker, word counter, and then print preview command every time you're ready to print a document, macros can save you a lot of unnecessary keystrokes — so that you don't suffer from repetitive stress syndrome.

Essentially, macros let you store complicated keyboard sequences under a unique name. When you need to type that information again, just tell Word which macro name to use, and Word types the information for you instead.

Working with macros involves two primary steps:

1. Recording (creating) the macro

2. Running the macro

Creating a macro

To create a macro, follow these steps:

1. **Choose Section⇨View Outside. (Skip this step if you're using Word as a separate program.)**

2. **Choose Tools⇨Macro.**

   The Macro dialog box appears.

3. **Type a name for your macro in the Macro Name box.**

   The name must begin with a letter and consist of a single word, such as **USC**.

4. **Type a description of your macro in the Description box.**

5. **Click Record.**

   The Record Macro dialog box appears, as shown in Figure 6-20.

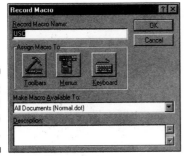

Figure 6-20:
The Record
Macro
dialog box.

6. **Click OK.**

   The two-button Macro Record toolbar appears (shown in Figure 6-21), indicating that all keyboard sequences and actions taken in dialog boxes are now being recorded.

Figure 6-21:
The Macro
Record
toolbar.

7. **Press the keystrokes that you want to record in your macro (such as typing** The United States Department of Censorship and Other Unconstitutional Acts **or choosing menu commands from the pull-down menus).**

8. **Click the Stop button (marked with a black box) in the Macro Record toolbar to stop recording your macro.**

9. **Choose File⇨Close and Return to. (Skip this step if you're using Word as a separate program.)**

Running a macro

After you record a macro, it only makes sense to use it once in a while. To run a macro, follow these steps:

1. **Choose Tools⇨Macro.**

   The Macro dialog box appears.

2. **Click the macro name that you want to run.**

3. **Click Run.**

   Watch in awe as Word effortlessly repeats your prerecorded steps.

Deleting a macro

If you want to delete your macros for whatever reason, follow these steps:

1. **Choose Tools⇨Macro.**

   The Macro dialog box appears.

2. **Click the macro name that you want to delete.**

3. **Click Delete.**

   Word displays a dialog box, asking if you really want to delete the macro.

4. **Click Yes.**

   The Macro dialog box appears again.

5. **Click Close.**

Chapter 7

Desktop Publishing with Word

• •

In This Chapter

▶ Adding headers and footers

▶ Setting up multicolumn documents

▶ Using frames

▶ Adding drop caps to attract attention

• •

*W*ord is more than just a word processor. With a little bit of creativity and a lot of patience, you can also turn Word into a fairly decent desktop publishing program to create your own newsletters, brochures, and flyers.

Keep Your Footers off My Headers!

Headers and footers can improve both the appearance and the readability of your documents by adding white space to the tops and bottoms of your pages. This white space provides a pleasing contrast to the grayness of your text and focuses your reader's attention on your words and accompanying graphics (while also giving the page a less cluttered look).

Headers appear at the top of the page, and footers appear at the bottom. Both headers and footers typically contain repetitive information on each page, such as the publication title, the section or chapter title, the page number, and the author's name.

Adding headers and footers

To add headers and footers, follow these steps:

1. **Choose <u>V</u>iew⇨<u>H</u>eader and Footer.**

   Word displays a Header and Footer toolbar along with a Header box where you can type a header. Figure 7-1 shows the toolbar and the Header box.

Switch between   Page   Date   Page setup
header and footer numbers   Time

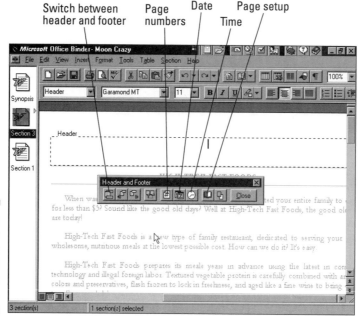

Figure 7-1:
The Header
and Footer
toolbar and
the Header
box.

2. **Type your header text in the Header box. (If you just want to type a footer, skip this step.)**

   You can click the Page Numbers, Date, or Time icon to insert the page number, date, or time in your header.

3. **Click the Switch Between Header and Footer icon, which appears as the far left button on the Header and Footer toolbar.**

   Word displays the Footer box.

4. **Type your footer text in the Footer box.**

5. **Click the Page Setup icon, which appears as an open book icon in the Header and Footer toolbar.**

   The Page Setup dialog box appears.

6. **Click the Layout tab (see Figure 7-2).**

7. **Click the Different Odd and Even check box if you want to define different headers and footers for odd and even pages. (For example, many books display the book title on all even numbered pages and the chapter title on all odd numbered pages.)**

8. **Click in the Different First Page check box if you want to define a different header or footer for your first page.**

9. **Click OK.**

The Header and Footer toolbar reappears.

10. **Click Close.**

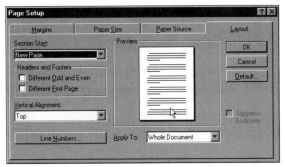

Adding white space above and below headers and footers

You can use headers and footers to control the amount of white space between the top of the header and the top of the page. You can also control the distance between the bottom of a footer and the bottom of the page.

To adjust the distance between the top and bottom edges of a page and the headers and footers, follow these steps:

1. **Choose View⇨Header and Footer.**
2. **Click the Page Setup button in the Header and Footer toolbar.**

The Page Setup dialog box appears.

3. **Click the Margins tab (see Figure 7-3).**
4. **Click the up/down arrows in the Header and Footer boxes located in the From Edge group (or just type a number, such as** 1.5).
5. **Click OK.**
6. **Click Close.**

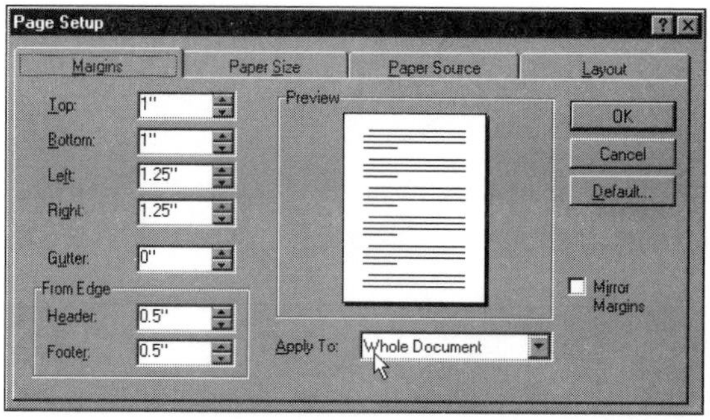

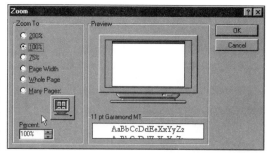

Figure 7-3:
The Page
Setup dialog
box's
Margins tab.

You also can adjust the distance between text and adjacent headers and footers in Page Layout view by following these steps:

1. Choose View⇨Zoom.

The Zoom dialog box appears, as shown in Figure 7-4.

Figure 7-4:
The Zoom
dialog box.

2. Click Whole Page and click OK.

Word displays your document as a full page.

3. If the rulers aren't displayed, choose View⇨Ruler.

The white area of the ruler indicates the top and bottom text margins.

4. Move the mouse pointer over the white and gray boundary on the ruler to the left of the screen.

The mouse pointer turns into an up- and downward-pointing arrow.

5. Drag the top- or bottom-margin boundary up or down to extend or reduce the text area.

Figure 7-5 shows the top margin being dragged.

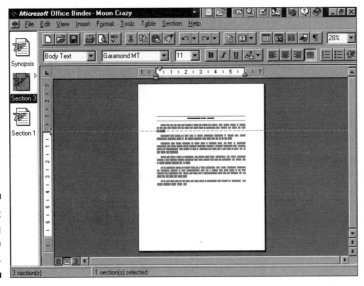

Figure 7-5:
Dragging
the top
margin.

Adding border rules to headers and footers

In addition to building white space into your documents and providing space for the publication name, section and chapter titles, author name, and page numbers, you can use headers and footers to add top and bottom borders to your pages.

To add a top or bottom border to your pages, follow these steps:

1. **Choose View⇨Header and Footer.**

2. **Choose View⇨Toolbars.**

   The Toolbars dialog box appears.

3. **Click the Borders check box to display the Borders toolbar and click OK.**

   Word displays the Borders toolbar, shown in Figure 7-6.

4. **Click a line of the desired thickness from the line list box (such as 4¹/₂ pt).**

   The Line list box displays your chosen line thickness.

Line list box   Top border   Bottom border   Borders toolbar

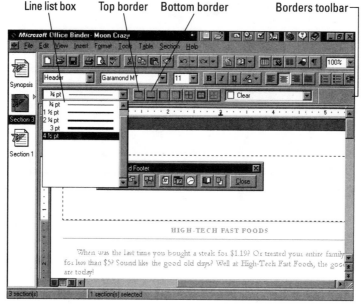

Figure 7-6:
The line list
box on the
Borders
toolbar.

5. **To add a border below the header text, click anywhere in the header text and then click the Bottom Border (or Top Border) button, which appears to the right of the line list box.**

   The line appears below (or above, if you clicked Top Border) the text, as shown in Figure 7-7. Note that the size of the Header or Footer text box determines the amount of white space that appears between the header (or footer) and the body text in your document.

6. **Click Close (or the Close box) in the Header and Footer toolbar.**

7. **Choose View⇨Header and Footer.**

   The Header and Footer text boxes appear dimmed.

8. **Choose View⇨Toolbars.**

   The Toolbars dialog box appears.

9. **Click the Borders check box to hide the Borders toolbar and click OK.**

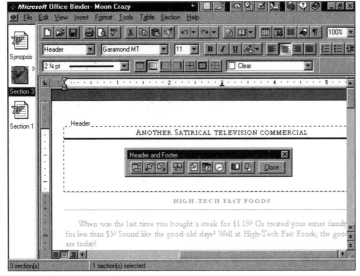

Figure 7-7:
A line appearing as a bottom border in a header.

Setting Up Multicolumn Documents

To create a newsletter or brochure, you'll probably want to display text in two or more columns to give it that professional look that can hide the fact that you really have nothing to say. Here are some reasons to use multicolumn documents:

- ✔ Multicolumn documents permit you to use a smaller type size, which means that you can fit more words on a page.

- ✔ Multicolumn documents make it easy to build white space into each page, permitting you to include columns of white space that form a pleasing contrast with the text.

- ✔ Multicolumn documents offer more opportunities for creative placement of photographs and other graphics. Small illustrations, scanned images, and charts can be placed in the narrow columns of white space. Larger graphics can begin in a text column and extend into the adjacent column of white space. Likewise, large, horizontal graphics can extend across multiple columns; a large photo, for example, can extend over two columns of a three-column grid.

To set up a multicolumn document quickly, follow these steps:

1. Click the Column button in the Standard toolbar.

The Column menu appears (see Figure 7-8).

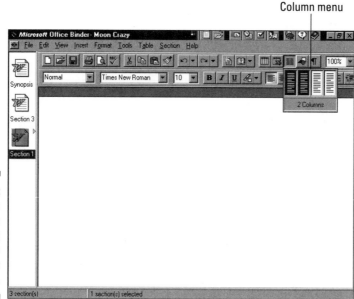

Column menu

Figure 7-8:
The Column
menu
appearing
beneath the
Column
button.

2. Hold down the left mouse button and drag the mouse to select the number of columns you want.

Word immediately converts your document into a multicolumn document.

Creating columns this way is fast and easy, but it creates columns of uniform size. This is why you may want to customize column widths.

To create customized columns, follow these steps:

1. Choose Format⇨Columns.

The Columns dialog box appears (see Figure 7-9).

2. In the Presets group, click the type of column you want. (Or type the number of columns you want in the Number of Columns box.)

3. Clear the Equal Column Width check box if you want to create columns of different widths. Then define those widths in the Width and Spacing group.

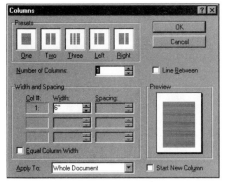

Figure 7-9:
The
Columns
dialog box.

4. **Click the Line Between check box if you want to add vertical lines between the columns.**

5. **Click OK.**

   Word displays your document in multiple columns.

I'm Innocent! This Is a Frame-Up!

If you're serious about using Word for desktop publishing, you'll want to use frames. Think of a frame as a container that can display text, illustrations, scanned photographs, charts, or tables.

The advantage of frames is that they offer a combination of flexibility and accuracy that otherwise is unavailable. Unlike text, a frame can be dragged anywhere on the page — even beyond the text area.

Creating, moving, and resizing frames

To insert a frame into a document, follow these steps:

1. **Choose Insert⇔Frame.**

   The mouse pointer turns into a cross.

2. **Click the spot in your document where you want to insert the top left corner of the frame (keeping the left mouse button held down) and create a rectangle of the desired size by dragging (the mouse) diagonally down from left to right.**

3. **Release the mouse button when you finish drawing the frame.**

   The frame appears in your document as a border of diagonal lines, as shown in Figure 7-10.

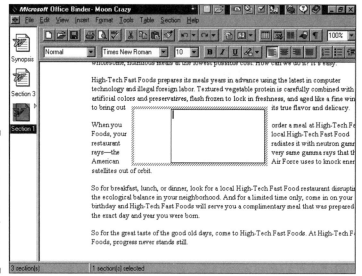

Figure 7-10:
A frame
plopped in
the middle
of a
perfectly
good
document.

Notice the blinking insertion point. If you want, you can begin typing text in immediately.

Also notice the diagonal lines that create the border of the frame. When you move the mouse pointer over the border, the mouse pointer changes to a four-headed arrow, and you then can drag the frame anywhere in the document or (if more than one page is visible on-screen) to a different page.

The first time you click the border, eight resizing handles appear around the frame. By dragging one of the side handles, you can make the frame wider. You can drag the frame beyond the boundaries of a column so that the frame extends over two or more columns.

Formatting and positioning frames

To format a frame, follow these steps:

1. **Click the frame that you want to format.**

2. **Choose Format⇨Frame.**

   The Frame dialog box appears, as shown in Figure 7-11.

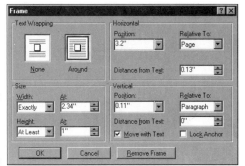

Figure 7-11:
The Frame
dialog box.

3. **Change whatever options you want from the bewildering selection available and click OK.**

   • **Text Wrapping options:** Define how text appears around your frame

   • **Horizontal options:** Define a new horizontal position for your frame

   • **Vertical options:** Define a new vertical position for your frame

   • **Size options:** Define (what else?) the size of the frame

4. **Choose Format⇨Borders and Shading.**

   The Paragraph Borders and Shading dialog box appears (see Figure 7-12).

5. **Change whatever options you want and click OK.**

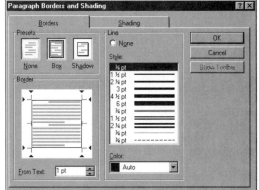

Figure 7-12:
The
Paragraph
Borders and
Shading
dialog box.

If you click the Shading tab in the Paragraph Borders and Shading dialog box, you can choose shading to make your frame stand out as a sidebar, as shown in Figure 7-13.

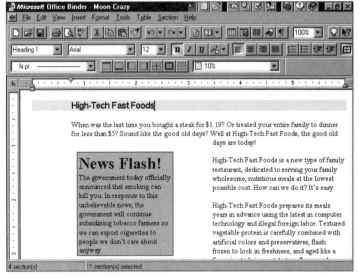

Figure 7-13:
An example
of a shaded
frame used
to create a
sidebar.

Become an importer of fine art!

Not only can frames contain text, but they can hold graphics as well. Graphics can be any of the following:

- ✔ The extensive clip art collection included with Word
- ✔ Custom illustrations created with drawing programs such as Adobe Illustrator, Aldus Freehand, CorelDRAW!, Visio, and ABC Flow Charter
- ✔ Scanned photographs

To insert graphics in a frame, follow these steps:

1. **Create your frame and click inside it.**

2. **Choose Insert⇨Picture.**

   The Insert Picture dialog box appears, as shown in Figure 7-14.

3. **Click the graphics file that you want to import into the frame. (You may have to dig through several folders to find the file you want.)**

4. **Click OK.**

   Word displays your picture in the frame.

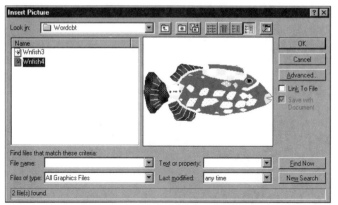

Figure 7-14:
The Insert
Picture
dialog box.

To resize the graphic image, first click it to display the eight resizing handles and then drag the handles as desired.

  ✔ To stretch the image horizontally or vertically, drag one of the middle handles. Drag into the image to make it smaller; drag away from the image to make it larger. The distortion is likely to become very noticeable.

  ✔ To increase or decrease image size proportionately, drag one of the corner handles. This method maintains the illustration's original aspect ratio (height-to-width relationship). Dragging toward the illustration makes it smaller; dragging away from the illustration makes it larger.

Cropping lets you adjust the size of your frame without adjusting the graphic image at the same time. To crop a graphic, hold down the Shift key while dragging one of the middle handles into the illustration.

Reformatting imported images

Click the graphic image with the right mouse button to display a shortcut menu that offers the following options:

  ✔ **Cut:** Removes a graphic image
  ✔ **Copy:** Copies a graphic image
  ✔ **Paste:** Inserts a previously cut or copied graphic image
  ✔ **Edit Picture:** Lets you edit the graphic image, add text to the image, combine images, recolor an image, or change its fill patterns

  ✔ **Borders and Shading:** Adds a line around the graphic to separate it from adjacent text

  ✔ **Caption:** Adds an automatically numbered caption to identify the graphic. Clicking the Caption option displays the Caption dialog box, where you can type the caption text and indicate where you want the caption to appear (see Figure 7-15). Word automatically updates caption numbers as you add or delete graphics.

  ✔ **Format Frame:** Displays the Frame dialog box (refer to Figure 7-11) so that you can change the size and position of the frame

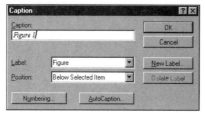

Figure 7-15:
The Caption dialog box.

Adding Drop Caps to Attract Attention

Drop caps are oversize letters that typically are found at the beginning of an article, helping to create a transition between the headline and the body text.

To add a drop cap, follow these steps:

1. **Highlight the first letter of the paragraph in which you want the drop cap to appear.**

2. **Choose Format⇨Drop Cap.**

   The Drop Cap dialog box appears, as shown in Figure 7-16.

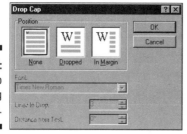

Figure 7-16:
The Drop Cap dialog box.

3. Choose a position.

In most cases, the appropriate choice is <u>D</u>ropped. If you are working on a single-column document with a deep left-hand margin, however, and if sufficient space is available, you can choose In <u>M</u>argin instead.

4. Click the <u>F</u>ont list box and choose a font.

5. Specify the size of the drop cap by entering a number in the <u>L</u>ines to Drop box or by clicking the up or down arrow.

6. Click OK and behold your new drop cap!

In many cases, you may need to select the drop cap and reposition it so that it aligns properly with the adjacent paragraph.

You often can improve the appearance of paragraphs that contain initial caps by setting the first line of text in uppercase text. Uppercase text provides a smooth transition between the drop cap and the rest of the paragraph.

Part III

How to Excel at the Numbers Game

"These two-color handouts are really going to give our presentation style!"

In this part...

*I*t's time to put away your adding machine and move into the modern age of electronic spreadsheets that can calculate results for you at the touch of a button. Whether you've used a spreadsheet before or don't have the slightest idea what a spreadsheet can do for you, this section can gently guide you through your fears and teach you how to master the premiere spreadsheet in the world, Microsoft Excel.

Not only will you learn what spreadsheets are good for and how they can make your life easier, but you'll also learn shortcuts to make Excel a snap to master. With Excel you can help track your expenses, plan your investments, or manage your company's entire cash flow from the convenience of your personal computer. If you're the type who was never good at math, Excel can do the hard work for you and make you look good in the process.

Chapter 8
Look, Ma! I'm an Accountant!

*M*ost folks who've been around computers for a few years credit (or blame) the first spreadsheet program for getting the computer revolution off the ground. Who cares? You just want to get your work done faster and with fewer errors. Excel allows us non-rocket scientists to work with numbers as though we were NASA engineers. (Well . . . almost.)

What Is a Spreadsheet, Anyway?

If you use, or have seen your accountant use, those green sheets of ledger paper with lines that make it easy to enter information in neat rows and columns, you know what a spreadsheet is. A computer spreadsheet is just the electronic equivalent of green ledger paper.

Like ledger paper, a computer spreadsheet displays rows and columns in the form of a grid, where the intersection of a row and a column creates a cell. Each cell can hold a number, text, or a formula.

So what's so wonderful about electronic spreadsheets? Why not just use the paper variety?

Are you kidding? With that icky old paper-and-pencil method, you have to perform calculations by hand. Blech! The worst part is that when you change numbers that affect one calculation, you have to perform any related calculations — by hand — all over again.

Laziness is the mother of invention

Back in 1979, two business students, Dan Bricklin and Bob Frankston, decided to spend less time with their homework so that they'd have more time for more important activities, like partying.

What to do? Perhaps they could put their new computers to work recalculating their business homework. So they did what any lazy business student would do: They wrote the world's first spreadsheet program and called the program VisiCalc, as in Visible Calculator. Pretty clever, huh?

Every spreadsheet program since then, including Excel, owes its existence to Dan and Bob. So if you don't like Excel, now you know who to blame.

That's why you want to use a spreadsheet like Excel. The moment you change one number in your spreadsheet, Excel automatically calculates a new result and recalculates any related formulas as well. Change a number, and — zap! — all the calculations are updated faster than you can say $E=mc^2$.

Basically, to use a spreadsheet, you need the three following items:

- ✔ Numbers
- ✔ Labels
- ✔ Formulas and Functions

Numbers can represent amounts, lengths, or quantities, such as $50.54, 309, or 0.094.

Labels simply identify what your spreadsheet numbers mean, in case you forget. Typical labels are "May," "Western Sales Region," or "Total Amount We Lost Through Fred's Stupidity."

Formulas let you calculate new results based on the numbers you've typed in. Formulas can be as simple as adding two numbers together or as complicated as calculating third order differential equations that nobody really cares about. *Functions* are predefined formulas that are built-in to Excel, such as calculating a square root.

Although spreadsheets mimic boring paper ledgers, they offer forecasting and budgeting capabilities that let you experiment with a variety of "what-if" scenarios. After entering all your budget figures, you can ask questions like, "What would happen if the cost of goods goes up 10 percent?" or "What would happen if our sales plummet 90 percent?" or "What would happen if I gave myself a million-dollar raise?"

Spreadsheets also are handy places to store lists. Because creating a name and address list in Excel is so easy, you may decide that it's the tool of choice for simple data management. Excel provides most of the tools you'll need for manipulating simple databases, such as sorting and searching.

To make Excel easy to use, Excel offers similar menus and toolbars to Word (and PowerPoint, for that matter), so you should feel pretty much at home as soon as you start Excel (see Figure 8-1). Speaking of starting Excel . . .

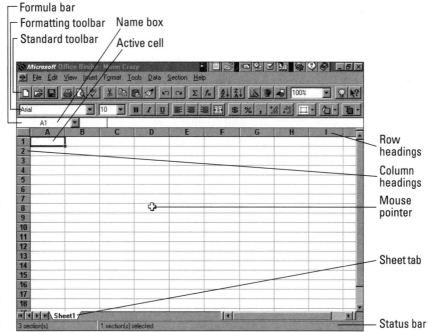

Figure 8-1:
The initial Excel screen, showing a blank worksheet.

You can start Microsoft Excel in three easy ways:

- ✔ Click the Start button in the Windows 95 Taskbar and choose Programs⇨Microsoft Excel. (This action starts Microsoft Excel as a separate program.)

- ✔ Click the Start a New Document button on the Microsoft Office Shortcut Bar and create a new Excel worksheet.

- ✔ Choose Section⇨Add and select Microsoft Excel Worksheet to open an Excel worksheet from within a binder.

After you've got Microsoft Excel started, get acquainted with the screen by staring at it and pretending you're in deep thought. Then browse through the following items:

- If you're not sure which toolbar button does what, you can just move the mouse pointer over the button to display a ToolTip that shows the name of the button. The left side of the status bar displays a longer description of the button's function.

- Excel spreadsheet files are called *workbooks,* each of which may include up to 256 individual *worksheets.* Each worksheet contains up to 256 vertical columns and 16,384 horizontal rows.

- Worksheets are identified by their sheet tabs; you can use the shortcut menu to rename them. To rename a sheet, right-click the sheet tab, and then click Rename. Enter a new, more descriptive name in the Rename Sheet dialog box, and then click the OK button.

- Columns are designated with letters (A, B, C, and so on), and rows are numbered (1, 2, 3, and so on).

- The intersection of a row and a column is called a *cell.* Any data that you enter into a worksheet — whether that data is numbers or text — is entered into cells.

- Cells are designated by their column letter followed by their row numbers. For example, the cell at the intersection of column G and row 12 is cell G12.

- Because your computer screen can display only a small portion of a worksheet, you'll use the scroll bars and other navigation techniques to get to the far reaches of larger worksheets.

Putting Stuff in a Worksheet

To enter data into a worksheet, just click in the cell where you want to place the data and start typing. (If you hate mice, use the cursor keys to move the cursor to a cell and then start typing. Or press Ctrl+G and type a cell address, such as A5.) It's just that simple. As you type, the data appears both in the cell and in the formula bar.

Three little buttons appear in the formula bar as soon as you start typing. The button marked with the red X is the Cancel button, the one with the green check mark is the Enter button, and the one with the fx symbol is the Function Wizard button.

Excel's no dummy. Whether you enter text, numbers, or even dates, it knows what you want and responds appropriately (usually).

- ✔ Text is automatically aligned at the left side of the cell, and numbers (including dates, such as Feb. 10, 1996) are aligned at the right side.

- ✔ Complete a cell entry by clicking the Enter button, pressing an arrow key to move to another cell, or pressing Enter on your keyboard.

- ✔ When you press the Enter key to complete a cell entry, the cell pointer moves down one row. This method is best for entering a column of data.

- ✔ You can cancel a cell entry before completing it by pressing the Esc key or clicking the Cancel button in the formula bar.

- ✔ Press the Backspace key to erase cell data one character at a time before completing the cell entry.

- ✔ You can correct data that has already been entered by typing a new entry or by pressing the F2 key, which puts you in Edit mode. In Edit mode, you can correct the data just as you would before completing a cell entry. When you are in Edit mode, you must complete the cell entry by clicking the Enter button or pressing Enter; you can't complete the edit by pressing an arrow key, as you can when you first enter data in the cell.

- ✔ Press the Delete key to erase the contents of a cell.

Names, ranges, and addresses

When a cell becomes active, its address (column letter and row number) appears in the name box to the left of the formula bar.

The name box isn't called the name box for nothing. You can use the name box to assign descriptive names to cells and ranges. (A *range* is a group of two or more cells.) In addition, you can use the name box to move to named cells and ranges that you specify.

Assigning names can make finding portions of a worksheet much easier. For example, figuring out where your budget's 1995 income area is a lot easier if the budget is called *95income* instead of *F22 through J43*.

Excel is an easy date

If you've worked with older spreadsheet programs that require you to enter dates in a very rigid format — such as @DATE(96,2,10) for February 10, 1996 — you can thank your lucky stars (or Bill Gates) that you have Excel.

In Excel, you can enter dates just about any way that you'd normally write them. For example, you can enter 2/2/96, Feb 2, 1996, or February 2, 1996. You may still want to format the dates so that they appear the way you want, but at least getting the dates into your worksheets is easy. (Formatting is covered later in this chapter.)

To assign a range name, follow these steps:

1. **Select the range of cells you want to name by dragging (holding down the left mouse button while dragging the mouse).**

   The range is highlighted, and the first cell in the range becomes the active cell. The active cell's address appears in the name box.

2. **Move the mouse pointer into the name box (the left box in the formula bar).**

   The mouse pointer assumes the shape of an I-beam.

3. **Click the name box.**

   The cell address is highlighted and moves to the left side of the selected range.

4. **Type the name that you want to assign to the range.**

5. **Press Enter.**

The name that you assigned appears in the name box.

To jump to a named range, follow these steps:

1. **Click the name box.**

2. **Click the downward pointing arrow in the name box to display a list of named ranges and click the named range you want. (Or type the name of the range to which you want to move and press Enter. Make sure that you don't type any spaces in the range name.)**

The range name that you entered is highlighted, and the cell in the upper left corner of the range is the active cell.

- ✔ Use the name box to jump to any cell address or range. Just click the name box and then enter the address or range. To move to range W5 through X15, for example, click the name box, type **W5:X15**, and press Enter. (Or press Ctrl+G and type the cell address or range.)

- ✔ Range addresses are always separated by a colon (:), as in B3:C8.

- ✔ You don't have to remember, or even type, range names. You can find a list of the names that you've assigned in the current workbook by clicking the down arrow on the right side of the name box in the Formula toolbar. A list of names appears; you can just click the name of the range you want.

- ✔ You'll find that a lot of the time you spend working with spreadsheets involves selecting ranges before formatting and performing other types of worksheet manipulation.

Copying text and numbers

All the Office programs use the same methods to copy data. In Excel, select the cell or range that you want to copy, click the Copy button in the Standard toolbar, move to where you want to deposit the copied data, and then click the Paste button. Easy.

There's an even easier way to copy data if you're copying to adjacent cells; just follow these steps:

1. **Position the mouse pointer over the fill handle (the little black box in the lower-right corner of the cell pointer).**

   The mouse pointer turns into a black cross.

2. **Hold down the left mouse button and drag in the direction in which you want to copy.**

- Excel is so smart, it usually knows when a cell entry should be incremented. For example, if you enter **January** or **Monday** (or **Jan** or **Mon**) and use the fill handle to drag to the right or down, Excel creates an incremented series, such as January, February, March or Mon, Tues, Wed.

- If you drag the fill handle up or to the left, Excel creates a decremented series: for example, January, December, November.

- Hold down the Ctrl key as you drag the fill handle to increment a cell entry that Excel isn't smart enough to figure out on its own. If you enter 1 in a cell and use the fill handle without Ctrl, you'll get 1, 1, 1. With Ctrl, you'll get 1, 2, 3.

- The Ctrl key has the opposite effect when you use it to copy a cell that Excel normally would increment. If January is entered in a cell, Ctrl causes Excel to copy the cell without incrementing.

Help, Mr. TipWizard!

To help make Excel easier to use, Excel provides a TipWizard. The TipWizard is like a coach who watches what you do and suggests more efficient ways of doing it. This feature is watching all the time, so you don't need to do anything to activate it.

You do, however, need to do something to see the advice that the TipWizard has to offer. When the TipWizard has a suggestion, the light bulb on the TipWizard button in the Standard toolbar "lights up," turning yellow. Click the TipWizard button, and the suggestion appears in its own TipWizard toolbar below the Formatting toolbar.

Suppose that you didn't know about Excel's incrementing capability, and you typed **Jan**, **Feb**, and **Mar**. The TipWizard would tell you that there is a better way to create a series, as shown in Figure 8-2.

Tip Wizard toolbar

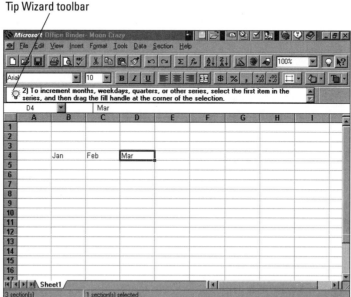

Figure 8-2:
The
TipWizard,
offering
help.

✔ To remove the TipWizard toolbar and reclaim some screen real estate, click the TipWizard button in the Standard toolbar.

✔ It's not a bad idea to leave the TipWizard toolbar on-screen all the time so that you can see new tips as they arise. If you leave the TipWizard on-screen when you exit Excel, it will be there waiting for you with a random Tip of the Day the next time you start Excel.

Save, save, save

In case you missed it in the Word section, you better save your documents on a regular basis, or you'll be sorry.

To save a workbook, including all its worksheets, choose one of the following:

✔ Click the Save button (the one marked with a picture of a disk) in the Standard toolbar.

> ✔ Press Ctrl+S.
>
> ✔ Choose File⊏>Save (if you're using Excel as a separate program).
>
> ✔ Choose File⊏>Save Binder (if you're using Excel within a binder).

Click the Save button at regular intervals — say, every 10 or 20 minutes — just to make sure that you don't lose everything, in case the power goes out.

To have Excel save your data automatically, choose Tools⊏>Add-Ins and choose AutoSave. Then specify a time interval to save your data by choosing Tools⊏>AutoSave.

Calculating by Using Formulas and Functions

Without the capability to perform calculations, Excel wouldn't have much of an advantage over the paper-and-pencil alternative. To get Excel to do your mathematical bidding, you create formulas or use one of its zillions of pre-defined formulas, called *functions*.

To create simple formulas, move to the cell where you want the result of the formula to appear on the spreadsheet and enter the appropriate cell references and math operators. The operators that you'll use most often are:

- + (addition)
- – (subtraction)
- * (multiplication)
- / (division)

Suppose that you want to multiply the contents of cell C4 by the contents of cell C3 and display the results in C5. In this case, to create a formula in C5 to multiply the contents of C4 by the contents of C3, you would follow these steps:

1. **Click cell C5 and then type = (the equal sign).**

   All formulas start with an equal sign—that's the way spreadsheets seem to work.

2. **Type** C3, **or click cell C3.**

   It's often easier to click on cell references than it is to type them.

3. Press * (asterisk)

The asterisk is the multiplication symbol.

4. Type C4, or click cell C4.

5. Press Enter.

The result of the formula instantly appears in C5, as shown in Figure 8-3. The formula in the formula bar should look like this: =C3*C4.

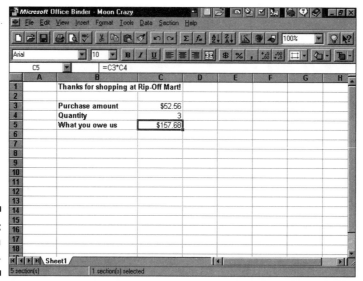

Figure 8-3:
Entering a
formula.

✔ The way that Excel normally displays data on-screen, you can't tell which cells contain formulas and which contain only numbers. The formula bar is the giveaway. You can tell whether a cell contains a formula by looking at the formula bar.

✔ Be very careful not to delete or edit cells that contain formulas by mistake; that can really ruin your day.

✔ If you do accidentally wipe out a formula, click the Undo button in the Standard toolbar before you do anything else.

✔ It's easy to enter formulas incorrectly, so it's important to proofread your worksheets to find out whether the numbers make sense. If you have a formula that should be multiplying 5 by 100 and the answer you get is 48,673, something is wrong!

Editing formulas

After you create a formula, you may need to edit it in case you screwed up typing it the first time, or in case you just need to change it for some unknown reason. To edit a cell containing a formula, follow these steps:

1. **Click on the cell containing the formula you want to change.**

2. **Press F2.**

    The cell displays the formula. Use the Backspace and Delete keys to erase part of your formula and type any new part of the formula.

3. **When you're done, press Enter to see your newly edited formula calculate a result.**

Copying formulas

The procedure for copying formulas generally is the same as for copying any other kind of data. When you copy formulas, however, Excel understands that you normally want the copies to be relative to their new location.

Suppose that the numbers in row 3 are the number of hours your employees worked last month and that the numbers in row 4 are their wages, in dollars per hour. If you copy the formula in C5 (=C3*C4) to cell D5, you'd want the copy to change to =D3*D4. And that's exactly what happens.

Excel uses relative addressing, so when you copy a formula, Excel copies the logic of the formula rather than the formula itself. The logic that Excel uses when you copy =C3*C4 from C5 to D5 is "Multiply the contents of the cell two rows up by the contents of the cell one row up."

It's especially important to look at the formulas that Excel creates as you copy. Excel makes assumptions when you copy formulas. And you know what can happen when you assume.

Having SUM fun

The most frequently used Excel function is the SUM function, which adds a range of two or more cells. Functions have a slightly different syntax from that of the formulas that you create; functions begin with the equal sign, but that's where the similarity ends.

After the equal sign comes the name of the function, followed by parentheses that contain the function's arguments. *Arguments* are the data or cell references that the function needs to perform its calculations. In the case of the SUM function, the only argument is the range of cells to be summed.

To sum a range of cells, follow these steps:

1. **Click the cell where you want the result of the function to appear and type =SUM(.**

2. **Type the range of cells to be summed (for example, F12:F24), or drag the mouse over the range that you want to sum.**

3. **Type) and press Enter to complete the entry.**

The sum of the range appears instantly.

- You can include more than one range in the SUM argument by separating the ranges with a comma. For example, the function =SUM(F12:F24,G18:G33) returns the sum of both ranges.

- The easiest way to sum a range is to have Excel do all the work for you. Just move to the result cell, and click the AutoSum button (it looks like a sideways *M*) in the Standard toolbar. Excel creates a formula with the SUM function and includes the adjacent contiguous range. The program doesn't always guess the correct range, but it's worth a try.

- As you start using functions, you'll find that you don't have to remember their syntax if you use the Function Wizard button (the one with fx on it) in the Standard toolbar. (To really learn how to use the Function Wizard button, pick up a copy of *Excel For Windows 95 For Dummies*.)

Making Your Numbers Pretty: No-Sweat Formatting

Although entering a bunch of numbers, text, and formulas can provide you needed feedback, you may not end up with anything very attractive. Changing various formatting attributes can turn a dull, lifeless worksheet into a powerful persuader. And persuasion, after all, often is what worksheets are designed for. You want your boss to approve your budget proposals, and a beautiful worksheet will give the boss the impression that you gave it more thought than you really did.

Excel offers an almost unlimited variety of formatting options. Fonts, borders, number styles, and alignment are just some of the tools that you can use to prettify your worksheet.

As a general rule, formatting follows this sequence: Select the cell or range of cells to be formatted and then choose the formatting you want to apply. For example, if you want to make the entries in a range of cells bold, drag the mouse over the range, and then click the Bold button in the Formatting toolbar.

✔ Most formatting affects cells or ranges of cells. Choose Format⇨Cells to display the Format Cells dialog box, which contains all the cell-formatting options. Notice the tabs for the formatting categories at the top of the dialog box. Click a tab to move to the portion of the dialog box that contains that category's options.

✔ The Formatting toolbar contains buttons for many of the most common formatting tasks, including fonts and sizes; bold, underline, and italic; alignment options; and common number styles. With most of these buttons, you're just a click away from formatting happiness.

✔ If you apply any formatting by mistake, immediately click the Undo button to remove the formatting.

✔ After applying a variety of formatting attributes to a range, you may wonder how you'll remember exactly what you did so that you can format another range the same way. No problem — just click one of the formatted cells, click the Format Painter button in the Standard toolbar, and then drag across the range that you want to format like the original range. *Voilà!*

✔ With all the formatting options at your disposal, it's easy to get carried away. You may be tempted to use too many options in a worksheet — 15 fonts, 10 border styles, all the colors in the rainbow. You can create a real mess. If you're not a professional designer, keep your worksheets simple.

Using AutoFormat

If you're not a designer, but you long for fancier formatting than you can pull off on your own, Excel provides some professional help in the form of AutoFormat.

To use AutoFormat, follow these steps:

1. Select the data that you want to format.

2. Choose Format⇨AutoFormat.

The AutoFormat dialog box appears (see Figure 8-4).

Figure 8-4:
The
AutoFormat
dialog box.

AutoFormat			? X

Table Format:

Simple
Classic 1
Classic 2
Classic 3
Accounting 1
Accounting 2
Accounting 3
Accounting 4
Colorful 1
Colorful 2
Colorful 3

Sample

	Jan	Feb	Mar	Total
East	7	7	5	19
West	6	4	7	17
South	8	7	9	24
Total	21	18	21	60

OK
Cancel
Options >>

3. Choose a format in the Table Format box and click OK.

From within the AutoFormat dialog box, you can browse through the different types of formats by clicking on the Table Format list. Each time you click on a different table format, the Sample box shows you how it will format your data.

✔ After using AutoFormat, you still may need to apply some specific formatting to portions of the worksheet. If you want to call attention to a particular cell or range, for example, you could increase the size or change the color of the data in those cells.

✔ If you want to restrict the types of formatting that AutoFormat will apply, click the Options button in the AutoFormat dialog box; then deselect the Formats to Apply options that you don't want AutoFormat to use. If you carefully selected the fonts that you want to use, for example, remove the check from the Font check box by clicking it.

Adjusting column widths

It won't be too long before you find that a lot of your data is truncated, scrunched, weird, or otherwise not displayed the way you intended. This problem often is the result of columns that are too narrow.

You can adjust columns by positioning the mouse pointer on the right border of the column heading (column headings are the letters above the cells) and dragging left to decrease the column width or right to increase it.

✔ You can let Excel figure out the optimal width for the column by double-clicking the border line in the column heading. You'll end up with a column that's just a bit wider than its longest entry.

✔ You may not want a particular column to be adjusted for its longest entry if, for example, one of its entries is a long title. If you use the automatic column width feature, you could end up with a column that is way too wide. To get around this little problem, click the column heading to select all the cells in the column; then hold down the Ctrl key and click the cell that you want to exclude from the automatic adjustment. Finally, from the menu bar, choose Format⇨Column⇨AutoFit Selection.

Sending Your Numbers to the Printer

After you finish putting together your masterpiece worksheets, the next step is getting them on paper. That way people don't have to crowd around your computer to see your worksheet and all the fancy formulas and numbers you've created.

Before printing your numbers, you might want to consider the following tips:

✔ Click the Page Setup button in the Print dialog box to change additional print options, such as orientation, margins, and grid lines.

✔ The Header/Footer tab of the Page Setup dialog box also allows you to add headers (text that appears at the top of a page) and footers (text that appears at the bottom of a page).

✔ After you change specifications in the Print and Page Setup dialog boxes, click the Print toolbar button to use the new settings the next time you print, therefore bypassing any dialog box interruptions.

✔ Before sending the document to the printer, check it out with Print Preview. You can get to Print Preview by clicking the Print Preview button in the Print dialog box or the one in the Standard toolbar. Using Print Preview can save you a lot of paper.

To print your worksheet, choose one of the following:

✔ Click the Print button on the Standard toolbar.

✔ Press Ctrl+P.

✔ Choose File⇨Print (if you're using Excel as a separate program).

✔ Choose File⇨Print Binder (if you're using Excel within a binder).

Chapter 9

And This Chart Proves Conclusively...

· ·

In This Chapter

▶ Turning numbers into charts

▶ Using the ChartWizard

▶ Changing chart types

▶ Picking the best chart type for the job

▶ Printing charts

· ·

A picture may be worth a thousand words, but unless your picture makes sense, the only words it's likely to evoke will be four-letter ones. Fortunately, Excel can help you make pretty-looking charts almost effortlessly so that you won't have to say a thing.

Turning Numbers into Charts

Excel can create gorgeous (or ugly) charts that graphically represent the numbers in your worksheets. As with every other aspect of Excel, the number of charting options can be overwhelming. But take heart — after you have your data entered in a worksheet, creating a chart is just a matter of letting Excel know which information you want to use, what type of chart you want, and where to put it.

Although you don't need to know much charting lingo to create charts, familiarity with a few terms will help keep you on the right track.

All charts contain at least one data series. A *data series* is just a set of values for a particular category. Sales figures for January, February, and March, for example, are one data series. The cost-of-goods figures for the same period are another data series.

Most charts also have an x-axis and a y-axis. The *x-axis* is the horizontal plane, and the *y-axis* is the vertical plane.

In most worksheets, the x-axis (sometimes called the category axis) plots the values in the data series over time. The y-axis (sometimes called the value axis) plots the amount of the numbers.

✔ You'll find that it's easiest to create Excel charts if your data is set up in normal table format, using contiguous rows and columns. Don't insert any blank rows or columns into the table.

✔ You can create a chart in the same sheet that contains the worksheet data or in a different sheet. There is no particular advantage to placing the chart in its own sheet, unless you are creating an on-screen presentation.

✔ Adding a new data series to a chart is as easy as dragging and dropping. Select the data in the new series, position the mouse pointer on the bottom border of the selection so that the pointer becomes an arrow, drag the series into the chart, and release the mouse button.

✔ Don't go nuts and chart everything in sight. Chart only the data that can really benefit from graphical representation.

Using the ChartWizard

To help you create charts (almost) automatically, Excel has something called a *ChartWizard*, which acts like a kindly computer guru who gently guides you through the process of creating charts from your data.

To create a chart with the ChartWizard, follow these steps:

1. **Select all the cells, including the column and row headings, containing the data you want to chart, as shown in Figure 9-1.**

   The column headings will be used as x-axis labels, and the row headings will be used in the chart legend.

2. **Click the ChartWizard button in the Standard toolbar.**

   The mouse pointer becomes a crosshair with a tiny chart attached. (If you want to create the chart in its own worksheet, instead of clicking the ChartWizard button, click Insert⇨Chart⇨As New Sheet. The remaining steps are the same.)

3. **Drag the mouse down and to the right to select the portion of the worksheet you want the chart to occupy (see Figure 9-2).**

Row headings   Chart Wizard button

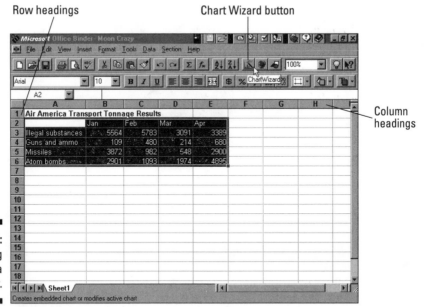

Column headings

Figure 9-1:
Selecting
data in a
worksheet.

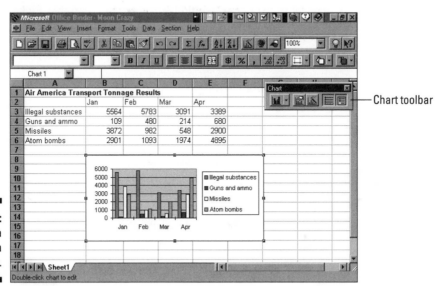

Chart toolbar

Figure 9-2:
Placing a
chart on a
worksheet.

4. Release the mouse button.

The first ChartWizard dialog box appears, as shown in Figure 9-3.

(The dollar signs in the range just mean that Excel is using absolute cell addressing; no need to give them a second thought.)

Figure 9-3:
The first
ChartWizard
dialog box.

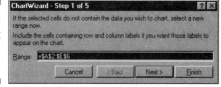

5. Click <u>N</u>ext >.

The second ChartWizard dialog box appears, as shown in Figure 9-4, to let you choose the chart type. Don't spend too much time worrying about the chart type now since you can change the chart type at any time.

(If you want to change a chart later, you can always follow the instructions listed in the "Changing chart types" section. If you don't have the slightest clue what type of chart would be best to use, read the "Picking the best chart type for the job" section.)

Figure 9-4:
The second
ChartWizard
dialog box.

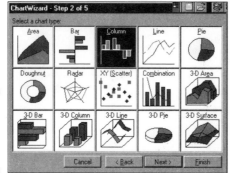

6. Click the picture of the chart type that you want to use, and then click <u>N</u>ext >.

The next ChartWizard dialog box appears, as shown in Figure 9-5, letting you choose specific formats of your chosen chart.

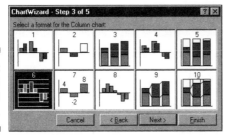

Figure 9-5:
The third
ChartWizard
dialog box.

7. **Click the picture of the chart format that you want to use, and then click _Next_ >.**

The fourth ChartWizard dialog box appears, shown in Figure 9-6. As you make option changes in this dialog box and the next one, your changes are reflected in the preview of the chart.

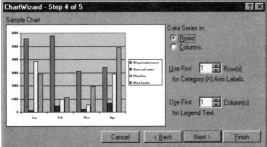

Figure 9-6:
The fourth
ChartWizard
dialog box.

8. **Make any necessary changes and then click _Next_ >.**

The fifth (and final) ChartWizard dialog box appears, as shown in Figure 9-7. This dialog box allows you to specify whether you want to add a legend, as well as chart and axis titles.

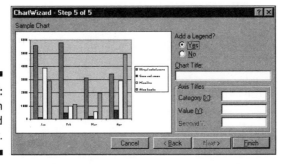

Figure 9-7:
The fifth
ChartWizard
dialog box.

9. Type a title in the Chart Title box.

10. Click the Finish button to insert the finished chart into the worksheet.

The Chart toolbar pops up, as shown in Figure 9-8.

11. Click anywhere in the worksheet to remove the Chart toolbar.

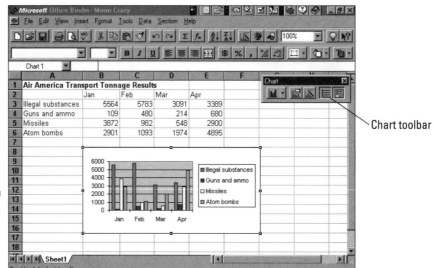

Chart toolbar

Figure 9-8:
A sample
chart in a
worksheet.

As you can see, with the Wizard's help, you can create eye-catching charts quickly and easily. So feel free to experiment and see what types of charts display your data best.

✔ The little black rectangles on the corners and the sides of the chart's border are called *handles,* which indicate that the chart is selected.

✔ To resize the chart, position the mouse pointer on one of the handles, and click and drag.

✔ You can reposition the chart by placing the mouse pointer inside the chart and clicking and dragging.

✔ You can edit a chart's appearance by double-clicking on it. After editing a chart, get out of Edit mode by clicking outside the chart.

✔ Any changes that you make to the numbers in the worksheet are reflected immediately in the chart.

Changing chart types

If, after expending all that brainpower to create a chart with all the elements just the way you want them, you realize — horror of horrors — that you've selected the wrong chart type, don't worry: Excel lets you change your chart type any time you want.

To change the chart type, follow these steps:

1. Click on the chart that you want to change.

2. Click the down arrow in the Chart Type button on the Chart toolbar.

The Chart Type menu appears, as shown in Figure 9-9. It should look pretty familiar because its buttons look similar to the chart type choices displayed in the second ChartWizard dialog box.

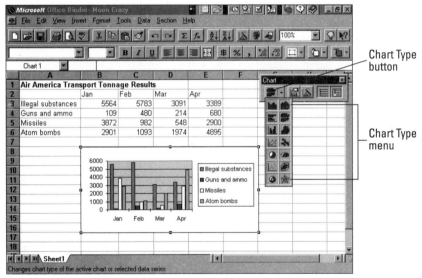

Figure 9-9:
Using the Chart Type menu to change your chart type.

3. Click on the picture of the chart type you want to use.

4. Click OK and — poof! — the chart type changes.

Figure 9-10 displays a chart that has changed from a column chart to a bar chart.

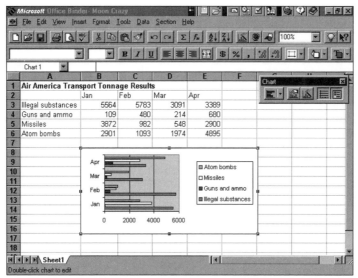

Figure 9-10:
A changed
chart.

✔ Changing the chart type can produce unexpected and disastrous results. If the chart looks really messed up after you change its type, click the Undo button in the Standard toolbar right away. It's also not a bad idea to save your workbook before making any major change such as this.

✔ You may need to reposition or resize the chart after changing its type.

Picking the best chart type for the job

In case you haven't noticed, some types of charts are better for presenting certain information than others. Just to give you some basic rules of thumb, the following is a quick description of the more common chart types, which you can review by looking back at Figure 9-4.

Column charts — Excel's default chart type — often are used for comparing two or more related data series at a specific point in time or a small amount of data over time. For example, you might use a column chart to display two data series (sales versus cost of goods) over time (a three-month period).

Bar charts are column charts turned on their sides; the columns are horizontal instead of vertical.

Pie charts are great for displaying proportional relationships among data items, such as the share that each month's sales contribute to sales for the quarter. The pie chart's primary limitation is that it can display only one data series.

Doughnut charts are similar to pie charts and are used for the same purpose (displaying proportional relationships among data items). They have one major advantage over pie charts, however: They can be used to plot more than one data series. A doughnut chart that contains more than one data series uses a separate ring for each series.

Line charts are used to emphasize the continuity of data over time. These charts are also a good choice for showing trends. They are especially useful for showing large sets of data, such as sales of a product over a five-year period. Several of the line-chart formatting options are particularly useful for charting data that experiences highs and lows, such as snowfall amounts or stock prices, and sometimes are referred to as high-low and high-low-close charts.

Area charts are essentially line charts with the spaces between the lines filled in.

Radar charts are similar to line charts but are often used to compare the whole value of several data series.

XY charts use both axes for values. This arrangement allows you to plot relationships between two data series, such as the effect of temperature on an electronic component's failure rate.

Combination charts allow you to combine two chart types to contrast multiple data series. For example, you might use the column-chart portion of a combination chart to plot store sales and a line chart to show the store's projected sales.

- ✔ Many of the chart types are available in 3-D, which just gives you a different look for the chart. Use this option if you like it.

- ✔ There are no hard and fast rules about which chart type must be used in each situation. Experiment with different types and the many other options for making your charts to get your point across as effectively as possible.

Printing Charts

Once you have a chart, it only makes sense to print it out so that you can show your wonderful work of art to others. (Of course, if you don't have a color printer, your charts are going to appear in boring black and white.)

- ✔ Before clicking the OK button, it's a good idea to click the Print Preview button so that you'll know whether you're about to print the right stuff. If the preview looks good, click the Print button in the Preview window.

- ✔ Make sure that your printer is turned on, paper is loaded, and the on-line light is on. To print your chart in a worksheet, choose one of the following:
- ✔ Press Ctrl+P.
- ✔ Click the Print button in the Standard toolbar.
- ✔ Choose File➪Print (if you're using Excel as a separate program).
- ✔ Choose File➪Print Binder (if you're using Excel within a binder).

Chapter 10

Excel Features That Make Economists of Us All

● ●

In This Chapter

▶ Finding answers with Goal Seek

▶ Sorting tables and other cool database stuff

▶ Analyzing data with PivotTables

▶ Adding cell notes

● ●

*A*lthough you can use Excel as a simple spreadsheet, it really contains loads of special commands that allow you to do all sorts of weird calculations. To get the most out of Excel, you need to go beyond the obvious and expected features. For a glimpse into some useful and unexpected features, read on.

Finding Answers with Goal Seek

The typical worksheet works something like this: enter data, create formulas, get answers. Bor-ring! Wouldn't it be great if you could just tell Excel what answer you want and have it adjust the data so that you get that answer? Your wish is Excel's command.

The feature that performs this magical feat is called Goal Seek. Just tell Goal Seek what result you want and which cell value to change to get that result.

To use Goal Seek to find the answer that you've been seeking, follow these steps:

1. Click the cell in which you want the new answer to appear. (This cell must contain a formula.)

2. Click Tools⇨Goal Seek.

The Goal Seek dialog box appears, with the address of the selected cell in the Set cell text box (see Figure 10-1). Remember: those dollar signs indicate that the cell reference is absolute instead of relative.

(Absolute reference means you're specifying a specific cell or range of cells. Relative reference means you're specifying the data stored in a cell or range of cells, but not the cell addresses themselves.)

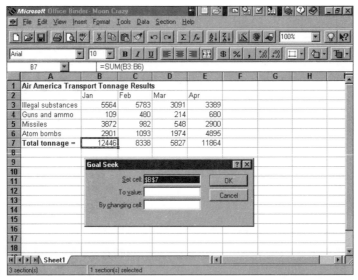

Figure 10-1:
The Goal
Seek dialog
box.

3. Click in the To value text box and type the answer you want.

For example, you may want to find out the tonnage of guns and ammo that would be required to generate a total January tonnage value of 14,000; you would type **14000** in the To value text box.

4. Click in the By changing cell text box.

This box is where you tell Excel which value to change to reach your goal.

5. Click the cell containing the value that you want Excel to change to get to your answer.

The cell to be changed must contain a value (a number), not a formula. Excel automatically types the cell address in the By changing cell box.

6. Click OK.

Excel automatically changes your chosen cell to provide the result that you requested. The Goal Seek Status dialog box shows the target value and the current value, which should be the same (see Figure 10-2).

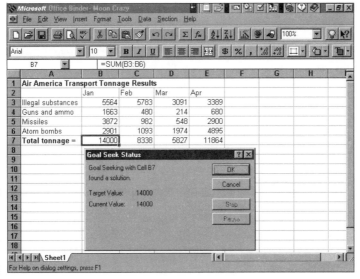

Figure 10-2:
The Goal
Seek Status
dialog box.

7. **Click OK to accept the changes or click Cancel to have the numbers revert to their original state.**

Excel's Goal Seeking feature may seem magical, especially when compared to doing the same calculations with an adding machine, but the Goal Seeking feature has a few flaws.

✔ In some cases, the goal you are trying to reach may be so complex that it takes your computer a while to find it. Be patient.

✔ In rare instances, Goal Seek may not be able to find the value that will give you exactly the answer you want, but it will get as close as possible.

✔ If you click the OK button in the Goal Seek Status dialog box by mistake and want the numbers back the way they were, click the Undo button in the Standard toolbar before you do anything else.

Sorting Tables and Other Cool Database Stuff

Although Excel is a spreadsheet, you can also torture it into a simple database. As far as Excel is concerned, a database is just a bunch of information in table format that you want to store and manipulate.

To create an Excel database table, start by entering column headings to label the items of information that you want to include. For a customer list, you might have items such as FIRST NAME, LAST NAME, and ADDRESS. Each of these items is called a *field*. All the items in a single row of the table are called a *record*. So the database consists of a bunch of records that consist of a bunch of fields.

Enter the data for the records just as you enter data in a normal worksheet, directly below the field-name labels.

TIP

✔ Enter the field names (column headings) in UPPERCASE so that Excel automatically detects them as field names.

✔ Don't worry about the order of the records; you'll learn how to sort them a bit later in this chapter.

Using an easier form of data entry

Entering data directly into the database table is easy enough, but it does have some drawbacks.

First, if you have lots of fields, you'll be scrolling back and forth, and you won't be able to see the first fields in the record as you enter the last. Second, each time you enter a new record, you'll have to find the next row after the end of the table. As your table grows, finding the last row can become more difficult.

To simplify typing data, Excel lets you type new records into a data form and automatically places each record at the end of the table.

To use a data form, follow these steps:

1. **Click in one of the cells in your data table.**

2. **From the menu bar, choose Data⇨Form.**

   A dialog box appears, asking whether you want to use the top row as the header row.

3. **Click OK.**

   The data-form dialog box — with the name of the current worksheet in the title bar — appears as shown in Figure 10-3, displaying the first record.

4. **Click New.**

   All the fields in the dialog box are cleared so that you can start entering a new record.

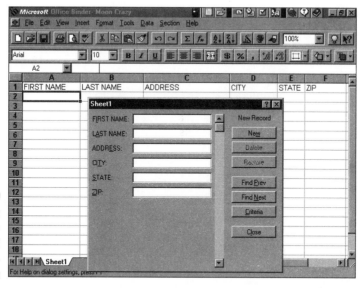

Figure 10-3:
The data-
form dialog
box.

5. **Type the data for the first field and then press the Tab key to move to the next field.**

6. **Continue entering data until all the fields for the record are entered and then click New again (or just press Enter).**

   Each time that you click New, the new record is placed at the bottom of the table, the text boxes are cleared, and you can start entering the next record.

7. **After entering all the records for this session using the data form, click Close.**

See how easy it is to enter data in records without having to use the scroll bar even once?

✔ Don't forget to save your work periodically (such as every 10 to 20 minutes) by clicking the Save button in the Standard toolbar. (To make Excel save your data automatically, choose Tools⇨AddIns, and click the AutoSave check box.)

✔ Format the fields in the existing records before using the data form. Each new record will use the formatting that you applied. If you format the Name fields with bold, for example, all new names will be bold.

✔ You can get into trouble if you enter ZIP codes as numbers. Before you enter new records with the data form, enter the ZIP code field in the first record as text so that Excel won't drop leading zeros. To do this, type an apostrophe (') in front of the ZIP code.

✔ You can duplicate the data from the preceding record by pressing Ctrl+' (apostrophe). If you're entering a series of records for people who live in the same city and state, press Ctrl+' when you get to the CITY field and press Ctrl+' again when you get to the STATE field. (The only drawback to this method is that you will lose any fancy formatting you may have done.)

✔ If you mess up a record, press Esc or click the Restore button if you catch your error before adding the record to the table. If you've already added the record, click the Find Prev or Find Next button until the offending record is displayed in the form and then edit the data or click the Delete button.

✔ Be consistent in the way that you enter records. You may want to merge some of the data with a Word document or another program. Use the same mixed-case format and don't use any spaces or punctuation in the fields.

✔ You can edit records in the data form. Display the record that you want to use by clicking the Find Prev or Find Next button, or click the Criteria button so that you can enter search criteria. If you mess up some of the data as you're editing, press Esc or click the Restore button.

Sorting it all out

Sorting databases is something that you'll do frequently. You may want to sort the list by last name to make it easier to find a particular person in the list; or you may want to sort by ZIP code (if you're creating mailing labels, for example).

Doing a simple table sort is just a click away. (Well, two clicks, really, but why quibble?) To sort the table, follow these steps:

1. **Click any cell in the column by which you want to sort the table.**

   If you want to sort the table by last name, for example, click in any cell in the column that contains the last names (see Figure 10-4). That's one click, if you're counting.

2. **Click the Sort Ascending button (to sort from A through Z) or the Sort Descending button (to sort from Z through A) in the Standard toolbar.**

See? Just two clicks, and the table is sorted (see Figure 10-5). Sorting doesn't physically change your data, just the way that data looks on-screen. When sorting, keep the following ideas in mind:

✔ You can undo a sort by clicking the Undo button in the Standard toolbar immediately after sorting.

✔ If you want to sort by more than one field at a time, you'll need to use the Sort dialog box, which you open by choosing Data⇨Sort from the menu bar. Then click Sort by last names and Then by first names so that all the Smiths, for example, would be listed together, alphabetized by first names.

Sort Ascending button   Sort Descending button

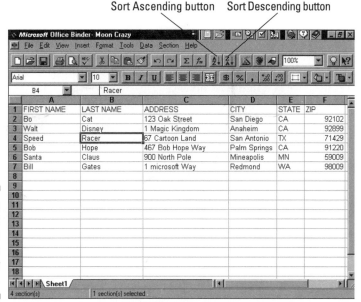

Figure 10-4:
An unsorted data table ready to be sorted by last name.

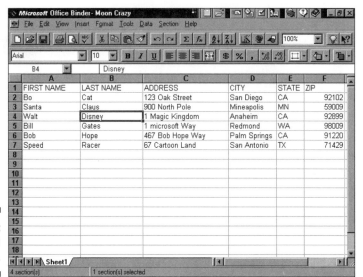

Figure 10-5:
The sorted data table.

Analyzing Data with PivotTables

A PivotTable lets you look at data in an Excel database in different ways (so at least one way will make sense). You can specify which fields from the database are used as page, row, and column headings, and which are used for calculations.

You could use a simple PivotTable to display how many customers live in each state. Although PivotTables can be quite complex, creating this sort of PivotTable with the PivotTable Wizard is a snap.

To create a PivotTable with the PivotTable Wizard, follow these steps:

1. **Click any cell in the database.**

2. **Choose Data⇨PivotTable.**

   The first PivotTable Wizard dialog box appears (see Figure 10-6).

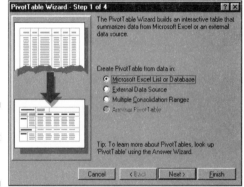

Figure 10-6:
The first
PivotWizard
dialog box.

3. **Click in the Microsoft Excel List or Database radio button.**

4. **Click Next >.**

   The second PivotTable Wizard dialog box appears (see Figure 10-7).

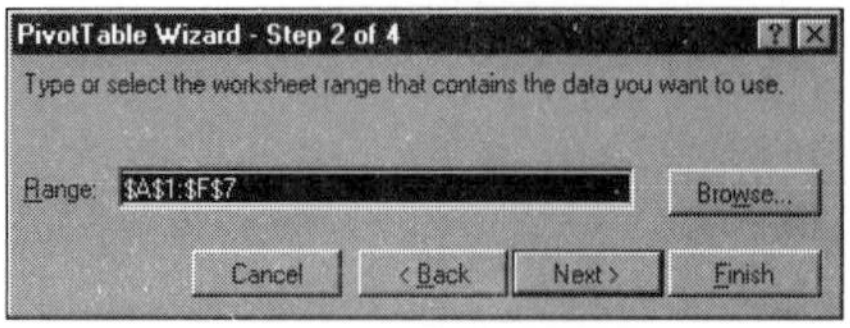

Figure 10-7:
The second
PivotWizard
dialog box.

5. **Highlight your database so that the <u>R</u>ange box contains the cell addresses of your database.**

6. **Verify that the range is correct and then click <u>N</u>ext >.**

The third PivotTable Wizard dialog box appears (see Figure 10-8). This dialog box is where you specify which fields to use in the PivotTable. The field names appear as buttons on the right side of the dialog box.

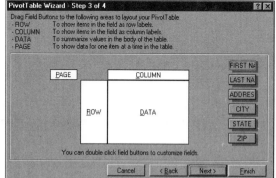

Figure 10-8:
The third
PivotWizard
dialog box.

7. **Drag the appropriate field-name buttons into the <u>P</u>AGE, <u>R</u>OW, <u>C</u>OLUMN, and <u>D</u>ATA portions of the dialog box.**

To create a simple PivotTable to count the number of customers in each state, drag the STATE button into the <u>R</u>OW portion and then drag STATE into the <u>D</u>ATA portion.

Notice that the STATE button becomes Count of STATE when it's dropped into the DATA portion of the dialog box (see Figure 10-9).

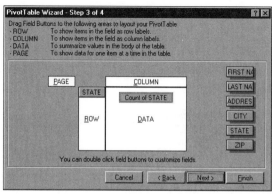

Figure 10-9:
The
PivotTable
set up to
count the
number of
people per
state in your
database.

8. Click <u>N</u>ext > to display the final PivotTable Wizard dialog box, as shown in Figure 10-10.

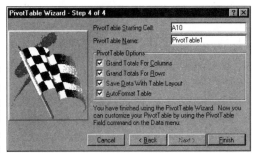

Figure 10-10:
The fourth
PivotWizard
dialog box.

9. In the PivotTable <u>S</u>tarting Cell text box, type a cell reference for the upper left corner of the new PivotTable, or just click in an empty cell on your worksheet.

10. Click <u>F</u>inish to finish creating the PivotTable.

Your finished PivotTable appears, as shown in Figure 10-11.

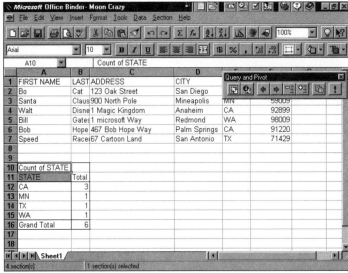

Figure 10-11:
The
completed
PivotTable.

✔ If you don't enter a reference for the PivotTable Starting Cell in the final PivotTable Wizard dialog box, the PivotTable displays a dialog box asking whether you want it to replace your database. Don't do it! (If you accidentally erase your database with a PivotTable, you can undo it by pressing Ctrl+Z immediately.

✔ The Query and Pivot toolbar that appears when you create a PivotTable gives you tools for manipulating the PivotTable. You can clear this toolbar by clicking its close box.

Adding Cell Notes

After typing numbers and creating formulas, you might suddenly wonder what assumptions you made when you entered data into a worksheet. Even worse, other people who are looking at the worksheet may have no idea what certain numbers mean or how you created certain formulas.

Fortunately, Excel lets you add hidden notes that can explain a cell entry — assuming, of course, that you have an explanation. By adding cell notes, you can at least explain what you did and why. That way others can question your assumptions or accept them (unlikely).

To add a cell note, follow these steps:

1. **Click in the cell to which you want to add a note.**

2. **Choose Insert⇨Note.**

   The Cell Note dialog box appears, as shown in Figure 10-12.

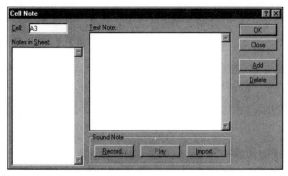

Figure 10-12:
The Cell Note dialog box.

3. Type the text of the note in the Text Note box.

You can add as much text as you want, but keep in mind that you want people to read the note. If it's too long, they may not bother (which may not always be such a bad thing at times).

4. Click OK.

A small red rectangle appears in the upper right corner of each cell that has a note attached.

5. To see a note for a particular cell, move the cursor over the cell.

The note appears as a tiny window near the cell, as shown in Figure 10-13.

Note indicator

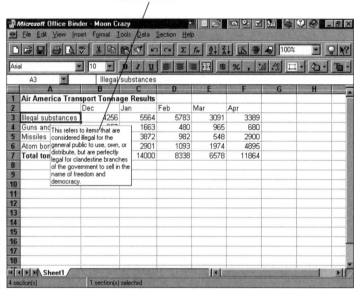

Figure 10-13:
A sample
cell note.

✔ You can edit notes by clicking on the cell containing the note and then choosing Insert⇨Note. Then click on the note you want to edit in the Notes in Sheet portion of the Cell Note dialog box.

✔ If your computer has sound-recording capabilities, you can record spoken notes to attach to your cells. You can play a recorded note by double-clicking the cell that contains the recorded note. (It just might make your day to hear your boss shouting, "What the h*** were you thinking here? Are you on some kind of new medication?")

Part IV
Suddenly It's Show Time

The 5th Wave   By Rich Tennant

"It's a Windows application that more fully reflects an actual office environment. It multi-tasks with other users, integrates shared data and then uses that information to network vicious rumors through an inter-office link-up."

In this part...

The third leg of Microsoft Office is PowerPoint, a specialized presentation graphics program that lets you create slides, outlines, and charts to help convince people that you really do know what you're talking about (even if you don't). So after you've written that killer report with Microsoft Word and crunched all the numbers with Microsoft Excel, it's time to present all of this information into one slick presentation with PowerPoint.

Chapter 11

What Do You Mean I Have to Make the Presentation?

*T*he number one fear of most Americans is public speaking. But giving a presentation can actually be easy if you use visuals. Visuals provide a framework for your presentation so that you don't have to memorize a speech. Instead, you can display pretty graphics and charts and talk about each one without having the entire audience staring at you the whole time.

To help you create powerful presentations, Microsoft Office includes a presentation program called PowerPoint. You can use PowerPoint to create all sorts of visuals, including 35mm slides, black-and-white or color overhead transparencies, or computer images displayed on a monitor or projected on a screen.

Creating Successful Presentations: Four Essential Elements

Speeches are usually heard (and quickly forgotten). On the other hand, presentations are both heard and seen. Basically, a presentation involves one or more of the following four elements:

✔ **Slides.** Slides are the primary speaker-support materials. The term *slide* can be misleading because it refers to four types of visuals: 35mm slides, black-and-white transparencies, color transparencies, and images displayed on a computer screen or placed on a screen by a projector driven by a computer.

✔ **Outlines.** PowerPoint allows you to print your presentation in Outline view. A printout of your presentation's outline contains slide titles and the text of bulleted lists. The outline is valuable because you can review your presentation at a glance to make sure that you have covered all the points and that your arguments appear in a logical sequence.

✔ **Notes.** Notes refer to printed pages containing *thumbnails,* or reduced-sized copies of each of your visuals, plus the 55 points you want to discuss while the presentation is being projected. Notes permit you to review and rehearse your presentation without referring to the actual slides or overheads.

✔ **Handouts.** Handouts permit you to provide your audience with a tangible reminder of your presentation and the points you covered. They also allow your audience to review your presentation and share it with others who were unable to attend.

A presentation is more than the sum of its parts. Your ability to inform, motivate, or persuade will be weakened if just one of the above elements is missing. For example, you may want to organize your presentation by creating a printed outline first.

Once you know what you want to say, you can create notes so you can rehearse your presentation and make sure that you don't omit any important points.

Finally, you may want to create handouts so your audience will have more than their scribbled notes to remind them of your sterling words.

But, never fear, PowerPoint makes it easy to prepare all four parts. Let's get started.

Getting Started with PowerPoint

Microsoft PowerPoint takes the work and the worry out of standing up in front of a group and opening your mouth (provided, of course, that you have a presentation worth looking at).

There are three ways to start PowerPoint:

- Click on the Start button on the Windows 95 taskbar and choose Programs⇨Microsoft PowerPoint.

- Choose Section⇨Add, choose Microsoft PowerPoint Presentation from the Add Section dialog box, and click OK.

- Click the Start a New Document button on the Office Shortcut Bar to create a new PowerPoint presentation.

The first method runs PowerPoint as a separate program. The second method runs PowerPoint as part of a Microsoft Office binder (see Chapter 3). The third method runs PowerPoint as a separate program and creates a new presentation.

When you run PowerPoint as a separate program, a Tip of the Day screen appears (see Figure 11-1). If you run PowerPoint within a binder, you can display the Tip of the Day screen by choosing Help⇨PowerPoint Help⇨Tip of the Day.

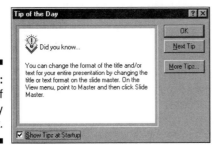

Figure 11-1:
The Tip of
the Day
dialog box.

Working with the AutoContent Wizard

PowerPoint's AutoContent Wizard presents the shortest distance between your ideas and a finished presentation. By using the AutoContent Wizard, you can immediately create decent-looking presentations without too much fuss or lost sleep.

To use the AutoContent Wizard, follow these steps (if you're using PowerPoint within a binder):

1. Choose Section➪View Outside.

2. Choose File➪New.

A New Presentation dialog box appears, as shown in Figure 11-2.

3. Click the Presentations tab.

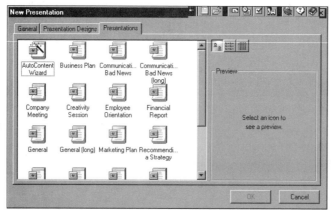

Figure 11-2: The New Presentation dialog box.

4. Click the AutoContent Wizard icon and click OK.

The AutoContent Wizard dialog box appears (see Figure 11-3).

5. Click Next >.

Another AutoContent Wizard dialog box appears asking for your name, what you are going to talk about, and what other information you want to display (see Figure 11-4).

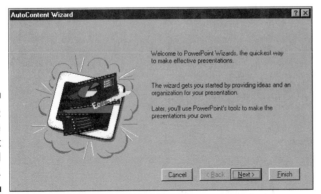

Figure 11-3:
The
AutoContent
Wizard
dialog box.

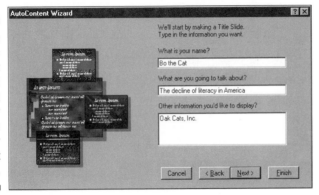

Figure 11-4:
The
AutoContent
Wizard
dialog box
asking for
your name
and other
pertinent
stuff.

6. **Type your name in the What is your name? text box.**

7. **Type your topic in the What are you going to talk about? text box.**

8. **Type any additional information in the Other information you'd like to display? text box.**

9. **Click Next >.**

   The AutoContent Wizard asks what type of presentation you want to give (see Figure 11-5).

10. **Click the option button of the presentation you want to give, such as Selling a Product, Service or Idea (which is the default selection).**

11. **Click Next >.**

    Still another dialog box appears, asking how long you want to present your information (see Figure 11-6).

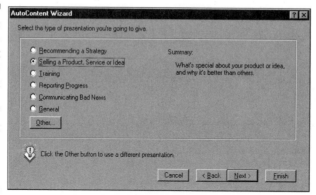

Figure 11-5:
The AutoContent Wizard dialog box gives you a choice of different presentations to choose from.

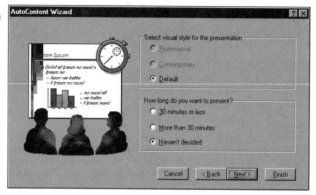

Figure 11-6:
The AutoContent Wizard dialog box asking how long you want to give a presentation.

12. **Click an option button representing the approximate length of time you want to give a presentation. If you don't know, click Haven't decided.**

13. **Click Next >.**

    Another dialog box appears, asking what type of output you will use, such as 35mm slides or an on-screen presentation (see Figure 11-7).

14. **Click the option button representing the type of output you want to use, such as On-screen presentation.**

15. **Click the Yes option button if you want to give out handouts.**

16. **Click Next >.**

    The final AutoContent Wizard dialog box appears, letting you know that you're finished answering questions from your computer and PowerPoint, as shown in Figure 11-8.

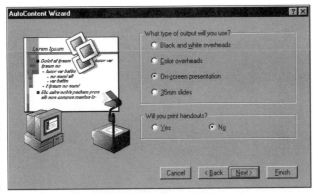

Figure 11-7:
Yet another
AutoContent
Wizard
dialog box,
asking what
type of
output you
want to use.

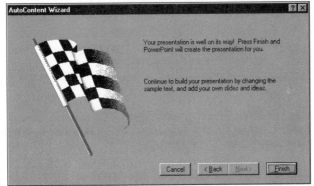

Figure 11-8:
The last
AutoContent
Wizard
dialog box.

17. **Click Finish.**

    PowerPoint displays your first slide for your review, as shown in Figure 11-9.

18. **Choose File⇨Save.**

    The File Save dialog box appears.

19. **Type a file name in the File name text box and click Save. (You may have to change folders to save your file in.)**

20. **Choose File⇨Exit.**

21. **Choose Section⇨Add from File.**

    The Add from File dialog box appears.

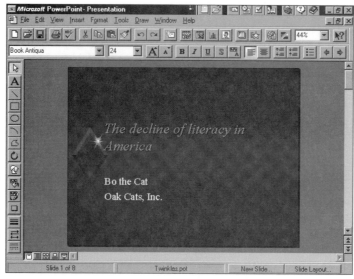

Figure 11-9:
An example
slide from
your
presentation.

22. Click the file name you typed in Step 19 and click A<u>d</u>d.

Microsoft Office adds your newly created PowerPoint presentation to your binder (and it keeps your original blank PowerPoint file in the binder), as shown in Figure 11-10.

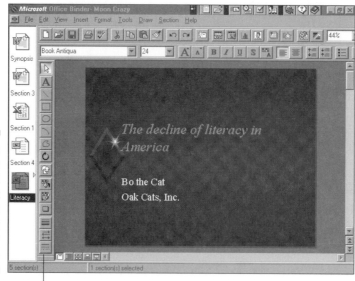

Figure 11-10:
The newly
created
PowerPoint
presentation
appears in
the binder
left pane.

Drawing toolbar

Switching Views

After you create a presentation, PowerPoint displays it as a series of slides. At any time, you can view your presentation in one of the following formats:

- ✔ **Slide:** Shows slides one at a time
- ✔ **Outline:** Shows an outline of your slide titles and text
- ✔ **Slide Sorter:** Shows multiple slides on the screen at once
- ✔ **Notes Pages:** Shows your slides along with your note text
- ✔ **Slide Show:** Lets you preview your slide show to make sure that everything works

When you're viewing your slides, you can see more of your presentation — the remaining slides — by choosing one of the following:

- ✔ Click the down arrow at the bottom of the vertical scroll bar located along the right edge of the screen.
- ✔ Click the scroll box in the vertical scroll bar and drag in it down.
- ✔ Click just below the scroll box.

Using the Slide view

Most people spend most of their time working in Slide view, fixing up their slides by editing and deleting text; adding new slides; and adding illustrations, regular charts, organization charts, or tables. When necessary, you can also choose a different presentation template (or combination of layout, colors, and typography).

The Slide view is best for viewing and editing individual slides. To switch to the Slide view, choose View⇨Slides.

Editing text

To edit text within the Slide view, follow these steps:

1. **Move the mouse pointer over the text that you want to edit.**

   The mouse pointer turns into an I-beam, also known as an insertion pointer (in the shape of an I).

2. **Click the left mouse button.**

   Diagonal lines surround your chosen text, as shown in Figure 11-11.

3. **Type new text or press Delete or Backspace to delete text.**

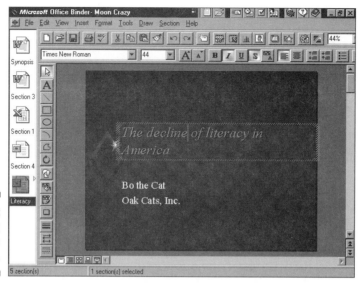

Figure 11-11:
Editing
text on a
slide.

Adding and deleting slides

In case you decide you need to add a slide, follow these steps:

1. **Use the vertical scroll bar to display the slide you want to appear immediately before your newly added slide.**

2. **Choose Insert⇨New Slide (or press Ctrl+M).**

   A New Slide dialog box appears, as shown in Figure 11-12.

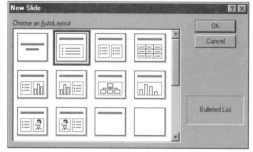

Figure 11-12:
The New
Slide dialog
box.

3. **Click the type of slide layout you want to use.**

4. **Click OK.**

   PowerPoint adds your new slide.

In case you decide to delete a slide, follow these steps:

1. Use the vertical scroll bar to display the slide that you want to delete.

2. Choose Edit⇨Delete Slide.

Using the Outline view

You can type and edit text in Slide view, but making those changes is easier in the Outline view, as shown in Figure 11-13. That way you can see how your entire presentation looks. To switch to the Outline view, choose View⇨Outline.

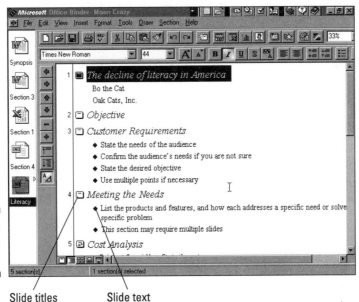

Figure 11-13:
The Outline
view.

Slide titles   Slide text

In the Outline view, the slide titles appear with an icon (shown as a rounded-corner box) and slide text appears indented with a black diamond next to it. Any text that you type next to a black diamond automatically appears on the appropriate slide when you switch to the Slide view of your presentation.

The title slide displays its text without the black diamond next to it. Unlike the slides that follow, title slides do not contain arguments or information. They are intended to appear on-screen while you introduce yourself and discuss your goals for the presentation.

Editing text

To edit slide text in the Outline view, follow these steps:

1. **Move the mouse pointer to the left of the title or bulleted item that you want to replace and select the words by dragging to the right.**

   The words now appear in reverse: white type against a black background.

2. **Type your new text and press Enter.**

3. **Repeat steps 1 – 2 for each slide text that you want to edit.**

Adding another bulleted item

To add another bulleted item under a heading, follow these steps:

1. **Move the mouse pointer to the far right of a heading (slide text marked by a black diamond).**

2. **Press Enter.**

   A new slide text heading appears.

3. **Type the text that you want to add.**

Rearranging slides

Rearranging the order of your presentation is easy when you are in Outline view. Simply follow these steps:

1. **Move the mouse pointer over the slide icon (the rounded-corner icon) that you want to move and click the left mouse button.**

   The slide icon turns black, all the text appears in reverse, and the mouse pointer turns into a four-headed "movement" arrow (see Figure 11-14).

2. **Click the Move Up or Move Down arrow button.**

   The renumbered slide appears in its new location.

Changing the level of outline points

You can promote or demote outline levels, making some points subordinate to others, by following these steps:

1. **Move the mouse pointer over the slide icon (the rounded-corner icon) or slide text (black diamond) that you want to move and click the left mouse button.**

   Your chosen text appears in reverse and the mouse pointer turns into a four-headed "movement" arrow.

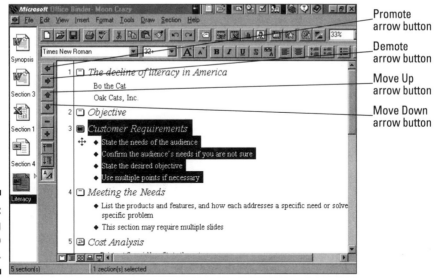

Figure 11-14:
Choosing
a slide to
move.

2. **Click the Demote button (the right arrow on the toolbar to the left of your screen) to make the new text appear at a lower level than the original text, or click on the Promote button (the left arrow) to make the new text appear at a higher level.**

Adding and deleting slides in Outline view

If you suddenly think of a new topic and you want it to have its own slide, you can easily insert a new slide in the outline by following these steps:

1. **Move the insertion pointer to the end of the line that you want the new slide to appear after.**

2. **Choose Insert⇨New Slide (or press Ctrl+M).**

   A new slide icon appears.

3. **Type the title of this new slide and press Enter.**

   Another new slide icon appears.

4. **Click the Demote button to convert this second slide icon into text and type your new text.**

To delete a slide or slide text, follow these steps:

1. **Move the mouse pointer over the slide icon (the rounded-corner icon) or slide text (black diamond) that you want to delete and click the left mouse button.**

   Your chosen text appears in reverse and the mouse pointer turns into a four-headed "movement" arrow.

2. **Choose one of the following:**

   - **Choose Edit⇨Cut if you want to place the deleted slide in the Clipboard and insert it into another outline.**
   - **Choose Edit⇨Clear if you're done with the slide forever.**
   - **Press Backspace.**
   - **Press Delete.**

   Instantly, the selected slide disappears and the remaining slides are renumbered.

Using the Slide Sorter view

The Slide Sorter view, shown in Figure 11-15, crams as many slides as possible on-screen so that you can see how your overall presentation looks. To switch to the Slide Sorter view, choose View⇨Slide Sorter. To rearrange slides, follow these steps:

1. **Move the mouse pointer over the slide that you want to move.**

2. **Hold down the left mouse button.**

   PowerPoint highlights the slide.

3. **Drag the mouse pointer to where you want to move the slide.**

You can increase or decrease the number of slides visible in PowerPoint's Slide Sorter by using the Zoom command. To adjust the number of slides in the Slide Sorter, choose one of the following:

- ✔ Choose View⇨Zoom and click the option button associated with the percentage that you want to display (such as 66 percent or 50 percent).

- ✔ Click the Zoom Control list box and choose a percentage (such as 400 percent or 25 percent).

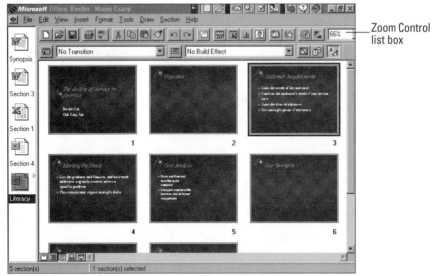

Zoom Control
list box

Figure 11-15:
The Slide
Sorter view.

Using the Notes Pages view

The Notes Pages view, shown in Figure 11-16, lets you see and add notes to each slide. To switch to the Notes Pages View, choose View⇨Notes Pages.

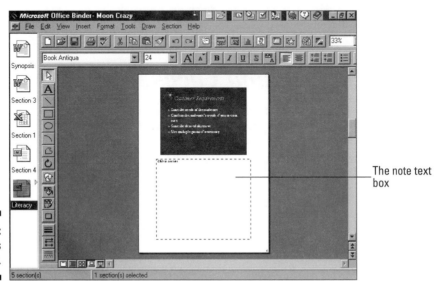

The note text
box

Figure 11-16:
The Notes
Pages view.

Using the Slide Show view

The Slide Show view lets you see how your presentation actually looks so that you can spot flaws, omissions, or missing graphics. To switch to the Slide Show view, follow these steps:

1. **Choose View⇨Slide Show.**

   The Slide Show dialog box appears (see Figure 11-17).

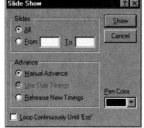

Figure 11-17:
The Slide
Show
dialog box.

2. **Click Show.**

3. **To see the next slide, press either the up- or right-arrow key on your keyboard. To see the previous slide, press either the down- or left-arrow key on your keyboard.**

4. **Press Esc to exit the slide show. (PowerPoint exits the slide show automatically when you reach the end.)**

Using the Spelling Checker

PowerPoint's spelling checker can make sure that you don't have embarrassing typographical errors in either your presentation visuals or your handouts. Any spelling mistakes in your slides can immediately and completely undermine your credibility. To prevent this problem, check your spelling before you let anyone else see your presentation.

To check your spelling, choose Tools⇨Spelling (or press F7).

Reformatting Your Presentation

If you want to change the way your slides look, you can change them yourself one at a time, or you can use a design template to change your entire presentation in one quick click of the mouse button.

When you change design templates, switch to the Slide view first so that you can immediately see the result of your changes.

To choose a different design template, follow these steps:

1. Choose Format⬃Apply Design Template.

The Apply Design Template dialog box appears, displaying a preview of each template (see Figure 11-18).

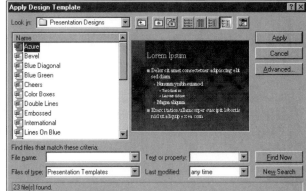

Figure 11-18:
The Apply
Design
Template
dialog box.

2. Click the design template you want to use and click Apply.

PowerPoint changes your entire presentation, as shown in Figure 11-19.

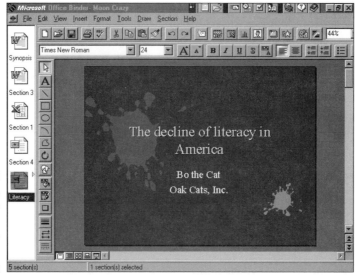

Figure 11-19:
The new
look of a
slide show
presentation.

Saving Your Work

After you get your outline in the shape you want it in, you should save the file.
To save your work, choose one of the following:

- ✔ Press Ctrl+S.

- ✔ Choose File⇨Save (if you're using PowerPoint as a separate program).

- ✔ Choose File⇨Save Binder (if you're using PowerPoint within a binder).

Chapter 12
Adding Pictures to Your Slides and Overheads

- -

In This Chapter

▶ Pasting clip art in your presentations

▶ Adding tables to your presentation

▶ Working with PowerPoint's drawing tools

▶ Placing text directly on PowerPoint slides

- -

*A*lthough most of your presentations will probably consist of words, your audience may get bored watching slides containing words alone. To enhance your presentations, add pictures such as the clip art provided with PowerPoint, illustrations created with other software programs, or illustrations you can create by using PowerPoint's drawing tools.

The key to using pictures is to ask yourself, "What function does this visual perform? How does it support the conclusion I want my audience to accept?" Your skill as a presenter increases when you restrict your use of visuals to those that contribute to the arguments you are presenting (rather than including a picture just because it happens to look nice).

Pasting Clip Art in Your Presentations

Even if you can't draw a straight line, don't worry. PowerPoint includes hundreds of high-quality predrawn illustrations that you can easily add to your presentation.

PowerPoint's clip art library contains a wide variety of useful images. Most have strong symbolic meaning, which can greatly enhance your presentation. Airplanes, for example, nonverbally suggest travel; microscopes, scientific study; and telephones or fax machines, communication (or busy signals).

Some illustrations provide a background or framework for words or presentation titles. Other PowerPoint clip art, such as maps of the United States or international maps, is accurate and representational and can both enhance the communicating power of your presentation as well as save you time and money. (Ever try drawing Hawaii's boundaries?)

Selecting and importing clip art

To add clip art to your slides, follow these steps:

1. **Choose View⇨Slides to switch to the Slide view.**

2. **Choose Insert⇨Clip Art (or click the Insert Clip Art button in the Standard toolbar).**

   The Microsoft ClipArt Gallery dialog box appears (see Figure 12-1). When you click each picture, the dialog box displays a description of what each picture represents.

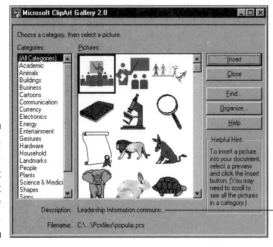

Figure 12-1: The Microsoft ClipArt Gallery dialog box.

Descriptions of pictures

3. **Click a category (such as Animals or Currency).**

4. **Click a picture that you want to insert on your slide and click Insert.**

   PowerPoint displays your chosen picture on the slide with eight white handles surrounding the picture.

5. **Move the mouse pointer over one of the white handles to change your picture to the desired size.**

6. **Place the mouse pointer in the middle of the picture, hold down the left mouse button, and drag the mouse to move the picture to the desired location.**

Manipulating artwork

You can modify imported illustrations in the following six ways:

- Resize
- Move
- Crop
- Recolor
- Add borders and backgrounds
- Ungroup and delete portions of the drawing

Resizing a picture

To resize the picture, follow these steps:

1. **Click the picture you want to resize.**

   White handles appear around the picture.

2. **Move the mouse pointer over a white handle.**

   The mouse pointer turns into a two-headed arrow.

3. **Hold down the left mouse button and drag the mouse until the picture is the size you want it.**

   Dotted lines appear to show how large (or small) the picture will be when you release the mouse button.

4. **Release the mouse button.**

You can also proportionately resize a picture by choosing <u>D</u>raw⇨<u>S</u>cal<u>e</u>. When the Scale dialog box appears, type a desired percentage of increase or reduction, or click the Up or Down arrows in the dialog box to select a desired percentage. For those who want a really fast way to resize a picture, click and drag on any corner handle of the picture, as shown in Figure 12-2.

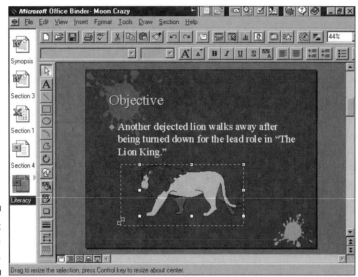

Figure 12-2:
Resizing a picture.

Moving a picture

To move a picture, follow these steps:

1. **Click the picture you want to move and hold down the left mouse button.**

   Dotted lines and white handles appear around the picture.

2. **Drag the mouse to a new location.**

   The dotted line of the picture shows where the picture will appear when you release the left mouse button.

3. **Release the left mouse button.**

Cropping pictures

Cropping means cutting out certain parts of a picture along the top, bottom, or sides. To crop a picture, follow these steps:

1. **Click the picture you want to crop.**

   Dotted lines and white handles appear around the picture.

2. Choose Tools➪Crop Picture.

The mouse pointer turns into a pair of overlapping "carpenter's squares," similar to a picture frame.

3. Choose one of the following:

- **To crop the top, bottom, or sides of the illustration, place the cropping tool over one of the middle handles and drag into the illustration.**

- **To crop from both the sides and the top or bottom of the illustration, place the cropping tool over one of the corner handles and drag into the illustration.**

Figure 12-3 shows a typical cropped picture.

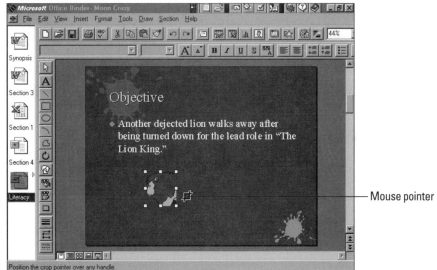

Mouse pointer

Figure 12-3:
A cropped
picture.

Color coordinating your clip art and presentation color scheme

Sometimes your clip art pictures may clash with the background colors of the slide. For you artistic types, PowerPoint gives you the freedom to modify the colors of clip art so you can display a purple dinosaur or a green hot dog if you want.

To change the colors of clip art, follow these steps:

1. Click the picture that you want to modify.

Dotted lines and white handles appear around the picture.

2. **Choose Tools⇨Recolor.**

The Recolor Picture dialog box appears, as shown in Figure 12-4.

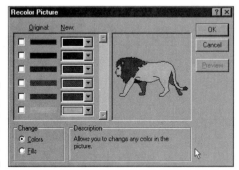

Figure 12-4:
The Recolor
Picture
dialog box.

3. **Click the Colors option button in the Change group if you want to replace solid colors.**

4. **Click the Fills option button if you want to change pattern fill colors.**

5. **Click the check box of the color that you want to change under the Original heading.**

6. **Click the list box, under the New heading, to select a new color to use.**

PowerPoint shows your changes right away.

7. **Clear the check box, under the Original heading, if you want to return to the original color.**

8. **Click OK when you finish coloring your clip art.**

Adding borders, backgrounds, and shadows

If you think your clip art still looks a bit naked or uninspired, you can enhance the image by adding a border, a background fill, a shadow, or a combination of the three.

To add a border or a background fill, follow these steps:

1. **Click the picture that you want to add a border or background fill.**

Dotted lines and white handles appear around the picture.

2. **Choose Format⇨Colors and Lines.**

A Colors and Lines dialog box appears (see Figure 12-5).

3. **Click the Fill list box to choose a fill color. (You can also choose shading, patterns, or textures as well by choosing Shaded, Patterned, or Textured.)**

Figure 12-5:
The Colors
and Lines
dialog box.

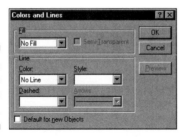

4. **Click the Color list box and choose a line color.**

5. **Click the Style list box and choose a line style.**

6. **Click the Dashed list box to choose a dashed style.**

7. **Click OK.**

PowerPoint displays your fill color and border.

Breaking up is hard to do

Sometimes you may want only part of a clip art illustration rather than the
whole thing. If you're creating a presentation that just requires a lion's head and
not its whole body, for example, you may want to break the lion's head off from
the rest of the body. In this case, you can customize a piece of clip art by
breaking it into its parts and then deleting the unwanted parts.

PowerPoint won't let you ungroup a picture and add a border, background,
or shadow at the same time. You can choose one technique or the other, but
not both.

You must recolor a PowerPoint picture before you ungroup it. You cannot
recolor a picture after it has been ungrouped. A prompt will appear, reminding
you that you are making an irreversible decision.

To ungroup a picture, follow these steps:

1. **Click the picture you want to ungroup.**

   Dotted lines and white handles appear around the picture.

2. **Choose Draw⇨Ungroup.**

   A dialog box appears, warning you that you'll lose any embedded data or
   linked information.

3. Click OK.

PowerPoint suddenly displays your chosen picture with several little
white handles, each one representing a different part of your picture (see
Figure 12-6).

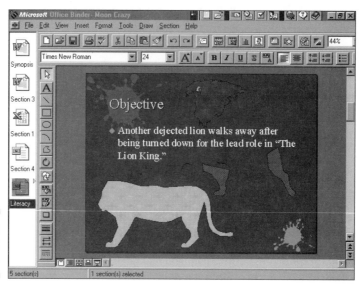

Figure 12-6:
A picture
ungrouped.

If you decide that ungrouping a picture isn't that useful after all, you can
regroup the separate parts of an ungrouped picture back together again. (Then
again, it's usually a whole lot easier just to find the original clip art file and use
that instead.)

To regroup the picture, follow these steps:

1. Move the parts of the picture the way you want them to be grouped.

**2. Place the insert pointer above and to the left of all the parts, and then
click and drag the mouse to the lower right below the picture.**

Little white handles appear around all the parts of the picture.

3. Choose Draw⇨Group.

Adding Tables to Your Presentation

Tables let you to visually display information in an understandable row-and-
column format. (For those of you familiar with creating tables in Word, you'll
notice that adding tables in PowerPoint isn't a whole lot different.)

Adding a table

To add a table to a slide, follow these steps:

1. Choose Insert⇨Microsoft Word Table.

An Insert Word Table dialog box appears, as shown in Figure 12-7.

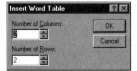

Figure 12-7:
The Insert
Word Table
dialog box.

2. Type the number of columns and rows you want for your table.

3. Click OK.

PowerPoint displays your table (see Figure 12-8).

4. Type the number of columns and rows you want for your table.

5. Click OK.

PowerPoint displays your table.

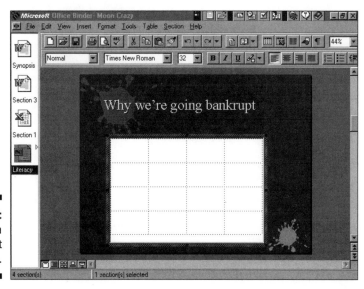

Figure 12-8:
A table in a
PowerPoint
slide.

Moving and resizing a table

Chances are good that your table won't be the right size or in the right position after you create it. To move a table, follow these steps:

1. **Move the mouse pointer to the edge of the table so that an four-headed arrow appears below the mouse pointer.**

2. **Hold down the left mouse button and drag the mouse.**

   As shown in Figure 12-9, dotted lines appear to show where the table will appear when you release the mouse button.

3. **Release the left mouse button.**

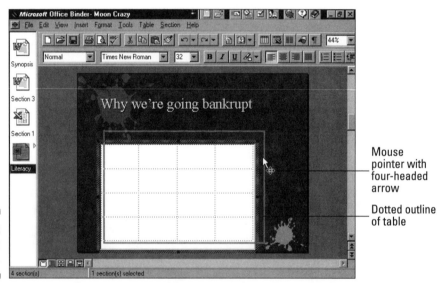

Mouse pointer with four-headed arrow

Dotted outline of table

Figure 12-9:
Moving a table.

To resize a table, follow these steps:

1. **Place the mouse pointer on top of one of the table handles so that the mouse pointer turns into a double-pointing arrow icon.**

2. **Hold down the left mouse button and drag the mouse.**

   Dotted lines appear to show where the table will appear when you release the mouse button.

3. **Release the left mouse button.**

Improving table appearance

When PowerPoint inserts a table, the table appears in dull black and white with no color or style whatsoever. If you want a more colorful or stylish table, follow these steps:

1. **Double-click the table you want to modify.**

2. **Choose Table⇨Table AutoFormat.**

   The Table AutoFormat dialog box appears (see Figure 12-10).

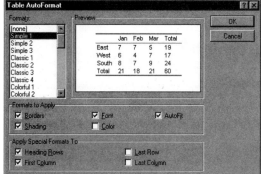

Figure 12-10: The Table AutoFormat dialog box.

3. **Click a table format.**

4. **Click OK.**

Figure 12-11 shows the result of a nicely formatted table, ready for prime time viewing.

A Number of Ways to Avoid Boring Numbers

Long lists of numbers can be boring, which is why Hollywood never makes a movie based on the *Wall Street Journal*. To spice up plain numbers, PowerPoint lets you add graphs to your slides.

To add a graph to your slide, choose Insert⇨Microsoft Graph.

A simple spreadsheet appears as shown in Figure 12-12, letting you type numbers and change the column and row headings.

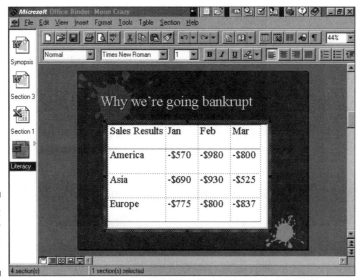

Figure 12-11:
A nicely
formatted
table.

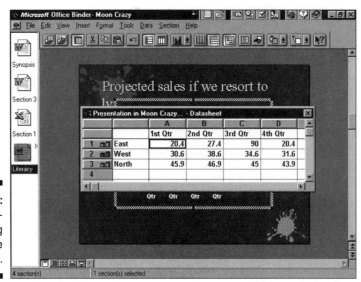

Figure 12-12:
A spread-
sheet, letting
you change
data around.

Entering data

You can enter data into a graph in two ways. You can enter data directly into the datasheet, or you can import data from a previously created spreadsheet.

To enter data in a datasheet, just click the cell that you want to change and type a new value.

If you want to copy data within a binder (from your Excel worksheet to your PowerPoint presentation), simply copy and paste the data from the Excel section to your PowerPoint section.

To enter data previously stored in a separate spreadsheet file, follow these steps:

1. **Click in the cell where you want to import the data.**

2. **Choose Edit⇨Import Data.**

   The Import Data dialog box appears, as shown in Figure 12-13.

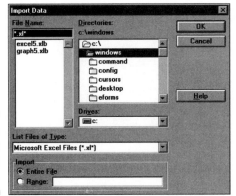

Figure 12-13:
The Import
Data dialog
box.

3. **Choose the file containing the data you want to import and click OK. (If you only want to import part of a spreadsheet's data, click the Range option button and specify the exact range you want to import.)**

   A dialog box appears, warning that your imported data will overwrite the existing data in the datasheet.

4. **Click OK.**

5. **Click the close box of the Datasheet window.**

   PowerPoint displays your graph (see Figure 12-14).

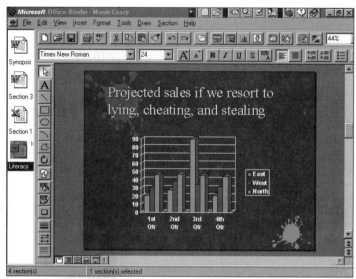

Figure 12-14:
A typical
graph.

Choosing the right type of graph

Out of sheer inertia and a fondness for repetition, PowerPoint always creates bar graphs. But you might decide that you want a different type of a graph.

To choose a different graph type, follow these steps:

1. **Double-click the graph you want to change.**

2. **Choose Format⇨Chart Type.**

   A Chart Type dialog box appears, as shown in Figure 12-15.

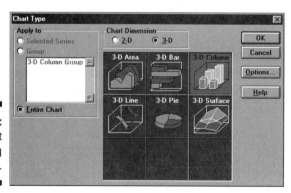

Figure 12-15:
The Chart
Type dialog
box.

3. Click the chart type that you want.

4. Click OK.

PowerPoint changes your graph. Figure 12-16 shows a different type of amazing graph that PowerPoint can display.

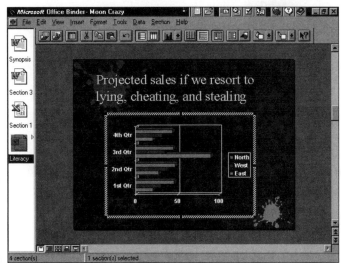

Figure 12-16:
A different
type of
graph.

Working with PowerPoint's Drawing Tools

All drawings, even those that seem very complicated, are ultimately based on a series of carefully assembled, but very basic, smaller drawings consisting of lines and shapes. When you need a custom drawing, you can use PowerPoint's drawing tools to create your own pictures.

Creating lines and shapes

PowerPoint provides six basic tools for creating your own drawings. These drawing tools appear in the Drawing toolbar when you're in the Slide view, as shown in Figure 12-17.

The Freeform tool turns the mouse pointer into a pencil point, letting you draw anything you can possibly draw using a clumsy mouse as a tool. The AutoShapes tool can draw predefined shapes such as crosses, stars, and arrows.

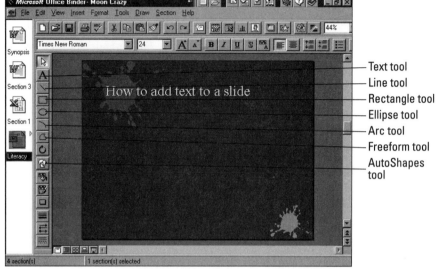

Text tool
Line tool
Rectangle tool
Ellipse tool
Arc tool
Freeform tool
AutoShapes tool

Figure 12-17:
The Drawing
toolbar
displayed
within the
Slide view.

To use any of these drawing tools, follow these steps:

1. **Click the drawing tool that you want to use (such as the Arc tool).**

   The mouse pointer turns into a cross-hair.

2. **Click the upper left location where you want to place the drawing, hold down the left mouse button, and drag the mouse down and to the right.**

   A dotted line appears, showing you where your drawn object will appear when you release the mouse button.

3. **Release the left mouse button.**

Aligning, layering, and rotating objects

After you've drawn a bunch of objects, you might like to adjust them so that they look pretty (or at least less obnoxious on the screen).

To align objects, follow these steps:

1. **Hold down Shift and click all the objects that you want to align.**

2. **Choose Draw⇨Align.**

3. **Choose one of the following:**

   - **Lefts:** Aligns objects along their left edges
   - **Centers:** Aligns objects along an imaginary vertical axis through the center of each object

- **Rights:** Aligns objects along their right edges

- **Tops:** Aligns objects along the topmost part of each object

- **Middles:** Aligns objects along an imaginary horizontal axis through the center of each object

- **Bottoms:** Aligns objects along the lowest part of each object

Sometimes one object can cover up another one. If you think an object is covering up another one, choose <u>D</u>raw⇨Send to Ba<u>c</u>k.

Turning words into art

Besides drawing odd geometric objects on your slides, you can also add additional text by using the Text tool (the tool with the large *A* on it). Text placed using the Text tool won't appear when you switch to the Outline view, however.

To place text directly on the slide, follow these steps:

1. **Click the Text tool.**

   The mouse pointer turns into a down arrow.

2. **Drag the mouse from upper left to lower right to define the area where you want the text to appear.**

3. **Type your text.**

To make your text look nice, highlight your text and choose one of the following buttons, as shown in Figure 12-18:

- ✔ Click the Increase Point Size button in the Formatting toolbar — the one with the large *A*. The size will increase each time you click the button.

- ✔ Click the Center Alignment button in the Formatting toolbar — the one with the lines of different lengths.

- ✔ Click the Text Shadow button, the one with the *S,* to add impact to the text.

To make your text box look nice, follow these steps:

1. **Click the text box that you want to modify.**

2. **Click the Fill Color tool.**

   A Fill Color menu pops up, as shown in Figure 12-19.

3. **Choose a color, shading, pattern, or texture.**

4. **Click the Line Color tool and choose a color for the border of the text.**

5. **Select the Line Style tool and choose a line style for your border.**

Now that you know how to make pretty presentations, use your time at work to make impressive resumes so that you can get a better job.

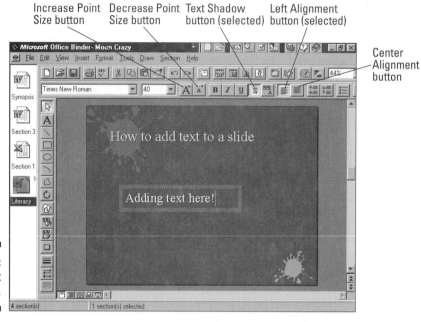

Figure 12-18:
Adding text
to a slide.

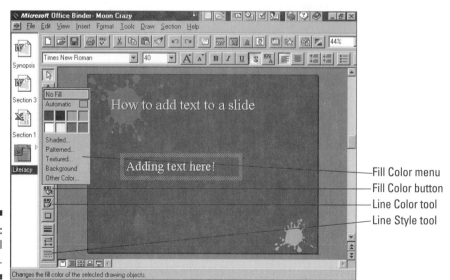

Figure 12-19:
The Fill
Color menu.

Part V
Keeping Track of Time with Schedule+

The 5th Wave   By Rich Tennant

"OH SURE, IT'LL FLOAT ALRIGHT, BUT INTEGRATION'S GONNA BE A KILLER."

In this part...

1 f you've ever lost a valuable name, address, or phone number because you forgot to write it down or (even worse) forgot where you put it, you'll appreciate having Microsoft Schedule+ around.

Not only can Microsoft Schedule+ store names and phone numbers, but it can also store your appointments, projects, and daily to-do tasks to help keep you looking like you actually know what you're doing.

If you're like most people who have a penchant for collecting information and wondering where to find it again, you'll find that Microsoft Schedule+ can rescue your data from ever getting lost again (unless, of course, you forget where you put your computer).

Chapter 13
Scheduling Your Time

● ●

In This Chapter

▶ Starting Microsoft Schedule+

▶ Making an appointment

▶ Printing your appointments out

▶ Exiting Microsoft Schedule+

● ●

*T*o help you keep track of appointments you'd rather not keep, tasks you'd rather not do, and names and addresses of people you may not like, Microsoft Office includes a special program called Microsoft Schedule+ (although no one knows what the "+" sign means).

Microsoft Schedule+ acts like an electronic version of the day-planner notebooks that busy people tend to carry around to keep track of what they're supposed to do at any given time. By tracking your appointments, tasks, and contacts on your computer, you can always be sure that your daily, weekly, or monthly tasks will never be forgotten (unless, of course, you forget to turn on your computer).

If the computer happens to be attached to a local area network, many people can share a single appointment book. That way everyone in the office can see when others are busy or out of the office, when time is available to waste in another meeting, and when the deadline that everyone will probably miss anyway is actually supposed to be met.

Starting Microsoft Schedule+

Unlike Word, Excel, or PowerPoint, Microsoft Schedule+ always runs as a separate program and never within a binder.

To start Microsoft Schedule+ from the Windows 95 taskbar, follow these steps:

1. **Click the Start button on the taskbar and choose Programs⇨Microsoft Schedule+.**

   A dialog box appears, asking whether you want to use Microsoft Schedule+ as a part of your network (see Figure 13-1).

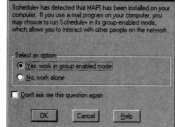

Figure 13-1: The Group Enabling dialog box.

2. **Click the No, work alone option button if you want to use Microsoft Schedule+ on your own computer.**

3. **Click OK.**

   The Schedule+ Logon dialog box appears (see Figure 13-2).

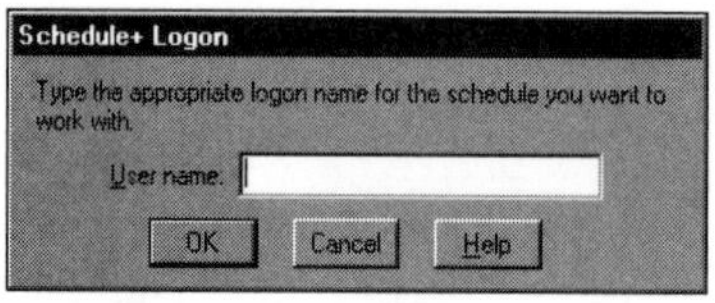

Figure 13-2: The Schedule+ Logon dialog box.

4. **Type a user name (such as your first name).**

5. **Click OK.**

   Another dialog box appears, asking whether you want to create a new file or use an existing one (see Figure 13-3).

6. **Click the option button to tell Microsoft Schedule+ to use an existing file or create a new one.**

   The Select Local Schedule dialog box appears (see Figure 13-4).

7. **If you're creating a new Schedule+ file, type its name in the File name list box and click Save. (If you're using an existing Schedule+ file, the Save button is replaced by an Open button. Just click the name of the file you want to use and then click Open.)**

The Microsoft Schedule+ screen appears (see Figure 13-5).

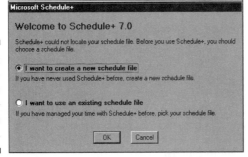

Figure 13-3:
The
Welcome to
Schedule+
7.0 dialog
box.

Figure 13-4:
The Select
Local
Schedule
dialog box.

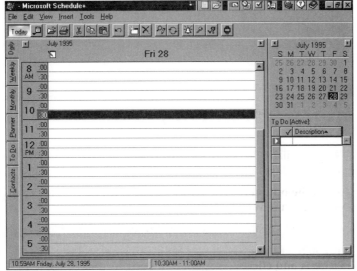

Figure 13-5:
The
Microsoft
Schedule+
screen.

You can quickly make an appointment, add a task, or add a contact by running Microsoft Schedule+ from the Office Shortcut Bar. Just click one of the following:

- ✔ Make an Appointment
- ✔ Add a Task
- ✔ Add a Contact

If you want to password-protect your Schedule+ files (just in case you have the names and addresses of people involved in a profession that could embarrass politicians and movie stars if publicized), follow these steps:

1. Choose Tools⇨Change Password.

The Change Password dialog box appears (see Figure 13-6).

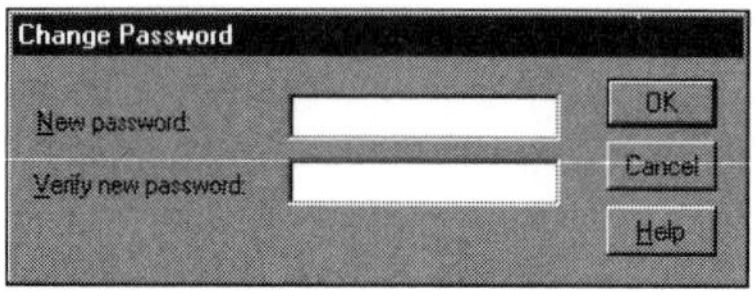

Figure 13-6:
The Change
Password
dialog box.

Change Password	
New password: [ ]	OK
Verify new password: [ ]	Cancel
	Help

2. Type your new password in the New password and the Verify new password text boxes.

3. Click OK.

The next time anyone tries to open this particular Schedule+ file, a password dialog box will appear.

Don't forget your password! If you do, Schedule+ won't let you access your own Schedule+ file.

Making an Appointment

Microsoft Schedule+ provides a Daily, Weekly, or Monthly view of your appointments. To switch views, click one of the following tabs:

- ✔ **Daily** — so you can see what appointments you've already missed (see Figure 13-7)
- ✔ **Weekly** — so you can see what appointments you have to avoid for the next seven days (see Figure 13-8)
- ✔ **Monthly** — so you can make long-range appointments that you will probably forget (see Figure 13-9)

Daily tab

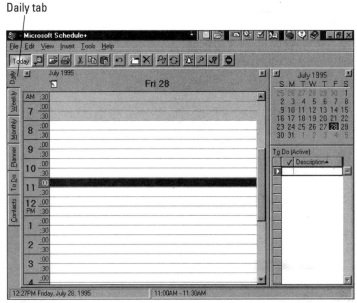

Figure 13-7:
The daily
view.

Weekly tab

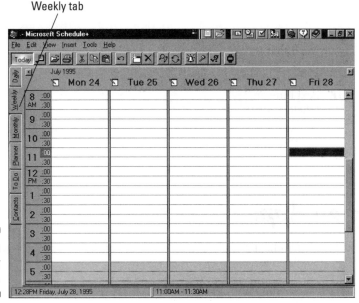

Figure 13-8:
The weekly
view.

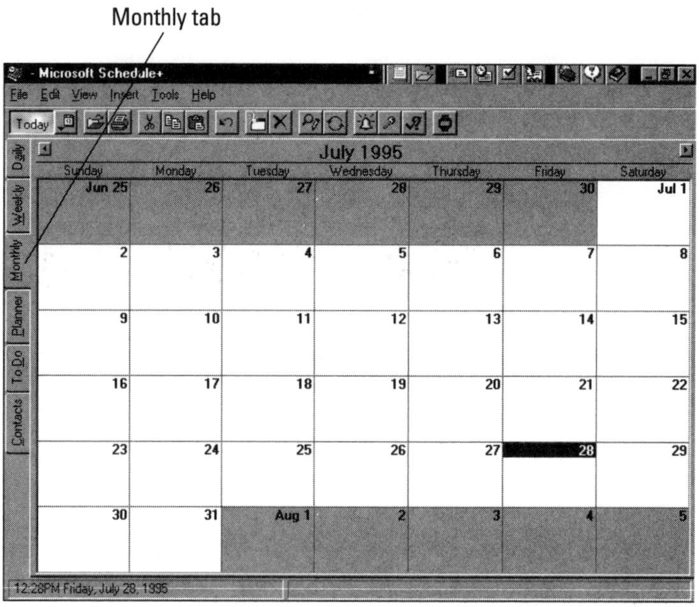

Monthly tab

Figure 13-9:
The monthly
view.

Both the daily and weekly views let you conveniently review, add, or edit your scheduled appointments. The monthly view is best for reviewing your appointments at a glance, although you can add and edit appointments in that view as well.

Making a new appointment

As soon as you make an appointment with someone else, try to enter that appointment into Microsoft Schedule+ as soon as possible before you forget.

To make a new appointment, follow these steps:

1. **Click a tab (Daily, Weekly, or Monthly).**

   Microsoft Schedule+ displays your chosen view.

2. **Click the time (for the Daily and Weekly views) or day (for the Monthly view) of an appointment.**

3. **Choose Insert⇨Appointment (or press Ctrl+M).**

   An Appointment dialog box appears.

4. **Click the General tab (see Figure 13-10).**

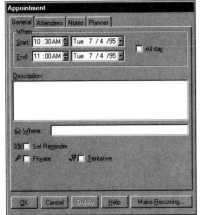

Figure 13-10:
The
Appointment
dialog box
with the
General tab
selected.

5. **Type a description of your appointment in the Description text box.**

   Unlike most day-planner notebooks, Schedule+ gives you enough space to really describe your appointment along with possible excuses you can create to get out of the appointment if necessary.

6. **Type the location of your appointment (if necessary) in the Where text box.**

   Schedule+ displays a little house icon beside the appointment to remind you that this appointment has a location specified.

7. **Click the Set Reminder check box to specify when you want Schedule+ to flash a reminder message to you.**

   Schedule+ displays a bell icon beside the appointment.

8. **Click the Tentative check box if you aren't sure whether the appointment is confirmed.**

   Schedule+ places the combination question-mark and check-mark icon beside tentative appointments.

9. **Click the Private check box if you're using Schedule+ on a network and don't want others to see your appointment.**

   Schedule+ uses a key icon to indicate that the appointment is private.

10. **Click OK.**

    Schedule+ displays your appointments on-screen, as shown in Figure 13-11.

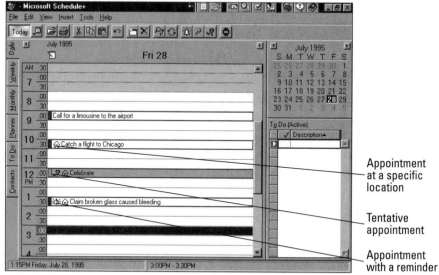

Figure 13-11:
Appointments
displayed in
the daily
view.

Appointment
at a specific
location

Tentative
appointment

Appointment
with a reminder

If you want to use the Reminder feature in step 7, make sure that you don't exit Schedule+. Keep it running or minimize it so that it doesn't clutter your screen. When the time for an appointment approaches, a Reminder dialog box like the one in Figure 13-12 pops up. If you quit Schedule+, you will not get those reminders.

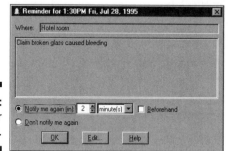

Figure 13-12:
A Reminder
dialog box.

Changing an appointment

Despite your best efforts to plan your schedule, things will always change and you may be forced to move or edit your appointments.

To edit an appointment, follow these steps:

1. **Click the appointment that you want to edit.**

2. **Choose Edit⇨Edit Item (or press Ctrl+E).**

   The Appointment dialog box appears.

3. **Make any changes you want to your appointment.**

   To change the starting and ending time or date for your appointment, for example, click the Start or End list box.

4. **Click OK.**

If you're in the Daily or Weekly view, you can change the time and date of an appointment by following these steps:

1. **Click the appointment you want to change.**

   Schedule+ displays the appointment with a dark bar at the top and a gray bar at the bottom.

2. **Move the mouse pointer over the dark bar on top of the appointment until the mouse pointer turns into an x-headed arrow.**

3. **Hold down the left mouse button and drag the appointment to a new time or day, as shown in Figure 13-13.**

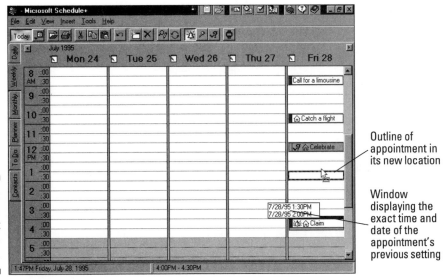

Figure 13-13:
Changing
the start
time of an
appointment.

Outline of
appointment in
its new location

Window
displaying the
exact time and
date of the
appointment's
previous setting

4. **Move the mouse pointer over the gray bar at the bottom of the appointment until the cursor turns into a two-headed arrow.**

5. **Hold down the left mouse button and drag the appointment up or down to increase or decrease the ending time (see Figure 13-14).**

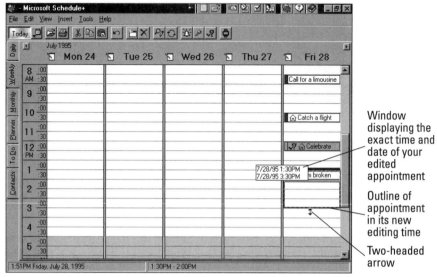

Window displaying the exact time and date of your edited appointment

Outline of appointment in its new editing time

Two-headed arrow

Figure 13-14:
Changing the end time of an appointment.

Deleting an appointment

After an appointment or if someone cancels on you, you can delete it to clear your schedule for more appointments that you probably won't want to keep either. To delete an appointment, follow these steps:

1. **Click the appointment you want to delete.**

2. **Choose Edit⇨Delete Item (or press Ctrl+D).**

Make sure that you really want to delete an appointment because Schedule+ deletes it as soon as you use the Delete Item command. If you suddenly change your mind after you've deleted, choose Edit⇨Undo or press Ctrl+Z.

Defining a recurring appointment

Many times you may have an appointment that occurs every day, week, or month (such as going to lunch with the boss, running an errand, or taking a nap). Rather than force you to keep entering recurring appointments,

Schedule+ lets you enter them once and define how often they occur. From that point on, Schedule+ automatically schedules your recurring appointments unless you specifically tell it otherwise.

To define a recurring appointment, follow these steps:

1. **Choose Insert⇨Recurring Appointment.**

   An Appointment Series dialog box appears.

2. **Click the General tab (see Figure 13-15).**

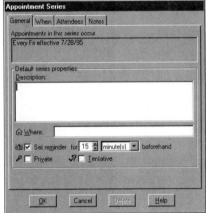

Figure 13-15:
The
Appointment
Series
dialog box
with the
General tab
selected.

3. **Type your recurring appointment in the Description box.**

4. **Type a location for your recurring appointment in the Where box.**

5. **Click the Set Reminder check box to specify when you want Schedule+ to flash a reminder message to you.**

6. **Click the Tentative check box if you aren't sure whether the appointment is confirmed.**

   Schedule+ displays confirmed and tentative appointments differently on-screen.

7. **Click the Private check box if you're using Schedule+ on a network and don't want others to see your appointment.**

8. **Click the When tab (see Figure 13-16).**

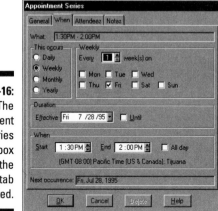

Figure 13-16:
The
Appointment
Series
dialog box
with the
When tab
selected.

9. **In the This occurs group, click the Daily, Weekly, Monthly, or Yearly option button to choose how often this appointment occurs.**

   Each time you click on either the Daily, Weekly, Monthly, or Yearly option button under the This occurs group, the box to the right displays different types of options.

10. **In the next group, define how often you want your appointment to occur (such as on every Friday or on the last Monday of every month).**

11. **In the Duration group, click the Effective list box to define the starting date of your recurring appointment.**

12. **Click the Until check box if you want to define when you want your recurring appointment to end.**

13. **In the When group, click the Start and End list boxes to define the time and length of your recurring appointment.**

14. **Click OK.**

   Schedule+ displays an icon that looks like two arrows chasing each other around in a circle beside recurring appointments. Think of this as a vicious cycle, especially if this recurring appointment is one that you really don't like.

To edit a recurring appointment, follow these steps:

1. **Choose Edit⇨Edit Recurring⇨Appointments.**

   The Recurring Appointments dialog box appears (see Figure 13-17).

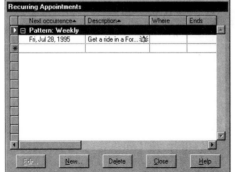

Figure 13-17:
The
Recurring
Appointment
dialog box.

   2. Click the recurring appointment you want to edit.

   3. Click Edit and then change the appointment, or click Delete to delete the appointment.

   4. Click Close.

Printing Your Appointments Out

Unless you carry a laptop computer around with you all day, you probably print out your appointment schedule so you can carry it easily. (Believe it or not, Microsoft Schedule+ can even download data to a Timex Data Link Watch. Then again, if you have enough time to figure out how to do this, you probably have plenty of time to waste anyway.)

To print your Schedule+ file, follow these steps:

   1. Choose File⇨Print (or press Ctrl+P).

     The Print dialog box appears (see Figure 13-18).

   2. Choose what to print from the Print layout list box.

   3. Click Preview to see if you like what you chose in step 2.

     Schedule+ displays a miniature version, shown in Figure 13-19.

   4. Click Close.

     The Print dialog box reappears.

   5. Under the Schedule range group, click the Starting and For list boxes to define what part of your schedule file to print.

   6. Click OK to start printing.

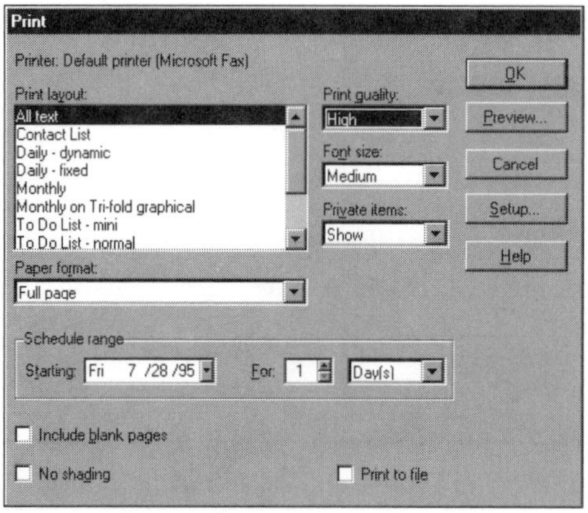

Figure 13-18:
The Print
dialog box.

Figure 13-19:
The
preview of
a monthly
appointment
list.

Exiting Microsoft Schedule+

After you use Microsoft Schedule+, you can exit it by choosing one of the
following:

- ✔ Choose File⇨Exit.

- ✔ Choose File⇨Close.

- ✔ Click the close box, which appears in the upper right corner of the
  Schedule+ window.

If you want Schedule+ to remind you of your upcoming appointments, don't exit Schedule+. Just click the minimize button to get it out of your sight. The only time you may want to exit completely out of Schedule+ is to free up memory to run other programs that come with manuals that don't make sense either.

The 5th Wave   By Rich Tennant

"I SAID I WANTED A NEW MONITOR FOR MY BIRTHDAY!
MONITOR! MONITOR!"

Chapter 14
Setting Tasks and Making Contacts

· ·

· ·

*B*esides letting you make (and break) appointments, Microsoft Schedule+ gives you the chance to create your own to-do lists (so you don't have to waste money buying special paper labeled "Things to do today"). You can also store names, addresses, and phone numbers of people who may come in handy.

Storing Names and Addresses

Nearly everyone has business cards for handing out to people who may be useful in the future. People stuck in the dark ages still store business card collections in Rolodex files, but you probably prefer to store names and addresses in Microsoft Schedule+.

By using Microsoft Schedule+, you can quickly copy (and share) your valuable business contacts with others, or just get rid of your cumbersome Rolodex file and put a much more cumbersome computer on your desk.

Storing a name

To store a name, follow these steps:

1. Choose Insert⇨Contact.

The Contact dialog box appears.

2. **Click the Business tab to display fields such as names and addresses (see Figure 14-1).**

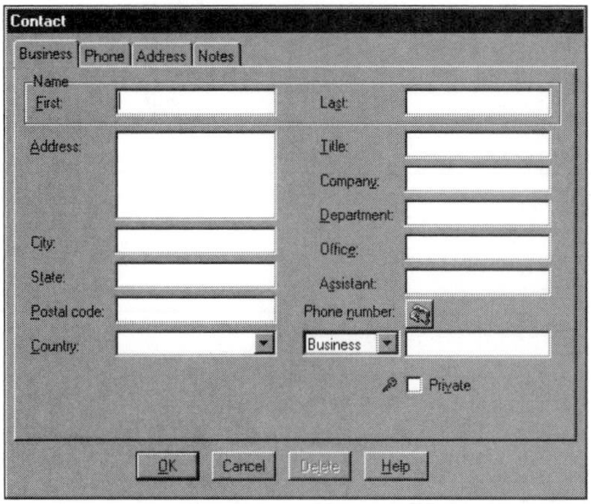

Figure 14-1:
The Contact
dialog box
with the
Business
tab
selected.

3. **Type the name, address, city, company, and any other information you want in the appropriate list boxes.**

4. **Click the Phone tab (see Figure 14-2).**

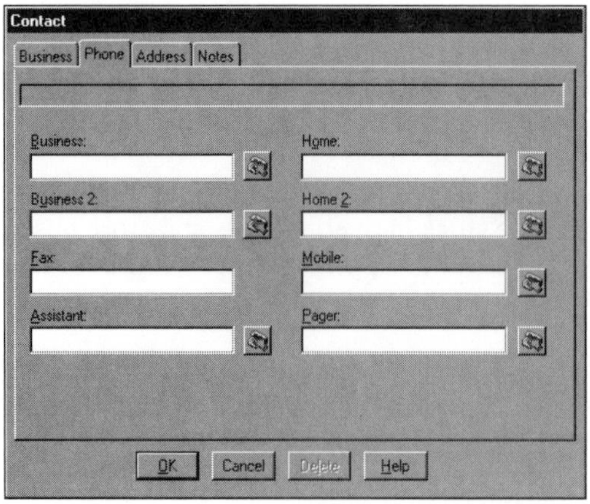

Figure 14-2:
The Contact
dialog box
with the
Phone tab
selected.

5. **Type all the phone numbers you care to store (such as Business, Home, Pager, and Mobile phone numbers).**

6. **Click the Address tab (see Figure 14-3).**

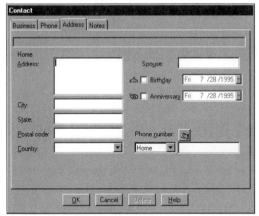

Figure 14-3:
The Contact
dialog box
with the
Address tab
selected.

7. **Type all the information you care to store about the person (such as the spouse name, birthday, or anniversary date).**

8. **Click the Notes tab (see Figure 14-4).**

   Click in the text box and type information about your contact that you didn't store anywhere else. (The Notes text box is a good place for information to be used in blackmailing.)

9. **Click OK.**

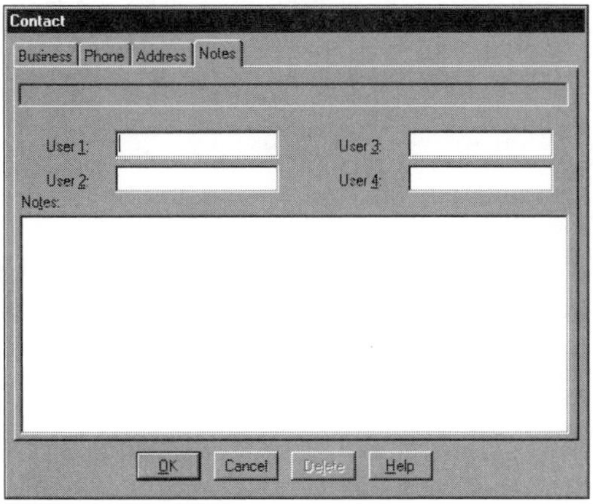

Figure 14-4:
The Contact
dialog box
with the
Notes tab
selected.

Viewing and editing multiple names

Without any prompting or help from you, Schedule+ automatically organizes your names alphabetically within the Contact view, as shown in Figure 14-5. To view your stored contacts, click the Contacts tab.

Go to   Last name   First name
text box   sort button   sort button

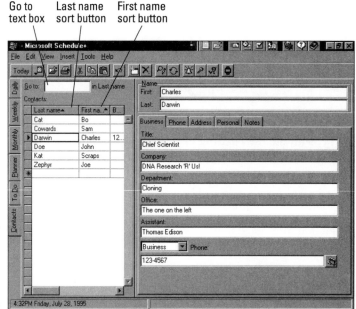

Figure 14-5:
The
Contacts
view.

To edit contact information, follow these steps:

1. **Click the Contacts tab.**

   The Contact dialog box appears.

2. **Under the Contacts group (the left side of the screen), click on the contact name that you want to edit.**

   The contact name and business information appears to the right of the screen.

3. **Click the tab containing the data that you want to edit (Business, Phone, Address, Personal, or Notes).**

4. **Type any changes you want to make in the appropriate boxes.**

Sorting your contacts

If you have a long list of contacts, you may have trouble finding information about the person you want to reach. To help you sort through your list of contacts, Schedule+ lets you sort alphabetically by last name, first name, or by other criteria such as by company name. To sort by last name, click the Last name sort button. To sort by first name, click the First name sort button.

To choose your own peculiar way to sort your contacts, follow these steps:

1. **Choose View⇨Sort.**

   The Sort dialog box appears (see Figure 14-6).

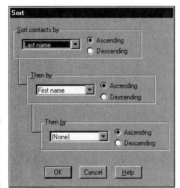

Figure 14-6:
The Sort
dialog box.

2. **Click the Sort contacts by list box and choose a category to sort by (such as last name, title, birthday, and so on).**

3. **Click the Ascending or Descending option button next to the list box.**

4. **Click the Then by list box and choose a secondary category to use.**

   If you sort by last name and Schedule+ finds two people with the last name of Doe, this secondary category determines how to sort those contacts.

5. **Click the Ascending or Descending option button next to the second category.**

6. **Click the Then by list box and choose a third category to sort by.**

7. **Click the Ascending or Descending option button next to the third category.**

8. **Click OK.**

   Schedule+ automatically sorts your entire contact list by your chosen criteria.

Searching for your contacts

Sorting is great when you want to organize your entire contact list, but many times you don't care about 99 percent of your contacts; you just want to find one contact. (Most likely the one who owes you money.)

To help you search for a specific contact, follow these steps:

1. **Click the column heading of the category you want to search (such as Last name or First name).**

2. **Click the Go to list box.**

   When you click the Last name column heading in step 1, the text `in Last name` appears next to the Go To list box.

3. **Type the first letter in the name of the contact (first name, last name, and so on) that you want to find.**

   Schedule+ moves the cursor to the first entry that contains the letter you just typed.

4. **Type a second and a third letter to narrow down the search.**

Creating a To-Do List

Many people spend a fortune buying special pads of paper labeled "Things to do today," and yet still never get anything done. Rather than waste money and paper, let Microsoft Schedule+ help you create a daily to-do list and check off your tasks as you complete them.

To create a to-do list, follow these steps:

1. **Click the Daily tab to display the Daily view.**

2. **Click the Description column in the To Do (Active) area.**

3. **Type a description of your task.**

4. **After you complete a task, click the check mark box next to the description.**

   Schedule+ displays a check mark and draws a line through your task, letting you know that it's finished (or at least you claimed it's finished). Figure 14-7 shows you what the To Do list looks like after checking off certain tasks as being complete.

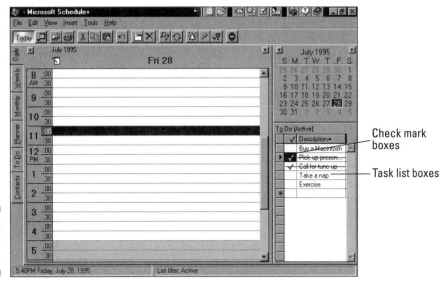

Figure 14-7:
The To-Do
list.

Check mark boxes

Task list boxes

If you don't check off a completed task, Schedule+ keeps displaying your uncompleted tasks until you do them or until you delete them and pretend that you never intended to do them in the first place.

Setting Goals and Achieving Them

While to-do lists are great for accomplishing daily tasks, you may have a larger task that you want to complete. Fortunately, Microsoft Schedule+ can help you define projects and the specific tasks needed to complete them on time and under budget (something Hollywood studios have never done in years of film making).

Creating a project

A project is a goal that usually requires lots of hard work and dedication, which explains why most of them never get done. However, if you have some projects that desperately need to be completed (or you'll get fired), let Microsoft Schedule+ help you define and plan them.

To create a project, follow these steps:

1. **Choose Insert⇨Project.**

   The Project dialog box appears (see Figure 14-8).

Figure 14-8:
The Project
dialog box.

2. **Type the name of your project in the Name list box.**

3. **Click the up and down arrows to define a priority for this project in the Priority list box.**

   Priorities can range from 1 to 10 or *A* to *Z* for those who prefer letters rather than numbers.

4. **Click OK.**

If you're hooked up to a network but don't want anyone to see what projects you're working on (or how late you are in completing them), click in the Private check box. If the Private check box is clean, anyone connected to your network can sneak a peek at your projects.

Creating a task

After you've defined a project, you need to specify the tasks for completing that project (otherwise you tend to ignore the project). To create a task, follow these steps:

1. **Choose Insert⇨Task (or press Ctrl+T).**

   The Task dialog box appears.

2. **Click the General tab (see Figure 14-9).**

3. **Click the Ends list box and click an ending date for this task (set as late as possible so you don't have to pressure yourself!).**

4. **Click the Starts list box and choose when you want to start the task (defined by the number of days before the ending date).**

5. **Click the Mark as done after end date check box.**

6. **Type a description of your task in the Description text box.**

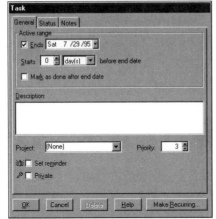

Figure 14-9:
The Task
dialog box
with the
General tab
selected.

7. **Click the Project list box and define the project this task belongs to.**

8. **Click the Priority list box and set a priority for this task.**

9. **Click the Set reminder check box and define when you want Schedule+ to flash you a reminder message about starting this task.**

10. **Click the Private check box if you're using Schedule+ on a network and don't want others to see what tasks you've scheduled for yourself.**

11. **Click OK.**

After you define a task, Schedule+ automatically displays it in the Daily view of your to-do list.

Viewing and editing your tasks

When you create projects and divide them into easy-to-accomplish tasks, you then want to see the progress of all your projects and associated tasks. To view a list of your projects, click the To Do tab, shown in Figure 14-10.

To edit a task, follow these steps:

1. **Click the task that you want to edit.**

2. **Choose Edit⇔Edit Item (or press Ctrl+E).**

   The Task dialog box appears, letting you edit your task.

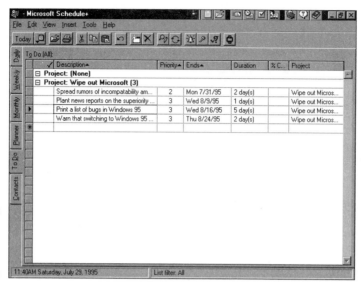

Figure 14-10:
The To Do
view.

To display the percent of the task that you've completed, follow these steps:

1. Click the %C column of a task.

A percentage scroll box appears (see Figure 14-11).

2. Click the up or down arrow in the percentage scroll box to display a percentage.

The moment a task becomes 100 percent complete, Schedule+ crosses the task off with a check mark.

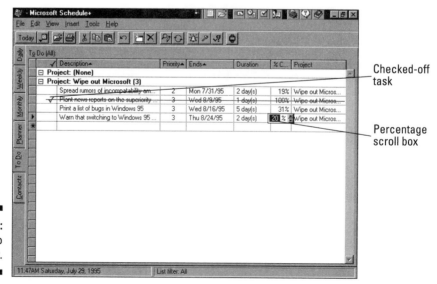

Figure 14-11:
The To Do
view.

Learning Effective Habits

If you've read the book *The Seven Habits of Highly Effective People* by Dr. Stephen R. Covey, you may wonder how you can apply its principles to your own life with Microsoft Schedule+. Lucky for you, Microsoft Schedule+ has a special feature just to do that.

To begin changing your life by adopting more effective habits, choose Tools⇨Seven Habits Quick Start. By answering a series of questions, the Seven Habits Tools can help you define what's important in your life, what goals you want to achieve in your lifetime, and what specific tasks you can do right now to achieve your dreams. Figure 14-12 shows one of the many screens that can help you think about what you're doing with your life and whether you're really doing what you want after all.

After you know what you want to do, you can begin to quickly recognize which daily tasks help (or hinder) your eventual progress towards that goal. Who knows? Maybe you will discover that you really hate your job after all and that you want to do something more creative and interesting. If Microsoft Schedule+ helps you change your life for the better, be sure to send Microsoft a thank-you letter.

Figure 14-12:
One of many dialog boxes from the Seven Habits Tools.

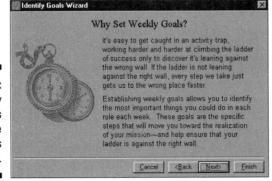

Part VI
Making the Most of Your Data

The 5th Wave   By Rich Tennant

YEAH, BUT YOU SHOULD SEE HOW NICELY IT CENTERED EVERYTHING.

In this part...

*1*f you need to store information like inventory part numbers, employee IDs, or stamp collecting data, you need to create your own custom database. You could create such a database by using index cards, but it's a whole lot easier to use Microsoft Access instead.

Microsoft Access lets you decide what type of data to store, how to display it, how to sort it, and even how to print it in a report. With Microsoft Access, your data will always be within a fingertip away — just as long as your computer is nearby as well.

Microsoft Office also provides several ways to exchange data between Word, Excel, Access, Schedule+, and PowerPoint. By combining words with spreadsheets, data, and graphs, you can create sophisticated reports that will look pleasing to the eye, even if you have nothing important to say.

Chapter 15

Organizing Your Assets (and Other Stuff)

• •

In This Chapter
▶ Database 101
▶ Using a database
▶ Searching a database
▶ Sorting a database

• •

*D*espite the sophistication of personal computers, many people still insist on storing important names, addresses, and phone numbers in Rolodex files, on index cards, or on sheets of paper stuffed into folders. Although effective, paper solutions are terrible for storing and analyzing information. Just look at a typical Rolodex file, and ask yourself how long it would take to find all the names and phone numbers of people who live in Missouri.

As the database portion of Microsoft Office, Microsoft Access allows you not only to store and retrieve information but also to sort, manipulate, and analyze that information to spot trends or patterns in your data. And the more you know about your information, the better off you'll be when dealing with your less knowledgeable, computer-illiterate competitors.

Microsoft Access only comes with the Professional edition of Microsoft Office. If you own the Standard edition of Microsoft Office, you'll have to buy Microsoft Access separately.

Database 101

Microsoft Access is nothing more than a fancy filing cabinet that allows you to dump information in and yank it back out again. Before you can dump information into Access, however, you have to design your database structure. A database file consists of the following elements:

- One or more fields
- One or more database records
- One or more database tables

A *field* contains one chunk of data, such as a name or phone number.

One or more fields make up a single *record*. A record contains related information, such as name, address, and phone number.

One or more records make up a *database table*. For example, one database table might contain names and addresses of customers, and another database table might list all the products stored in your inventory.

One or more tables make up a *database file*. A database file is the physical file stored on your hard disk. (If you erase this file, you've just erased your entire database.)

Creating a database file

The *database file* is a file that physically exists on your hard disk (or floppy disk) and that has the funny file extension MDB, which stands for Microsoft DataBase. Think of a database as a filing cabinet devoted to holding one type of data, such as information related to taxes or business.

To create a database file, follow these steps:

1. **Click the Start button in the Windows 95 Taskbar and choose Programs⇨Microsoft Access.**

    Microsoft Access loads and displays a Microsoft Access dialog box, shown in Figure 15-1.

Figure 15-1:
The
Microsoft
Access
dialog box.

2. **Click the Database Wizard option button and click OK.**

   The New dialog box (shown in Figure 15-2) appears, offering a variety of databases you can use.

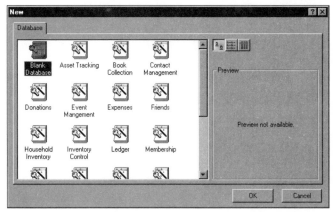

Figure 15-2:
The New
dialog box.

3. **Click the type of database that you want to use (such as Asset Tracking or Expenses) and click OK.**

   The File New Database dialog box appears.

4. **Type a name for your database in the File name box and click Create.**

   The Database Wizard dialog box appears, letting you know the type of information the database will store. Figure 15-3 lets you know that this particular database will store contact and call information.

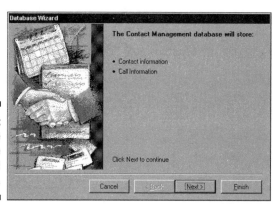

Figure 15-3:
The
Database
Wizard
dialog box.

5. Click Next >.

Another Database Wizard dialog box (shown in Figure 15-4) appears, giving you the chance to add additional fields.

Figure 15-4:
This
Database
Wizard
dialog box
gives you a
chance to
add
additional
fields.

6. Click in the check boxes of the additional fields you want to store in your database and click Next >.

Still another Database Wizard dialog (shown in Figure 15-5) appears, giving you the chance to select a screen display.

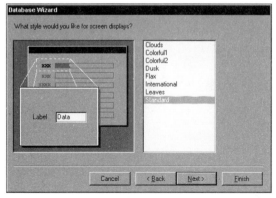

Figure 15-5:
This
Database
Wizard
dialog box
lets you
select a
screen
display.

7. Choose a screen display style (most likely Standard) and click Next >.

Another Database Wizard dialog box (shown in Figure 15-6) appears, asking what style you want to use for printed reports.

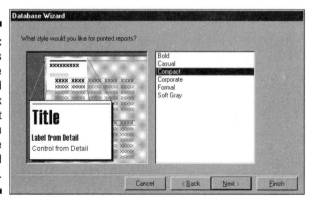

Figure 15-6:
This
Database
Wizard
dialog box
asks what
style you
want to use
for printed
reports.

8. Choose a style and click Next >.

(To help you pick the style best suited for your needs, click on different styles. Each time you choose a different style, the Database Wizard dialog box shows you what that style looks like in the left-hand window.)

One more Database Wizard dialog box (shown in Figure 15-7) appears, asking you for a title of the database.

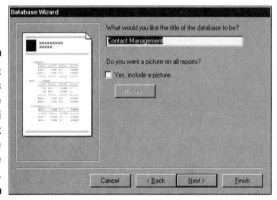

Figure 15-7:
This
Database
Wizard
dialog box
asks for the
title of the
database.

9. **Type a name for your database (such as** Valuable names **or** People I have to deal with**) and click** Next >.

The last Database Wizard dialog box, shown in Figure 15-8, appears.

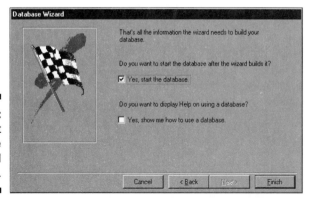

Figure 15-8:
The last
Database
Wizard
dialog box.

10. **Click Finish.**

Access displays your database (see Figure 15-9).

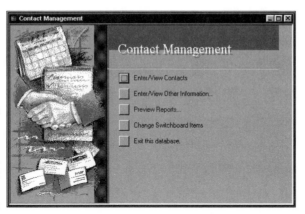

Figure 15-9:
A sample
contact
management
database.

Opening an existing database

If you want to open an existing database file, follow these steps:

1. **Click the Start button in the Windows 95 Taskbar and choose Programs⇨Microsoft Access.**

   Microsoft Access loads and displays a Microsoft Access dialog box.

2. **Click the Open an Existing Database option button and click the database name that you want to open.**

3. **Click OK.**

Just in case you've already started Access and want to load an existing database, follow these steps:

1. **Choose File⇨Open Database (or press Ctrl+O).**

   The Open dialog box appears.

2. **Click the database name that you want to open and click Open.**

Saving your database

As you edit, delete, and add new data, Access saves your database file automatically. However, if you've changed the structure of your database in any way, you must save your database file manually.

To save a database, choose one of the following:

  ✔ Choose File➪Save.

  ✔ Press Ctrl+S.

  ✔ Click the Save icon in the Standard toolbar.

Viewing the parts of your database

When Access creates a database, the database actually consists of two separate windows:

  ✔ The switchboard window

  ✔ The database window

The switchboard window (refer to Figure 15-9) provides a simple one-click interface to your database, letting you view, edit, and print your database information. The database window (shown in Figure 15-10) shows you all the separate reports, modules, forms, tables, and macros that make up your entire database.

Figure 15-10:
The
database
window.

To switch between the switchboard window and the database window, click the Window menu and choose the switchboard or database window from the bottom of the list.

The whole purpose of the switchboard window is to hide the ugly details of managing a database. If you really want to get involved with creating, modifying, and programming Access, switch to the database window. If you just want to use a database and could care less about the fine details, use the switchboard window instead.

Exiting from Access

Like all programs, you eventually want to exit Access so you can do something more exciting with your life than designing databases and typing in data. To exit from Access, choose File⇨Exit.

If you're the type who hates using the mouse and prefers using the keyboard, press Alt+F4 to exit from Access or any other Office 95 program.

There, now wasn't that easy?

Using a Database

After Access creates a database, it's completely empty (and also completely useless) until you start stuffing your own information into it.

(If you clicked the "Yes, include sample data" check box in Figure 15-4, your database will be filled with sample — and still useless — information.)

Stuffing data into a database

To stuff data into a new or existing database, it's easier to do it from the switchboard window. To use the switchboard window to add new data, follow these steps:

1. **If the Database window is visible, click on the Forms tab, click Switchboard and then click Open.**

   The Switchboard window appears.

2. **Click the Enter or look at button (the top button in the switchboard window). Refer to Figure 15-9.**

   Access displays the first record in your database, showing fields for you to type in information (see Figure 15-11).

3. **Choose Insert⇨Record (or click the Insert Record button).**

   Access displays a blank record.

4. **Click in the field where you want to add data and type in your data.**

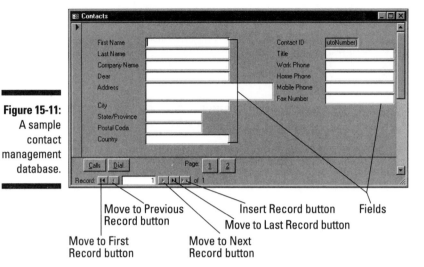

Figure 15-11:
A sample contact management database.

Move to Previous Record button

Insert Record button

Fields

Move to Last Record button

Move to First Record button

Move to Next Record button

If you just want to view the records stored in your database, click one of the following buttons:

- ✔ Move to First record button
- ✔ Move to Previous record button
- ✔ Move to Next record button
- ✔ Move to Last record button

Deleting data

Eventually, you need to delete individual field data or entire records. To delete data stored in a field, follow these steps:

1. **Click in the field containing the data that you want to delete.**

2. **Choose one of the following methods to delete the data:**

   - **Press Delete or Backspace**

   - **Drag the mouse to highlight the data, then press Delete or Backspace**

To delete an entire record, follow these steps:

1. **Click the Move First record, Move Previous record, Move Next record, or Move Last record buttons to display the record you want to delete.**

2. Choose Edit⇨Delete Record.

A dialog box appears, warning that if you continue, your deleted record will be lost for good.

3. Click Yes (but only if you're sure you want to delete your chosen record forever).

Searching a Database

After you create a database and stuff information into it, guess what? It's useless unless you can retrieve information from it again. Typical paper databases — such as filing cabinets, Rolodex files, and paper folders — are designed for storing and retrieving information alphabetically. By contrast, Access can find and retrieve information any way you want: by area code or ZIP code, alphabetically by last name or first name, by state, or by date.

Searching a database is great for retrieving specific information, such as a specific person's phone number, all the people who live in Minnesota, or all the people who live in a certain area code. Access provides two ways to search a database:

✔ Finding a specific record
✔ Finding one or more records by using a filter

Finding one specific record

To find a specific record, you have to know part of what you want. Access can't read your mind, so you have to give it clues, such as "Find all the addresses of people who live in Alaska," "Find the first names of people whose last name is Blake," or "Find the phone number of James Earl Jones."

When you want to find a specific record, you have to know at least one bit of data about that record. If you want to find a specific phone number, for example, you have to know the first or last name of the person you want to call. (Otherwise, what's the sense of looking up a phone number?)

The more specific the data that you already know, the faster Access can find the record you want. Asking Access to find the phone number of someone who lives in California is going to be a lot slower than asking Access to find the phone number of someone whose last name is Bangladore. Lots of people live in California, but how many people have such an odd last name as Bangladore?

When you want to tell Access to find something for you, you have to use a dialog box. This dialog box allows you to specify several options:

- **Find What:** Tells Access exactly what you want to find — a word, a single word, or an entire phrase.

- **Match:** Tells Access where to look for the data you specified in the Find What option. Here are your three choices:

  - **Any Part of Field** (a search for *Ann* would find both *MaryAnne* and *AnnMarie*)

  - **Match Whole Field** (a search for *Ann* would find only records containing *Ann*)

  - **Start of Field** (a search for *Ann* would find *AnnMarie* and *Ann* but not *MaryAnne*)

- **Search:** Tells Access which way to start looking for the data specified in the Find What option. Here are your choices:

  - **Up:** Tells Access to search all records, starting from the record that currently contains the cursor and going up to the first record in the table.

  - **Down:** Tells Access to search all records, starting from the record that currently contains the cursor and going down to the last record in the table.

  - **All:** Tells Access to search all records in the entire database.

- **Match Case:** For finicky people who only want exactly what's typed in the Find What box. Choosing this option means that if you search for *AnN*, Access will find records containing *AnN* but not records containing *Ann*, *ann*, or *aNN*.

- **Search Fields as Formatted:** For searching for data that appears in a different format from the one in which it was stored. For example, Access can display a date as 10/14/95 but store it as 14-Oct-95. Choosing this option tells Access to search for data only as it appears on-screen.

To find a specific record in a database table, follow these steps:

1. **Click in the field containing the data that you already know.**

   If you want to find a person's phone number but know only that person's last name, for example, click the LastName field.

2. **Choose Edit⇨Find (or press Ctrl+F).**

   The Find in Field dialog box appears (see Figure 15-13).

3. **Type the data that you want to find (such as a last name like Jefferson) and click the Find First button.**

   Access highlights the first record that contains your chosen data.

4. **Click the Close button to close the Find in a Field dialog box. (Or click Find Next if you want to see the next record that contains your chosen data.)**

Finding one or more records by using a filter

To find one or more records, you have to create a filter. A filter tells Access, "Show me all the people who live in Oregon and have the last name of Smith." Using this filter, Access rummages through your entire database and shows you the names, addresses, and phone numbers of all the Smiths who live in Oregon.

When you want to use a filter, you have to use the Filter dialog box, which allows you to specify several options:

✔ **Field:** Tells Access which fields you want to search. You can choose one or more fields.

✔ **Sort:** Tells Access to sort records in alphabetical order (ascending), to sort records in reverse alphabetical order (descending), or to not bother sorting at all (not sorted).

✔ **Criteria:** Tells Access what to look for. You can specify two or more criteria, such as "Find all the addresses of people who live in Oregon or California" or "Find all the addresses of people who live in Oregon and California."

To find one or more records using a filter, follow these steps:

1. Click in the field that you want to search by.

If you want to search by last name, for example, click in the Last Name field.

2. Choose Records⇨Filter⇨Filter by Form.

The Filter by Form dialog box appears (see Figure 15-14).

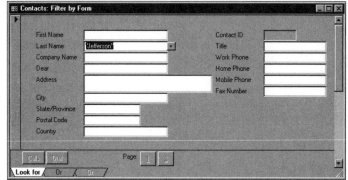

Figure 15-14:
The Filter by Form dialog box.

3. Click the downward-pointing arrow next to the field you chose in step 1.

A list appears, containing all the data available in that particular database field.

4. Click the data that you want to find.

5. Choose Filter⇨Apply Filter/Sort.

Access displays all records matching your search criteria.

6. Choose Records⇨Remove Filter/Sort.

After using a filter, make sure that you remove the filter; otherwise, Access displays only those records matching your last search, and you may think the rest of your data is gone.

Sorting a Database

To sort a database, you have to tell Access which field you want to sort and how you want to sort it (in ascending or descending order). For example, you can sort your database alphabetically by last name, by ZIP code, or by city. Unlike searching, which shows only part of your database, sorting simply shows your entire database from a different point of view.

To sort a database, follow these steps:

1. **Click in the field that you want to sort by.**

   If you want to sort by last name, for example, click in the Last Name field.

2. **Choose Records⇨Sort⇨Ascending (or Descending).**

   Ascending sorts alphabetically from A to Z. Descending sorts in reverse from Z to A.

   Access obediently sorts your records alphabetically.

3. **Choose Records⇨Remove Filter/Sort.**

To see your sorted records easier, choose View⇨Datasheet. This command displays all your records in rows and columns, as shown in Figure 15-15.

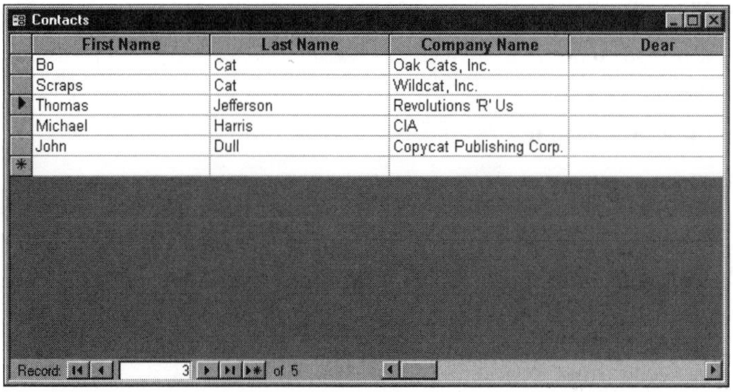

First Name	Last Name	Company Name	Dear
Bo	Cat	Oak Cats, Inc.	
Scraps	Cat	Wildcat, Inc.	
Thomas	Jefferson	Revolutions 'R' Us	
Michael	Harris	CIA	
John	Dull	Copycat Publishing Corp.	

Contacts

Record: 3 of 5

Figure 15-15:
The
Datasheet
view.

Chapter 16

Making the Most of Stored Information

S toring information in a database is okay, but the real fun comes when you have the data entered. After all, storing all the names and addresses of your customers is a waste if you don't use the information to help you make more money (which is what business is really all about).

To help you use your stored information effectively, Access provides different ways to view, print, and analyze your data. Information stored on Rolodex cards, in address books, or on paper forms is static; it remains the way you recorded it. Data stored in Access can be molded, shaped, and manipulated like Silly Putty.

Asking Questions with Queries

A *query* is a fancy term for a question you can ask Access. After you store information in a database, you can use queries to get the information back out again — and in different forms. A query can be as simple as finding the names and phone numbers of everyone who lives in Arkansas, or it can be as sophisticated as making Access retrieve the names of all sales people who made over $50,000 in sales and live in California, Nevada, or Arizona.

Because queries can be so flexible and powerful, they're a whole subject you can study all by themselves. (In fact, the Microsoft Access manual devotes several chapters to explaining queries, and many computer programmers spend entire semesters studying database queries, so don't feel bad if you don't master the topic of queries in twenty-one days or less.)

Do you need to use queries? No, but they can make life a great deal easier for you if you do. As an alternative, you can analyze your entire database yourself to try to make some sense out of it, but having Access dig through your database to find what you want is much easier.

For example, a query can list all the names and addresses of customers who haven't paid their bills in the past sixty days. Trying to find this information on your own is time-consuming and tedious. In comparison, having a query find it for you is fast and accurate. The whole secret to creating effective queries is knowing what you want and telling Access how to find it. (Not always an easy task. If you've ever told a child to bring you something cold to drink and he comes back with a jar full of pickle juice, you already know the problems of giving accurate commands.)

What's the difference between a query and the Find command?

Both queries and the Find command tell Access to retrieve and display certain data from your database. The main difference between the two is that the Find command can only search for specific data in one field while queries can search for data in one or more fields.

A second crucial difference is that you can save queries as part of your database file so that you can use them over and over again without

defining what you want to look for each time. When you use the Find command, you always have to define what you want to look at.

Use the Find command when you need to search through one field and you need to make this search only once. Use queries when you need to search through two or more fields and you routinely need to make this same search.

Creating a query

When you create a query, you must specify the *search criteria,* the type of data you want Access to find. Just to give you an idea how complicated queries can get, here are some of the more common types of search criteria options:

- ✔ **Exact matches:** Tells Access to find all records containing certain information, such as finding everyone with the last name of *Jones* who lives in Idaho and works as a lumberjack.

- ✔ **Partial matches:** Tells Access to find all records containing certain information, such as finding everyone whose last name begins with *B* and who works at any type of a job with the word *computer* in the title.

- ✔ **Less than:** Tells Access to find all records containing information that is less than a specific value, such as finding everyone who makes less than $30,000 a year, has been married less than three years, and flies on a commercial airline less than four times a year.

- ✔ **Greater than:** Tells Access to find all records containing information that is greater than a specific value, such as finding everyone who owns more than three yachts, earns over $50,000 a month, and hasn't paid any taxes in over five years.

- ✔ **Between:** Tells Access to find all records that fall between two specific values, such as finding everyone born between 1960 and 1970, who earns more than $30,000 a year but less than $90,000, and has more than two but less than five children.

Queries can get fairly complicated, such as asking Access to find the names of all people who earn less than $75,000 a year, live in either Seattle or Detroit, have owned their own houses for over six years, work in computer jobs, own personal computers, and subscribe to more than three but less than six magazines a year.

 Just remember that the quality of your answers depends heavily on the quality of your queries (questions). If you create a poorly designed query, Access probably won't find all the data you really need and may overlook important information that can impact your business or your job.

To create a query, follow these steps:

1. **Choose <u>W</u>indow and switch to the database window.**

2. **Click the Queries tab.**

3. **Click <u>N</u>ew.**

   A New Query dialog box appears (see Figure 16-1).

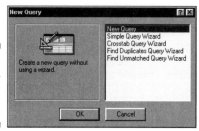

Figure 16-1:
The New
Query dialog
box.

4. **Click Simple Query Wizard.**

5. **Click OK.**

   The Simple Query Wizard dialog box appears (see Figure 16-2).

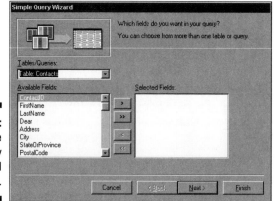

Figure 16-2:
The Simple
Query
Wizard
dialog box.

6. **Click the Tables/Queries list box and choose the table you want to search.**

7. **Click the Available Fields list box and choose the field you want your query to search.**

8. **Click the > button.**

   Access displays your field in the Selected Fields box. Repeat steps 7 and 8 for each field you want to use in your query.

9. **Click Next >.**

   Access asks what title you want to give your query, as shown in Figure 16-3.

10. **Type a name for your query in the Query list box.**

Figure 16-3:
The Simple
Query
Wizard
dialog box,
asking for a
query title.

11. **Click Finish.**

    Access shows you the result of your query — just so you can make sure
    that it does what you want it to do.

12. **Click the close box to remove the query result.**

13. **Choose Window and switch to the database window.**

    Access displays your newly created query on-screen.

Using a query

After you create and save a query, you can use that query as many times as you
want, no matter how much you add, delete, or modify the records in your
database. Since some queries can be fairly complicated ("Find all the people in
North Dakota who owe over $10,000 on their credit cards, own their own farms,
and have declared bankruptcy in the past 30 days or less."), saving and reusing
queries helps save you time, which is the whole purpose of computers in the
first place.

To use an existing query, follow these steps:

1. **Choose Window and switch to the database window.**

2. **Click the Queries tab.**

    A list of your available queries appears.

3. **Click the query you want to use and click Open.**

    Access displays the results of your query.

4. **Click the close box to remove the query result.**

Deleting a query

Eventually, a query may no longer serve its purpose as you add, delete, and modify the data in your database. To keep your database window from over-flowing with queries, delete the ones you don't need.

Deleting a query does not delete data. When you delete a query, you're just deleting the criteria you use to search your database.

To delete a query, follow these steps:

1. **Choose <u>W</u>indow and switch to the database window.**

2. **Click the Queries tab.**

   A list of your available queries appears.

3. **Click the query you want to delete.**

4. **Choose <u>E</u>dit⇨<u>D</u>elete (or press Delete).**

   A dialog box appears, asking whether you really want to delete your chosen query.

5. **Click <u>Y</u>es.**

   Your query disappears from the database window.

If you suddenly realize that you deleted a query by mistake, don't cringe in horror. Immediately, choose <u>E</u>dit⇨<u>U</u>ndo or press Ctrl+Z. Access undoes your last command and restores your query to its original state. (Whenever you do something by mistake, you can use the Undo command to correct it. Just make sure that you choose the Undo command immediately after you screw up; otherwise, Access may not be able to recover from your mistake.)

Making Your Data Look Good in Reports

If you have valuable information stored in your databases, you probably will need to show people your data. Instead of dragging them to your computer and showing them the data on your pretty new color monitor, you can print out your data in a report.

Besides being more convenient than making someone look at your computer, reports can display just the data you want seen, show the totals, and look so classy that others think that you put more effort putting it together than you really did.

Making a report

To make a report, follow these steps:

1. **Choose <u>W</u>indow and switch to the database window.**

2. **Click the Reports tab.**

3. **Click <u>N</u>ew.**

   A New Report dialog box appears (see Figure 16-4).

4. **Click Report Wizard.**

5. **Click the list box and choose a database table to use.**

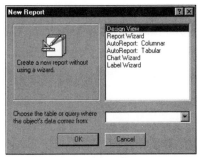

6. **Click OK.**

   A Report Wizard dialog box like the one in Figure 16-5 appears, asking
   `What Wizard do you want?`

7. **Click the <u>T</u>ables/Queries list box to select a database table to use.**

8. **Click the <u>A</u>vailable Fields list box and choose the field you want to print on your report.**

9. **Click the > button.**

   Access displays your field in the <u>S</u>elected Fields box. Repeat steps 7-8 for each field you want to use in your query.

10. **Click <u>N</u>ext >.**

   Figure 16-6 shows the Report Wizard dialog box that appears, asking whether you want any grouping levels in addition to the ones shown.

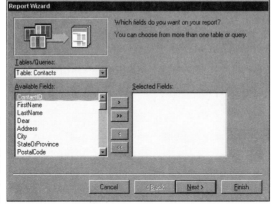

Figure 16-5:
The Report
Wizard
dialog box.

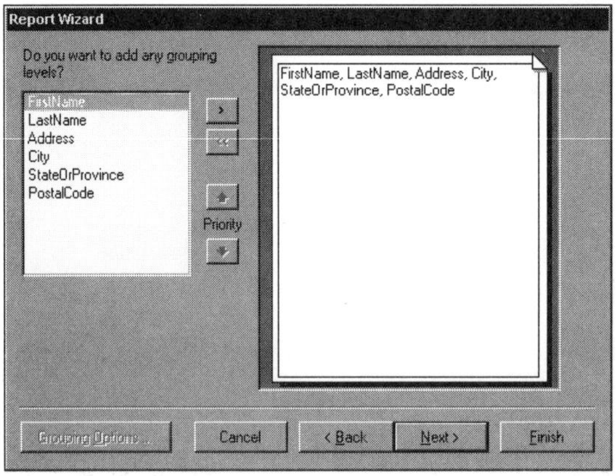

Figure 16-6:
Another
Report
Wizard
dialog box.

11. **Click Next >.**

    Figure 16-7 shows still another Report Wizard dialog box that appears, asking `What sort order and summary information do you want for detail records?`

12. **Choose the fields you want to sort by (if any), and then click Next>.**

    Figure 16-8 shows still another Report Wizard dialog box that appears, asking `How would you like to lay out your report?`

13. **Click the Layout (Vertical or Tabular) and Orientation (Portrait or Landscape) option buttons you want to use for your report.**

14. **Click Next >.**

    Another Report Wizard dialog box appears, asking for a style to use (see Figure 16-9).

15. **Click a style in the list box and click Next >.**

    Figure 16-10 shows another Report Wizard dialog box that appears, asking `What title do you want for your report?`

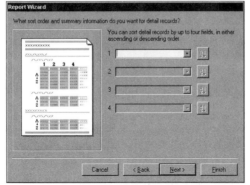

Figure 16-7:
Another
Report
Wizard
dialog box.

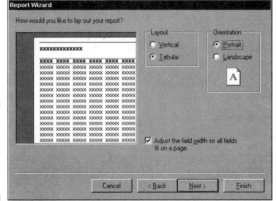

Figure 16-8:
Yet another
Report
Wizard
dialog box.

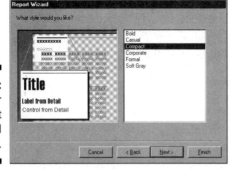

Figure 16-9:
Still another
Report
Wizard
dialog box.

16. **Type a title for your report and click Finish.**

   Access displays your report on-screen, as shown in Figure 16-11.

17. **Choose File⇨Print (or press Ctrl+P).**

   A Print dialog box appears.

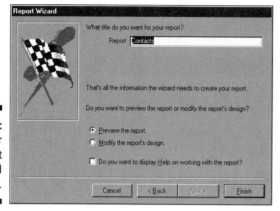

Figure 16-10:
Still another
Report
Wizard
dialog box.

Figure 16-11:
A preview of
your report.

18. **Click OK.**

Access prints out your report (just as long as your printer doesn't jam, which they tend to do whenever you need something in a hurry).

19. **Choose File⇨Save (or press Ctrl+S) to save your report.**

20. **Choose File⇨Close.**

Access displays the database window again.

Deleting a report

Eventually, a report may no longer serve its purpose as you add, delete, and modify the data in your database. To keep your database window from overflowing with useless reports, delete the ones you don't need.

Deleting a report does not delete data. When you delete a report, you're just deleting the way you told Access to print your data.

To delete a report, follow these steps:

1. **Choose <u>W</u>indow and switch to the database window.**
2. **Click the Reports tab.**

    A list of your available reports appears.

3. **Click the report you want to delete.**
4. **Choose <u>E</u>dit⇨<u>D</u>elete (or press Delete).**

    A dialog box appears, asking whether you really want to delete your chosen report.

5. **Click <u>Y</u>es.**

    Your report disappears from the database window.

If you suddenly realize that you deleted a report by mistake, don't cringe in horror. Immediately, choose <u>E</u>dit⇨<u>U</u>ndo or press Ctrl+Z. Access undoes your last command and restores your report.

Making Mailing Labels

Mailing labels are those little stickers you can paste on an envelope so you don't have to write the complete address yourself. If you periodically do mass mailings to the same people, you can save time by letting Access print mailing labels for you.

By storing names and addresses in an Access database, you can print mailing labels any time you want or sell your database to a mailing list company so that everyone in your database starts receiving junk mail from organizations nobody has heard of.

To make mailing labels, follow these steps:

1. **Choose <u>W</u>indow and switch to the database window.**
2. **Click the Reports tab.**

3. Click _New_.

The New Report dialog box appears.

4. Click Label Wizard.

5. Click the list box and choose a database table to use.

6. Click OK.

The Label Wizard dialog box appears (see Figure 16-12).

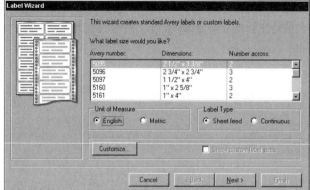

Figure 16-12:
The Label
Wizard
dialog box.

7. Choose a label size and click _Next_ >.

Another Label Wizard dialog box appears (see Figure 16-13).

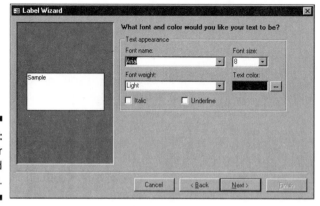

Figure 16-13:
Another
Label Wizard
dialog box.

8. **Choose a font name, size, color, and typeface (italics or underline) and then click Next >.**

   Yet another Label Wizard dialog box appears (see Figure 16-14).

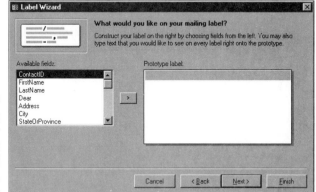

9. **Click a field you want to appear on your labels and then click the > button.**

   Repeat this step for each field you want to add to the label. (*Note:* Make sure that you insert spaces between each field or use the up/down arrow keys to display a field on another line.)

10. **Click Next >.**

    Figure 16-15 shows another Label Wizard dialog box that appears, asking `Which fields would you like to sort by?`

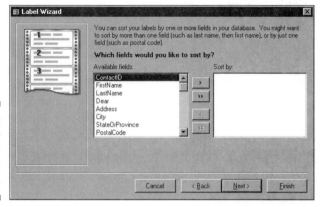

11. **Click the field (or fields) you want to use to sort and click the > button.**

12. **Click Next >.**

Still another Label Wizard dialog box appears, asking What name would you like for your report? (see Figure 16-16).

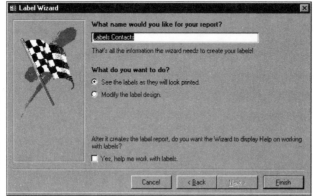

13. **Type a name for your report and click Finish.**

Access shows you what your mailing labels will look like if your printer doesn't screw up. Figure 16-17 shows a preview of your labels.

14. **Turn on your printer, shove in your mailing labels, and choose File⇨Print (or press Ctrl+P).**

    A Print dialog box appears.

15. **Click OK.**

    If your printer works, your mailing labels appear printed neatly on each label.

16. **Choose File⇨Close.**

    Access displays the name of your mailing label report in the database window.

Modifying Your Forms

A Form displays a single record of your database, such as someone's name, address, phone number, employee number, and so on. Although Access can create forms for you automatically through the magic of the Form Wizard, you may want to customize your form's appearance anyway, just to show Access that you still possess your own free will.

Forms consist of one or more fields and field labels. A field contains the information stored in your database, and the label simply identifies your data.

When you modify a form, you can

✔ Change the position, size, and text appearance of your fields and labels

✔ Add labels of your own

Moving fields and field labels on a form

Although Access's Form Wizard can create forms for you automatically, you may want to modify your form later. In this way you can let the Form Wizard do all the tedious work in creating a form for you, and then go back and pretty it up. For that reason, Access lets you move fields and field labels around in a form until the entire form looks exactly right to you.

To move fields and field labels on a form, follow these steps:

1. **Choose Window and switch to the database window.**

2. **Click the Forms tab.**

Access displays a list of your forms.

3. Click the form you want to modify and then click the Design button.

Access displays your form as labels and fields, as shown in Figure 16-18.

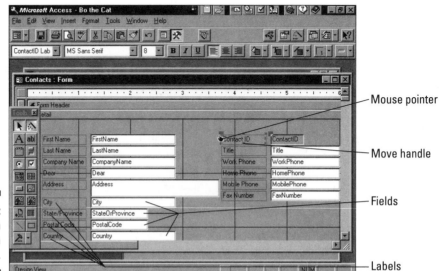

Figure 16-18: The Design view of a typical form.

Mouse pointer

Move handle

Fields

Labels

4. Click the field or label you want to move.

Access displays little gray handles around the field or label. The upper left gray handle, which appears larger than the rest, is the move handle.

5. Move the mouse pointer over the move handle.

The mouse pointer becomes a little black pointing hand with one finger sticking up.

6. Hold down the left mouse button and move the mouse pointer.

The field or field label moves along with the mouse pointer.

7. Move the field or field label where you want it and release the left mouse button.

Resizing fields and field labels

When Access creates a form for you, it tries to create fields and field labels that are large enough to show all your data. However, sometimes a field is too small (or too large). Rather than suffer with such imperfections, you can resize your fields and labels.

To resize a field or label, follow these steps:

1. **Choose Window and switch to the database window.**

2. **Click the Forms tab.**

    Access displays a list of your forms.

3. **Click the form you want to modify and then click the Design button.**

    Access displays your form as labels and fields.

4. **Click the field or field label you want to resize.**

    Access displays little gray handles around the field or field label. Tiny black boxes appear around the edges. These tiny black boxes are called the size handles.

5. **Move the mouse pointer over one of the size handles until it changes into a two-headed arrow.**

6. **Hold the left mouse button down and move the mouse.**

    The field or field label changes size.

7. **Release the mouse button when the field or label is the size you want.**

Changing the text appearance of fields and field labels

Because Access lacks an active imagination, it tends to create dull fields and field labels that appear in black and white, in 8-point size in the MS Sans Serif font, with left alignment.

To spice up your fields and field labels to highlight important information or just to give yourself something important to do while at work, Access lets you change background and foreground colors, fonts, size, and alignment (left, center, or right).

Don't alter the appearance of your fields and field labels too drastically. You can display data in shocking pink, 48-point size, and some bizarre font never before seen by humans, but such wildly creative fields and field labels may detract from the purpose of your form, which is to display data so that others can see and understand it.

To change the text appearance of fields and labels, follow these steps:

1. Choose _W_indow and switch to the database window.

2. Click the Forms tab.

Access displays a list of your forms.

3. Click the form you want to modify and then click the _D_esign button.

Access displays your form as labels and fields.

4. Click the field or label you want to change.

Access displays little gray handles around the field or field label.

5. Press the right mouse button.

A pop-up menu appears (see Figure 16-19).

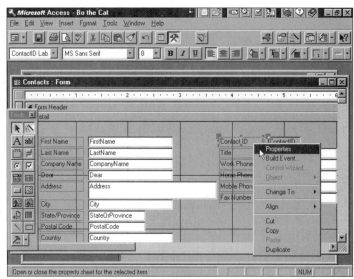

Figure 16-19: The right mouse button pop-up menu.

6. Choose Properties.

A Properties dialog box appears.

7. Click the Format tab (see Figure 16-20).

Figure 16-20:
The
Properties
dialog box
with the
Format tab
selected.

8. **Click the property you want to change (such as the Border Color or Back Color) and make any changes you want.**

9. **Click the close box of the Properties dialog box and admire the changes you've made.**

Adding labels of your own

Each field on a form has a corresponding field label. However, sometimes you may want to add labels of your own, which can contain company names, short instructions, or mischievous messages — just to see if your boss is paying attention.

To satisfy this creative urge, Access lets you create your own labels and plop them anywhere on a form. Such labels are purely decorative, so make sure that you really need them before messing up your form any more than you must.

To add your own labels to a form, follow these steps:

1. **Choose Window and switch to the database window.**

2. **Click the Forms tab.**

   Access displays a list of your forms.

3. **Click the form you want to modify and then click the Design button.**

   Access displays your form as labels and fields.

4. **Click the Label tool in the Toolbox.**

   The mouse pointer turns into a large *A* and a plus sign. (Just look at Figure 16-21 to see for yourself.)

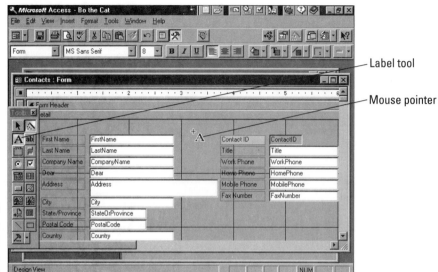

Label tool

Mouse pointer

Figure 16-21:
Drawing a
new label.

5. **Move the mouse pointer to the location on the form where you want the upper left corner of your label.**

6. **Hold down the left mouse button and move the mouse pointer to the location where you want the lower right corner of your label.**

7. **Release the mouse button.**

   Access draws your label on the form.

8. **Type the text you want to appear in the label and then press Enter.**

   Then you can modify the color, font, size, bold, italic, or alignment of your label.

Chapter 17

Using Form Letters and Address Labels to Get the Word Out Fast

∙ ∙

In This Chapter

▶ Getting Schedule+ and Word to cooperate

▶ Making mailing labels

▶ Printing addresses on envelopes

▶ Making form letters and other personalized mail

∙ ∙

*A*lthough Microsoft Word is perfectly capable of creating form letters and mailing labels all by itself, why store names and addresses in Microsoft Word if you have them available in Microsoft Schedule+?

Combining Schedule+ and Word gives you great flexibility in printing form letters. That way you can create personalized letters that may actually read like they were written by someone who cared.

Getting Schedule+ and Word to Cooperate

Creating a form letter or mailing label requires two separate files:

- ✔ A data source (a Schedule+ file)
- ✔ A document (a Word file)

The data source contains names and addresses while the document determines the appearance and position of the names and addresses on a mailing label or within a form letter.

First you must create a data source, which means storing names and addresses (or whatever else you want) in a Schedule+ file. After you have a data source, you can use Word to create the document to display this data.

Making Mailing Labels

Mailing labels are nothing more exciting than names and addresses that appear on stickers you paste on envelopes. Although you could print addresses directly on envelopes, it's usually a lot easier to use mailing labels so that you can print a sheet of names and addresses at one time, and paste them on anything from postcards and envelopes to big bulky packages that will probably get lost or damaged in the mail.

Merging Schedule+ data with Word

Since most of your important names and addresses are probably stored in a Schedule+ file anyway, you might as well use that information rather than re-enter them in Word.

To create mailing labels from within Word, follow these steps:

1. **Choose Section⇨View Outside. (Skip this step if you're running Word as a separate program.)**

2. **Load Word and choose Tools⇨Mail Merge.**

   The Mail Merge Helper dialog box appears (see Figure 17-1).

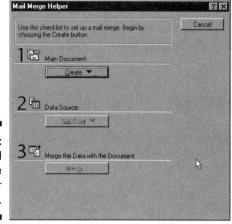

Figure 17-1:
The Mail
Merge
Helper
dialog box.

3. **Click the Create button.**

   A list box appears (see Figure 17-2).

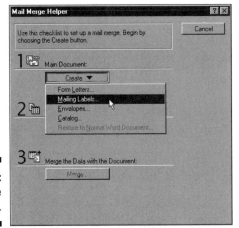

Figure 17-2:
The Create
list box.

4. **Choose Mailing labels.**

   A Microsoft Word dialog box appears.

5. **Click the Active Window button.**

6. **Click the Get Data button.**

   A list box appears.

7. **Choose Use Address Book.**

   The Use Address Book dialog box appears (see Figure 17-3).

Figure 17-3:
The Use
Address
Book dialog
box.

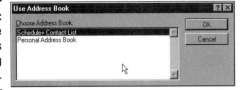

8. **Click the Schedule+ file you want and click OK.**

   A Microsoft Word dialog box appears, telling you that you must set up
   your main document (see Figure 17-4).

Figure 17-4:
A Microsoft
Word dialog
box.

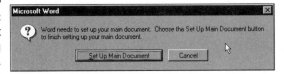

9. **Click the Set Up Main Document button.**

   The Label Options dialog box appears (see Figure 17-5).

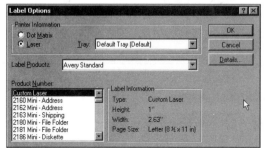

Figure 17-5:
The Label
Options
dialog box.

10. **Choose the label type you want and click OK.**

    The Create Labels dialog box appears (see Figure 17-6).

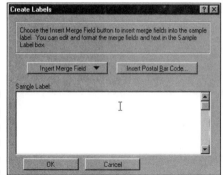

Figure 17-6:
The Create
Labels
dialog box.

11. **Click Insert Merge Field.**

    A pop-up menu appears, showing all the information you can print on your label.

12. **Click all the data you want to appear on your label. (Repeat this step as often as necessary to include all the data you want.)**

    Be sure to put spaces or commas between each field (such as Last Name and First Name) and press Enter to move to the next line.

13. **Click OK.**

14. **Click the Merge button.**

    The Merge dialog box appears.

15. **Click the Merge button again.**

    Word displays your labels on-screen (see Figure 17-7).

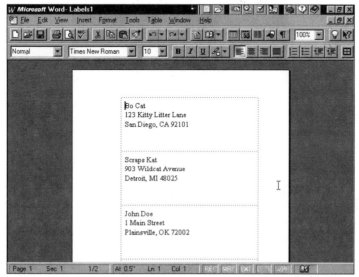

Figure 17-7:
The
appearance
of your
labels.

Printing Addresses on Envelopes

Instead of printing addresses on mailing labels and then wasting time pasting these mailing labels on an envelope, sometimes you may want Word to print the addresses on the envelope. If you have a few addresses to print and don't want to waste an entire sheet of mailing labels just to print two or three addresses, for example, print directly to envelopes.

To print envelopes from within Word, follow these steps:

1. **Choose Section⇨View Outside. (Skip this step if you're running Word as a separate program.)**

2. **Load Word and choose Tools⇨Mail Merge.**

    The Mail Merge Helper dialog box appears.

3. **Click the Create button.**

    A list box appears.

4. **Choose Envelopes.**

   A Microsoft Word dialog box appears.

5. **Click the Active Window button.**

   The Mail Merge Helper dialog box appears again.

6. **Click the Get Data button.**

   A list box appears.

7. **Click Use Address Book.**

   The Use Address Book dialog box appears.

8. **Click on the Schedule+ file you want and click OK.**

   A Microsoft Word dialog box appears, telling you that you must set up your main document.

9. **Click the Set Up Main Document button.**

   The Envelope Options dialog box appears (see Figure 17-8).

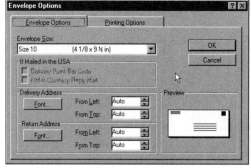

Figure 17-8:
The
Envelope
Options
dialog box.

10. **Choose the envelope size you want and click OK.**

    The Envelope Address dialog box appears.

11. **Click Insert Merge Field.**

    A pop-up menu appears, showing all the information you can print on your label.

12. **Click all the data you want to appear on your label. (Repeat this step as often as necessary to include all the data you want.)**

    Be sure to put spaces or commas between each field (such as Last Name and First Name) and press Enter to move to the next line.

13. **Click OK.**

   The Mail Merge Helper dialog box appears again.

14. **Click the Merge button.**

   The Merge dialog box appears.

15. **Click the Merge button again.**

   Word displays your envelopes on-screen (see Figure 17-9).

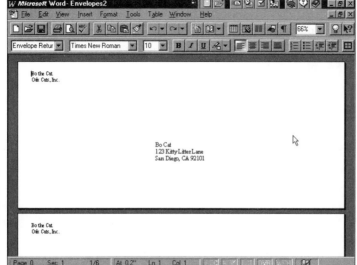

Figure 17-9:
The
appearance
of your
envelopes.

Making Form Letters and Other Personalized Mail

Everyone has received a form letter at some point in their lives, such as the Publisher's Clearing House Sweepstakes notifying you that *you* may have just won ten million dollars. Any time you need to write custom letters that contain different but predictable data, you can save time by writing a form letter. To create a form letter, follow these steps:

1. **Choose Section⇨View Outside. (Skip this step if you're running Word as a separate program.)**

2. **Load Word and choose Tools⇨Mail Merge.**

   The Mail Merge Helper dialog box appears.

3. Click the Create button.

A list box appears.

4. Choose Form Letters.

A Microsoft Word dialog box appears.

5. Click the Active Window button.

The Mail Merge Helper dialog box appears again.

6. Click the Get Data button.

A list box appears.

7. Click Use Address Book.

The Use Address Book dialog box appears.

8. Click the Schedule+ file you want.

9. Click OK.

A Microsoft Word dialog box appears, telling you that you must set up your main document.

10. Click the Edit Main Document button.

The Mail Merge toolbar appears (see Figure 17-10).

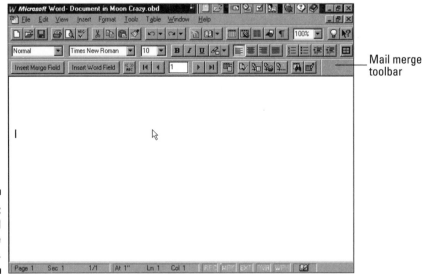

Mail merge toolbar

Figure 17-10:
The Mail Merge toolbar.

11. Type your form letter and click the Insert Merge Field button when you want to insert data from your Schedule+ file (such as a name, address, or ZIP code).

Figure 17-11 shows a sample form letter with merge fields highlighted.

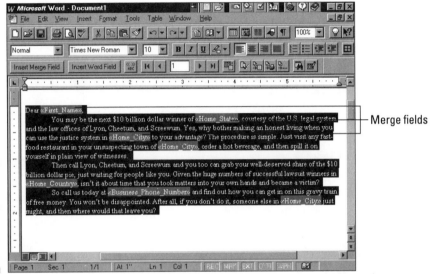

Figure 17-11:
A sample
form letter
with merge
fields
highlighted.

Merge fields

The 5th Wave   By Rich Tennant

"NO, THEY'RE NOT REALLY A GANG, JUST A PARTICULARLY AGGRESSIVE LAN."

Chapter 18

Exchanging Information within Microsoft Office

· ·

· ·

*T*he most popular type of program that most people use is a word-processing one. Despite the efficiency of telephones, televisions, and other nouns that begin with *tele*, writing still remains one of the more common ways that people communicate with each other (besides using obscene hand gestures).

No matter how classy you make your graphs in PowerPoint or how complex you make the calculations in Excel, you'll always need to write words that explain what the information means. And by combining words with spreadsheets, data, and graphs, you can create sophisticated reports that will look pleasing to the eye, even if you have nothing important to say. For that reason, Microsoft Office provides several ways to exchange data between Word, Excel, Access, Schedule+, and PowerPoint.

Exchanging Data between Programs

Microsoft Windows 95 makes exchanging data between different programs easy. Just copy the data you want from one program and paste the data in another.

Windows provides four different ways to share data between programs:

- ✔ Copy it
- ✔ Move it
- ✔ Link it
- ✔ Embed it

Copying data

Copying data is useful when you want certain data to appear in more than one program, such as having names and addresses in both an Access database and a Word form letter.

To copy data, follow these steps:

1. **Highlight the data you want to copy by holding down the mouse button and dragging the mouse pointer over the data you want to copy, or holding down Shift and using the arrow keys to move the cursor over the data you want to copy.**

2. **Press Ctrl+C or click the Copy button, as shown in Figure 18-1.**

   Although you can't see the Clipboard, Windows temporarily stores your highlighted data on it.

3. **Move the cursor to the window and the position where you want to paste the data you highlighted in step 1.**

4. **Press Ctrl+V or click the Paste button.**

TECHNICAL STUFF

The Windows Clipboard

When you copy or move data, Windows stores this information temporarily in an area of memory affectionately known as the *Clipboard*. The Clipboard can hold globs of data but only one glob at a time. The moment you copy or move another glob of data, the Clipboard immediately erases the data it's currently holding and replaces it with the new data.

After you've copied or moved data to the Clipboard, you can paste the data to a Word, Excel,

PowerPoint, or Access window as many times as you want. But the moment you copy or move new data to the Clipboard, the Clipboard forgets all the old data previously stored on it.

(One exception to this is if you save the contents of the Clipboard to a file by using the Clipboard Viewer program. Then you can retrieve the file using the Clipboard Viewer and paste its contents in another program.)

Copy button   Cut button   Paste button

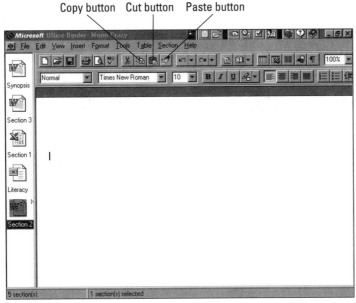

Figure 18-1:
The Copy,
Cut, and
Paste
buttons on
the toolbar.

Moving data

Moving data is useful when it's in one file but you want it in another file. You can move text from one Word document to another document, for example, or move a spreadsheet from Excel to Word.

To move data, follow these steps:

1. **Highlight the data you want to move by holding down the mouse button and dragging the mouse pointer over the data you want to move or by holding down Shift and using the arrow keys to move the cursor over the data you want to move.**

2. **Press Ctrl+X or click the Cut button (refer to Figure 18-1).**

   Although you can't see the Clipboard, Windows temporarily stores your highlighted data on it.

3. **Move the cursor to the window and the position where you want to paste the data you highlighted in step 1.**

4. **Press Ctrl+V or click the Paste button.**

When you cut data from a program, the data exists only on the Clipboard, so paste it to a new document or location right away. If you cut or copy additional data before pasting the first chunk of data, the Clipboard erases the first data cut and replaces it with the new data. You forever lose the first chunk of data you cut to the Clipboard.

When you use the Cut command, always follow it immediately with a Paste command unless you want to lose your cut data for good.

Linking data

Linking data lets you create a graph in PowerPoint and have that graph appear in a Word document. Linking is most useful when you need to share data with several people. If you have a graph that five other people need to use, for example, you can print five copies and pass them around the office, a time-consuming and inconvenient process.

As an easier alternative, link your graph to these five people's Word documents. That way when you change your graph in PowerPoint, linking automatically updates the graphs in their Word documents.

To link data, follow these steps:

1. **Open (or switch to) the program containing the data that you want to link.**

   If you want to link a graph from PowerPoint into a Word document, for example, open (or switch to) PowerPoint.

2. **Highlight the data you want to move by holding down the mouse button and dragging the mouse pointer over the data you want to move or by holding down the Shift key and using the arrow keys to move the cursor over the data you want to move.**

3. **Choose Edit⇨Copy (or press Ctrl+C).**

4. **Open (or switch to) the program where you want to link your data.**

   If you're linking a PowerPoint graph to a Word document, for example, open (or switch to) Word.

5. **Place the cursor where you want the linked data to appear.**

6. **Choose Edit menu⇨Paste Special.**

   The Paste Special dialog box appears (see Figure 18-2).

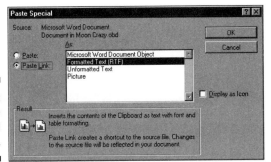

Figure 18-2:
The Paste
Special
dialog box.

7. **Click the Paste Link option button.**

8. **Choose the way that you want to link the data (such as Formatted Text or Unformatted Text).**

9. **Click OK.**

Now any time you change the data in the source file (the file you chose in Step 1), the data automatically changes in the destination file (the file you chose in Step 4).

Breaking links

You can break a link at any time. After you break a link, the linked data still remains but can never be updated or reconnected ever again for the rest of your life, so be careful before breaking a link.

You can break a link only from within the program containing the linked data. If you have a PowerPoint graph linked to a Word document, for example, you have to break the link from within Word.

To break a link, follow these steps:

1. **Open or switch to the program containing the linked data.**

2. **Choose Edit⇨Links.**

The Links dialog box appears (see Figure 18-3).

3. **Click the link that you want to break and click Break Link.**

A dialog box appears, asking if you're sure you want to break a link because, after you do, you cannot unbreak it.

4. **Click Yes.**

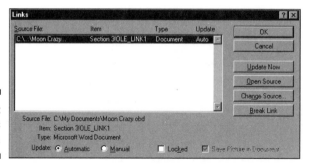

Figure 18-3:
The Links
dialog box.

To break a link within Microsoft Excel, highlight the linked data and press Delete. The above four steps won't work within Excel because Microsoft hasn't quite gotten the concept of integration to work smoothly within all programs in Microsoft Office, despite their advertising claims to the contrary.

Embedding data

When you embed data, you physically store data from one program in another, such as embedding an Excel spreadsheet in a Word document. The main difference between linking and embedding is that embedding creates a single document that contains all the data. With linking, the information is updated dynamically as the source file changes.

You can embed Excel, Access, and PowerPoint data in a Word document, and then view, edit, or print that document on another computer — even if that computer doesn't have a copy of Excel, Access, or PowerPoint. When you embed data, the data resides in a single file. When you link data, the data resides in two separate files.

The steps to embedding data are similar to the steps to linking data, except that you choose the option that has the word "Object" in it rather than the option that has "Link" in it.

To embed data, follow these steps:

1. **Open or switch to the program containing the data that you want to embed.**

   If you want to embed a graph from PowerPoint into a Word document, for example, open or switch to PowerPoint.

2. **Highlight the data you want to move by holding down the mouse button and dragging the mouse pointer over the data you want to move or by**

Linking versus Embedding

Should you link or embed data? Linking shares data between two or more separate files, but embedding crams the data into a single file. As a result, embedded files tend to get fat and large, and linked files stay lean.

On the other hand, sharing linked data files is a pain in the neck. Not only do you have to give each person a copy of all your linked data files, but each person must have a copy of each program that created the linked data. If you link an Excel spreadsheet to a Word document and want to share your work with others, for example, you have to give them your Excel spreadsheet file and your Word document file, in addition to

making sure that they have a copy of Excel and Word on their computers.

Sharing embedded data files is easy. Just give one file to the other people and you're done. Even if your embedded file contains Excel data and the others don't have Excel on their computers, the embedded files can still display the Excel spreadsheet data.

If you want to share files with other people who may not have the exact same programs you have, embed your data. If you want to keep your files small and separate, and you want to update data stored in multiple documents easily, link data.

holding down Shift and using the arrow keys to move the cursor over the data you want to move.

3. **Choose Edit⇨Copy (or press Ctrl+C).**

4. **Open or switch to the program where you want to embed your data.**

   If you're embedding a PowerPoint graph to a Word document, for example, open or switch to Word.

5. **Place the cursor where you want to embed the data.**

6. **Choose Edit⇨Paste Special.**

   The Paste Special dialog box appears.

7. **Click the Paste option button.**

8. **Choose the option that ends with the word *Object*, such as *Microsoft Word Document Object* or *Microsoft Excel Worksheet Object*.**

9. **Click OK.**

Editing embedded data

To edit embedded data, just double-click the embedded data. After you double-click embedded data, two changes immediately occur:

✔ The menu and toolbar change to match the program that created the embedded data. If you double-clicked an Excel spreadsheet that was embedded in a Word document, for example, Excel's menus and toolbar temporarily replaces Word's menus and toolbars (see Figure 18-4).

✔ The embedded data immediately changes to its format in the program that created it. For example, an embedded Excel spreadsheet shows row numbers, column labels, and worksheet tabs.

When you're finished editing embedded data, click anywhere outside the embedded data.

Row and column headings in Excel spreadsheet   Excel toolbar

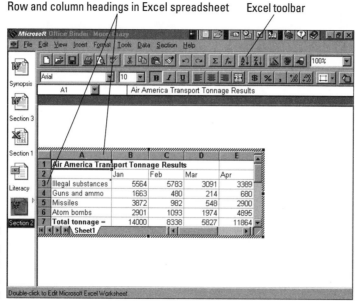

Figure 18-4: Embedded data.

Deleting embedded data

To delete embedded data, use the mouse or arrow keys to highlight it, and then press Delete. Simple, isn't it?

When you delete linked data, that data still exists in a separate file. When you delete embedded data, that data may or may not exist in another file. Before deleting embedded data, make sure that you won't need it again.

Sharing Text with Word

If you're creating a fancy report, you can write your text in Word and spruce it up with numbers from Excel, data from Access, and pretty pictures from PowerPoint.

Word and Excel

Word can display Excel worksheet data in four ways:

- ✔ As text
- ✔ As a picture
- ✔ As a table
- ✔ As a spreadsheet

Pasting Excel data as text

When you paste Excel data into Word as text, you have to align the numbers in neat rows and columns yourself. The main advantage of copying Excel data as text is to display numbers in a format other than in rows and columns.

To paste Excel data as text into Word, follow these steps:

1. **In an Excel file, highlight the data you want to import.**
2. **Choose Edit⇨Copy (or press Ctrl+C).**
3. **Open or switch to Word.**
4. **Place the cursor where you want the Excel data to appear.**
5. **Choose Edit⇨Paste Special.**

   The Paste Special dialog box appears.
6. **Click the Paste option button.**
7. **In the As list box, choose Unformatted Text.**
8. **Click OK.**

Pasting Excel data as a table

When you paste Excel data into Word as a table, the numbers display in neat rows and columns that you can edit, but you cannot use Excel formulas or functions to make calculations.

To import Excel data as a table into Word, follow these steps:

1. In an Excel file, highlight the data you want to import.

2. Choose Edit⇨Copy (or press Ctrl+C).

3. Open or switch to Word.

4. Place the cursor where you want the Excel data to appear.

5. Choose Edit⇨Paste (or press Ctrl+V).

Pasting Excel data as a picture

When you import Excel data as a picture, the numbers display in neat rows and columns, but you cannot edit the data in any way. Importing data as pictures is most useful when you don't want someone to edit your data by mistake (or on purpose).

To import Excel data as a picture into Word, follow these steps:

1. In an Excel file, highlight the data you want to import.

2. Hold down Shift and choose Edit⇨Copy Picture.

The Copy Picture dialog box appears (see Figure 18-5).

Figure 18-5:
The Copy
Picture
dialog box.

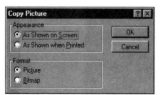

3. Click OK.

4. Switch to Word.

5. Place the cursor where you want the Excel data to appear.

6. Choose Edit⇨Paste (or press Ctrl+V).

Linking Excel data into Word

When you import Excel data into Word as a spreadsheet, the numbers display in neat rows and columns, and you can use Excel formulas or functions to calculate results. The only two ways to display a spreadsheet in Word is to link or embed data from Excel to your Word document.

To link Excel data into Word, follow these steps:

1. **In an Excel file, highlight the data you want to link.**

2. **Choose Edit⇨Copy (or press Ctrl+C).**

3. **Open or switch to Word.**

4. **Place the cursor where you want the Excel data to appear.**

5. **Choose Edit⇨Paste Special.**

   The Paste Special dialog box appears.

6. **Click the Paste Link option button.**

7. **Choose Microsoft Excel Worksheet Object from the As list box.**

8. **Click OK.**

Embedding Excel data into Word

To embed Excel data into Word, follow these steps:

1. **In an Excel file, highlight the data you want to embed.**

2. **Choose Edit⇨Copy (or press Ctrl+C).**

3. **Open or switch to Word.**

4. **Place the cursor where you want the Excel data to appear.**

5. **Choose Edit⇨Paste Special.**

   The Paste Special dialog box appears.

6. **Click the Paste option button.**

7. **Choose Microsoft Excel Worksheet Object from the As list box.**

8. **Click OK.**

Creating spreadsheets within Word

Sometimes you may need to create a spreadsheet from scratch that you want to appear in a Word document. You can load Excel, create your spreadsheet, and then copy and paste it into Word. But that's clumsy, and we all know that computers make life easier than that (except when you try reading the manuals).

A shortcut is to create the Excel spreadsheet directly within Word, complete with all Excel's formulas and functions. When you save your Word document, Office saves (embeds) the Excel spreadsheet within your Word document file.

To create Excel data in Word, follow these steps:

1. **In a Word document, place the cursor where you want to create an Excel spreadsheet.**

2. **Click the Insert Microsoft Excel Worksheet button on the toolbar.**

   A grid appears, as shown in Figure 18-6.

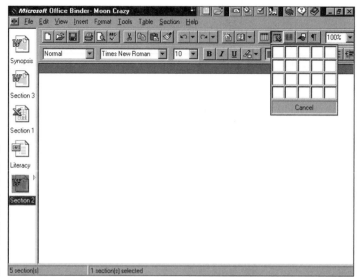

Figure 18-6:
The Insert
Microsoft
Excel
Worksheet
button and
its grid.

3. **Move the mouse pointer down the boxes on left side of the grid, indicating the number of rows you want and to the right, indicating the number of columns; click the mouse button.**

   If you click the box in the bottom right corner of the grid, for example, Excel creates a spreadsheet consisting of four rows and five columns. The embedded Excel worksheet appears in your document along with the Excel toolbar and menus at the top of the screen.

4. **Type any numbers, functions, or formulas you want in the spreadsheet.**

When the cursor appears inside a spreadsheet embedded in Word, Excel's menus and toolbar temporarily replace Word's menus and toolbar.

To resize your spreadsheet, drag the resize handles of the spreadsheet. Excel creates a bigger or smaller spreadsheet for you to use.

Word and Access

Normally, Access data is most useful for storing information that you think you'll need again at a later date. However, you can also paste Access data as a table in a Word document.

To paste Access data as a table in Word, follow these steps:

1. **Choose Section⇨View Outside if you're running Word within a binder. (Skip this step if you're running Word as a separate program.)**

2. **Choose Insert⇨Database.**

   The Database dialog box appears (see Figure 18-7).

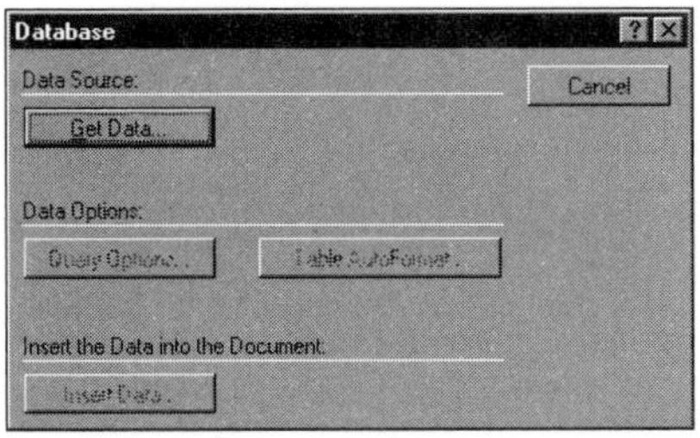

Figure 18-7:
The
Database
dialog box.

3. **Click the Get Data button.**

   The Open Data Source dialog box appears (see Figure 18-8).

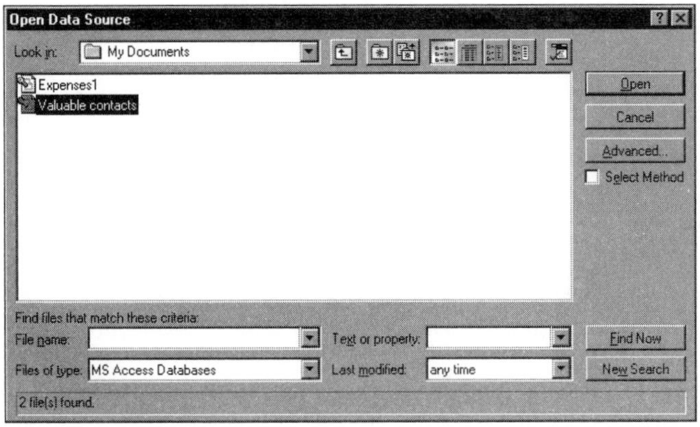

Figure 18-8:
The Open
Data Source
dialog box.

4. **Click the arrow in the Files of type list box and choose MS Access Databases.**

5. **Click the Access file you want to import into your Word document and then click the Open button.**

   The Microsoft Access dialog box appears (see Figure 18-9).

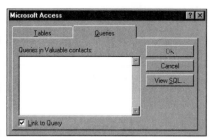

Figure 18-9:
The
Microsoft
Access
dialog box.

6. **Click the Tables tab and choose the table you want to insert into your Word document.**

7. **Click OK.**

   The Database dialog box appears again.

8. **Click the Table AutoFormat button.**

   The Table AutoFormat dialog box appears (see Figure 18-10).

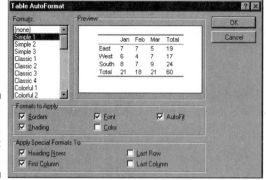

Figure 18-10:
The Table
AutoFormat
dialog box.

9. **Choose the table format you want to use.**

10. **Click OK.**

    The Database dialog box appears again.

11. **Click the Insert Data button.**

    The Insert Data dialog box appears (see Figure 18-11).

Figure 18-11:
The Insert
Data dialog
box.

Figure 18-11:
The Insert
Data dialog
box.

12. **Click the All option button (or type the range of records you want to insert, such as records 1 through 12).**

13. **Click OK.**

Word and PowerPoint

PowerPoint is a great program for creating slides, overheads, and outlines. Word is useful for word processing, but its weak drawing program can't match PowerPoint's artistry. You can take advantage of both programs' capabilities, however. You can create a fancy, colorful PowerPoint presentation and paste either text or graphic objects into Word.

Pasting text from PowerPoint into Word

Text most commonly appears in PowerPoint as an outline, a slide title, or a text box. Any time you move the mouse pointer over text, PowerPoint helpfully turns it into an I-beam.

What appears to be text in a PowerPoint presentation may actually be a graphic object, such as fancy titles or headlines. If you move the mouse pointer over text but it doesn't change into an I-beam, chances are the text is really a graphic object.

To import PowerPoint text in Word, follow these steps:

1. **In a PowerPoint file, highlight what you want to import.**

2. **Choose Edit⇨Copy (or press Ctrl+C).**

3. **Switch to Word and place the cursor where you want to import the PowerPoint text.**

4. **Choose Edit⇨Paste (or press Ctrl+V).**

Pasting graphics from PowerPoint into Word

PowerPoint graphics appear in a Word document as an object you can resize, move, or even edit from within Word. That way you can make sure that your text flows nicely around the graphic object and use Word as a desktop publisher for creating simple newsletters, flyers, and other things that people will throw away the moment you're not looking at them any more.

To import PowerPoint graphics in Word, follow these steps:

1. **In a PowerPoint presentation file, click the graphic object that you want to import.**

   PowerPoint displays resize handles around any graphic object that you click.

2. **Choose Edit➪Copy (or press Ctrl+C).**

3. **Switch to Word and place the cursor where you want to import the PowerPoint graphic.**

4. **Choose Edit➪Paste (or press Ctrl+V).**

Exchanging Numbers with Excel

Although Excel's main purpose is for calculating numeric results, you can still copy and paste data from Word, PowerPoint, or Access into an Excel worksheet. You may find copying text from Word easier than typing text in a worksheet cell, for example.

Excel and Word

When you copy text from Word into Excel, you have three choices:

- ✔ Paste the text into a worksheet cell
- ✔ Paste the text into a worksheet text box
- ✔ Paste a Word table into multiple worksheet cells

Copying text into a worksheet cell

When you copy text from Word to an Excel worksheet, you can paste the text into a single worksheet cell. Unfortunately, if you paste a long phrase or paragraph into a worksheet cell, all the text tries to cram into the one cell. If the neighboring cells are empty, the text overflows into those neighboring cells and makes a complete mess.

To copy Word text into an Excel worksheet cell, follow these steps:

1. **In a Word document file, highlight the data you want to import.**

2. **Choose Edit⇨Copy (or press Ctrl+C).**

3. **Switch to Excel and place the cursor to the cell where you want to import the Word text.**

4. **Choose Edit⇨Paste (or press Ctrl+V).**

Copying a table from Word into Excel

When you copy a table stored in a Word document and paste it into an Excel worksheet, Excel thoughtfully places each cell of your Word table in corresponding cells in the worksheet.

To copy a Word table into Excel, follow these steps:

1. **In a Word document file, highlight the table that you want to import.**

2. **Choose Edit⇨Copy (or press Ctrl+C).**

3. **Switch to Excel.**

4. **Click the cell where you want the upper left corner of the table to appear.**

5. **Choose Edit⇨Paste (or press Ctrl+V).**

Linking Word text to an Excel worksheet

Linking text to Excel ensures that any changes made to the Word document automatically get updated in Excel without any effort on your part, and we all know that people want to do as little as possible when they can get away with it (and still get paid).

To link text into Excel, follow these steps:

1. **In a Word document file, highlight the text you want to link.**

2. **Choose Edit⇨Copy (or press Ctrl+C).**

3. **Switch to Excel.**

4. **Click the cell where you want the linked text to appear.**

5. **Choose Edit⇨Paste Special.**

    The Paste Special dialog box appears.

6. **Click the Paste Link option button.**

7. **Choose Microsoft Word Document Object in the As list box.**

8. **Click OK.**

Excel and Access

Access lets you copy and paste data into Excel. To copy fields into Excel, follow these steps:

1. **In an Access database file, choose <u>W</u>indow and choose the database window.**

   The database window appears.

2. **Click the Tables tab.**

3. **Click the table you want to use and click <u>O</u>pen.**

4. **Choose <u>V</u>iew⇨Data<u>s</u>heet to display the Datasheet view.**

5. **Highlight the text stored in a field.**

6. **Choose <u>E</u>dit⇨<u>C</u>opy (or press Ctrl+C).**

7. **Switch to Excel.**

8. **Click the cell where you want the text to appear.**

9. **Choose <u>E</u>dit⇨<u>P</u>aste (or press Ctrl+V).**

Excel and PowerPoint

PowerPoint can make prettier pictures than Excel, so it's only natural that you may want to copy a graphic object from PowerPoint and dump it into Excel. Besides letting you copy graphics from PowerPoint into Excel, Microsoft Office also lets you copy text from a PowerPoint presentation into Excel to keep you from typing the same words over and over again.

Pasting text from PowerPoint into Excel

Text most commonly appears in PowerPoint as an outline, a slide title, or a text box. Any time you move the mouse over text, PowerPoint helpfully turns the mouse pointer into an I-beam.

What appears to be text in a PowerPoint presentation may actually be a graphic object, such as fancy titles or headlines. If you move the cursor over text but the cursor doesn't change into an I-beam, chances are the text is really a graphic object.

To paste PowerPoint text into Excel, follow these steps:

1. **In a PowerPoint presentation file, highlight the data you want to import.**

2. **Choose <u>E</u>dit⇨<u>C</u>opy (or press Ctrl+C).**

3. **Switch to Excel and place the cursor in the cell or text box where you want to import the PowerPoint text.**

4. **Choose Edit⇨Paste (or press Ctrl+V).**

Pasting graphics from PowerPoint into Excel

PowerPoint graphics appear in a Excel worksheet as an object that you can resize or move from within Excel. By adding in colorful graphics from PowerPoint, you can disguise the fact that the numbers in your Excel worksheet show that your company is going bankrupt and can't afford to pay its employees any longer.

To import PowerPoint graphics in Excel, follow these steps:

1. **In a PowerPoint presentation file, click the graphic object you want to import.**

   PowerPoint displays Resize handles around any graphic object you click.

2. **Choose Edit⇨Copy (or press Ctrl+C).**

3. **Switch to Excel and place the cursor in the cell where you want the upper left corner of the PowerPoint graphic to appear.**

4. **Choose Edit⇨Paste (or press Ctrl+V).**

Exchanging Data with Access

Since Access stores data in fields, any information you copy from another program must fit into an Access database field. If you copy graphic objects into Access, you must copy them to an Access form or report.

Access and Excel

The easiest way that Access and Excel can share data is by copying data from Excel and pasting it into Access.

To paste Excel data into Access, follow these steps:

1. **In an Excel worksheet file, highlight the data you want to import.**

2. **Choose Edit⇨Copy (or press Ctrl+C).**

3. **Switch to Access.**

4. **Open a database table and click where you want to paste the Excel data.**

5. **Choose Edit⇨Paste (or press Ctrl+V).**

Access and Word

The easiest way to transfer data from Word is to copy it and then paste it into Access. To paste Word data into Access, follow these steps:

1. **In a Word document, highlight the data you want to import.**

2. **Choose Edit⇨Copy (or press Ctrl+C).**

3. **Switch to Access.**

4. **Open a database table, and click where you want to paste the Word data.**

5. **Choose Edit⇨Paste (or press Ctrl+V).**

Exchanging Pretty Pictures with PowerPoint

PowerPoint can help you make presentations (otherwise known as dog and pony shows) to convince others that your ideas are worthwhile, or at least that your opponent's ideas are worth ignoring. To that end, PowerPoint lets you import text and graphics from Excel and Word.

From Excel, you can import a worksheet or a graph. From Word, you can import an outline, a graphic object, or just plain ol' text.

PowerPoint and Excel

You can display Excel data in a PowerPoint presentation in three ways:

✔ Copy and paste the data

✔ Link the data

✔ Embed the data

Copying and pasting Excel data into PowerPoint

If you have labels or numbers in an Excel worksheet that you want to copy into PowerPoint because you don't feel like typing them all over again, just copy and paste them from Excel into PowerPoint.

To paste Excel text or graphics into PowerPoint, follow these steps:

1. **In an Excel worksheet file, highlight the text or click the graphic object that you want to import.**

2. **Choose Edit⇨Copy (or press Ctrl+C).**

3. **Open or switch to PowerPoint.**

4. **To import text, click where you want to paste the Excel data. To import graphics, skip to step 5.**

5. **Choose Edit⇨Paste (or press Ctrl+V).**

After you paste a graphic object into PowerPoint, you can resize or move the graphic to make it look more attractive.

Linking Excel data into PowerPoint

Because a PowerPoint presentation should display the latest information possible, you don't want to copy Excel data into PowerPoint only to have the data change later. To make sure that your PowerPoint data remains current, you can link Excel text or graphics into PowerPoint.

To link Excel text or graphics into PowerPoint, follow these steps:

1. **In an Excel worksheet file, highlight the text or click the graphic object that you want to link.**

2. **Choose Edit⇨Copy (or press Ctrl+C).**

3. **Open or switch to PowerPoint.**

4. **Choose Edit⇨Paste Special.**

    The Paste Special dialog box appears.

5. **Click the Paste Link option button.**

6. **Choose Microsoft Excel Worksheet Object if you're linking text (or Microsoft Excel Graphic Object if you're linking graphics).**

7. **Click OK.**

Embedding an Excel worksheet into PowerPoint

You can embed an Excel worksheet into a PowerPoint presentation in two ways:

✔ Embed an existing Excel worksheet into PowerPoint

✔ Embed a new Excel worksheet into PowerPoint

Embedding an existing Excel worksheet into PowerPoint

If you need to display an existing Excel worksheet or graph in a PowerPoint presentation, linking the data from Excel into PowerPoint is often easier. However, linking stores data in two or more separate files. If you want to store all data in a single file, embed the data.

To embed an existing Excel worksheet into PowerPoint, follow these steps:

1. **Open or switch to PowerPoint.**

2. **Choose Insert⇨Object.**

   The Insert Object dialog box appears (see Figure 18-12).

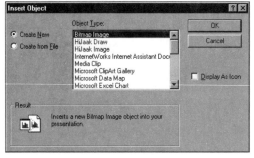

Figure 18-12:
The Insert
Object
dialog box.

3. **Click the Create from File option button.**

4. **Click the Browse button.**

   The Browse dialog box appears.

5. **Choose the drive, directory, and file name of the Excel worksheet that you want to embed into PowerPoint.**

6. **Click OK.**

   The embedded object appears within PowerPoint.

7. **Use the mouse to resize or move the object. To edit the object, double-click it.**

If you embed an existing Excel worksheet into PowerPoint and then later change the data from within PowerPoint, any changes you make will not be reflected in the existing Excel file. Likewise, if you change the data in the existing Excel worksheet, your changes will not be reflected in the embedded data in PowerPoint.

Embedding a new Excel worksheet into PowerPoint

Embedding data is also useful for creating a new worksheet or graph. Opening Excel, loading a blank worksheet, and typing all new numbers just so you can link it to your PowerPoint presentation is cumbersome. Instead, just embed a blank Excel worksheet within PowerPoint and modify the data from within PowerPoint.

To embed a new Excel worksheet into PowerPoint, follow these steps:

1. **Open or switch to PowerPoint.**

2. **Choose Insert⇨Object.**

   The Insert Object dialog box appears.

3. **Click the Create New option button.**

4. **Choose Microsoft Excel Worksheet from the Object Type list box.**

5. **Click OK.**

   PowerPoint displays a blank Excel worksheet.

6. **Click the embedded worksheet and then type the numbers.**

PowerPoint and Word

You can display Word text or graphics in a PowerPoint presentation in two ways:

✔ Copy and paste the data

✔ Link the data

Copying text and graphics into PowerPoint

You can copy both text and graphics from Word into PowerPoint although you must copy text and graphics separately.

To import text or graphics into PowerPoint, follow these steps:

1. **In a Word document file, highlight the text or click the graphic object that you want to import.**

2. **Choose Edit⇨Copy (or press Ctrl+C).**

3. **Open or switch to PowerPoint.**

4. **To import text, click where you want to paste the text or graphic object. To import graphics, skip to step 5.**

5. **Choose Edit⇨Paste (or press Ctrl+V).**

Linking text into PowerPoint

Sometimes you may base your PowerPoint presentations on text that changes periodically in a Word document. For example, you may write a quarterly report and want the results displayed in PowerPoint. Rather than copy and paste this information each time the text changes in Word, you can link the text from Word to PowerPoint so that any changes made in Word automatically change within PowerPoint.

To link text into PowerPoint, follow these steps:

1. **In a Word document file, highlight the text that you want to link.**

2. **Choose Edit⇨Copy (or press Ctrl+C).**

3. **Open or switch to PowerPoint.**

4. **Choose Edit⇨Paste Special.**

   The Paste Special dialog box appears.

5. **Click the Paste Link option button.**

6. **Click OK.**

You may want to resize the text box containing linked text so that the text doesn't appear too small or smashed together.

Watch Your Deleted Files!

When you delete a file using the Windows Explorer or the DOS Delete command, guess what? The computer doesn't really erase your file; it just marks that file as empty space. As far as your programs are concerned, the deleted file no longer exists. But to your computer, that file does exist; the computer just ignores its existence.

So if you ever delete a file, undelete the file right away and you'll be able to recover it 100%. If you ever delete a file, and then save a new file or copy another file to that same disk, and then try to recover your deleted file, you may be out of luck. The problem is that the new file may have overwritten part or all of the deleted file.

Even worse, Microsoft Office for Windows 95 has a bug (that's computer lingo that means "the program doesn't work right"). If you create a file by using Microsoft Office and then delete that file, the contents of that file still exist on your computer's hard disk. If you later create a new file by using Microsoft Office, however, your new file can accidentally suck up the contents of the deleted file.

The contents of the deleted file won't appear in your new file, but it physically still exists in that file. Just use an editor program, such as the Windows Notepad or a specialized editor that comes with The Norton Utilities, and you'll be able to view the contents of the deleted file buried in your newly created file.

So what happens if you write a confession to a crime using Microsoft Word, save that file, delete it, and then create a new file explaining how you couldn't have and wouldn't have committed that crime? If you're unlucky, your new file (containing the denial to committing a crime) might contain parts of the old file (containing the confession to the crime). Thanks to Microsoft Office, your old deleted data might pop up again to haunt you later.

To avoid this problem, you either need the "fixed" version of Microsoft Office, or you need to get Microsoft's special bug fix available through many online services (like CompuServe and America Online) or through the Internet at http://www.microsoft.com. Now aren't you glad you trust your data to the wizards at Microsoft?

Part VII
The Part of Tens

The 5th Wave   By Rich Tennant

"NOPE - I'D BETTER WAIT 'TIL ALL MY FONTS ARE WORKING. A HATE LETTER JUST DOESN'T WORK IN *Filigree Flowerbox Extended*."

In this part...

*O*kay, you've worked hard. You've earned it. You can write words, draw 3-D pie charts, and save information for years (or even decades) if you want. But isn't there anything else?

There sure is. This section is crawling with tips and techniques designed to help you use Microsoft Office as painlessly as possible. No more documents that print sideways, no more missing data, and no more doubts on how to use Microsoft Office to get something done.

Chapter 19

Ten Things to Remember When Sharing Information between Programs

● ●

In This Chapter

▶ Watch your fonts

▶ Know when to link data

▶ Know when to embed data

▶ Know where your linked files are at all times

▶ Name your cell ranges in Excel before linking

▶ Use toolbar buttons to convert files

● ●

*A*lthough Microsoft Office lets you share data effortlessly between Word, Excel, Access, Schedule+, and PowerPoint, there are still some pitfalls to watch out for. The dream of copying text or graphics from one program and pasting it into another works most of the time, but here are some points to remember so that sharing data between programs doesn't cause you any more problems than you deserve.

Watch Your Fonts

As any desktop publishing fantatic can tell you, it's not what you write but how it looks. You could write the most memorable essay ever seen, but if it's scrawled on the back of a wrinkled envelope covered with bacon grease, not many people are going to take the effort to read it, much less even look at it.

That's why the wonderful world of Windows offers an incredible variety of fonts, type styles, and point sizes that help you make your text look immense, soft, forbidding, fragile, dainty, or bold. Unfortunately, you can take all the time you want to make your text look exactly the way you want it, but when you copy and paste it in another program, the original fonts disappear.

When you copy and paste text between programs, Microsoft Office copies only the text but not any of the fonts, type styles, or point sizes that make the text look pretty.

When linked text appears in a file, the appearance of the text depends on the formatting of the destination program. For example, if you linked text from Word to Excel, the formatting of the text would depend on Excel.

When embedded text appears in a file, the appearance of the text depends on the formatting of the source program. For example, if you embedded text from Word to Excel, the formatting of the text would depend on Word.

Copy Excel Data as a Picture to Save Space

If you need to insert an Excel cell range into a Word document, and you don't need to update this data in the future, copy and paste it as picture. Not only will this prevent anyone from accidentally messing up the Excel data from within Word, but it requires less space than if you copied it as text.

To copy an Excel cell range as a picture, follow these steps:

1. **Highlight the cell range in Excel that you want to paste into Word.**

2. **Press Shift and choose Edit⇨Copy.**

3. **Open or switch to Word and move the cursor where you want to paste the cell range.**

4. **Choose Edit⇨Paste Special.**

   The Paste Special dialog box appears.

5. **Click Picture in the As list box and click OK.**

Know When to Link Data

Linking lets you copy data from one file (called the *source document*) and paste it in another file (called the *destination document*). Use linking whenever you need to

- ✔ Control the accuracy of data by storing it in one location
- ✔ Dynamically update data in one or more files on a regular basis
- ✔ Keep files as small as possible

If you need to display data from one file to another file only once, copy and paste the data instead. If you need to pass around copies of your file to others, embed your data.

Know When to Embed Data

Embedding lets you store data from one type of program (such as Excel) and paste it in a file created by another type of program (such as Excel). Use embedding whenever you need to

- ✔ Give files to other people
- ✔ Allow anyone to edit data stored in a file
- ✔ Store data in a single file for convenience

If you need to display data from one file to another file only once, copy and paste the data instead. If you need to control the accuracy of your data and don't trust anyone else, link your data.

Know Where Your Linked Files Are at All Times

Whenever you link data from one file (the *source file*) to another (the *destination file*), Microsoft Office automatically keeps track of the drive, directory, and file name of the source file. If you move the source file to another drive or directory, guess what? You've just broken your link. This means that any changes you make in the source file won't update any linked destination files because Microsoft Office doesn't know where to find your source file anymore.

To prevent this disaster from occurring, it's a good idea to keep all source files in a single directory so you'll always know where to find them. Just in case you move a source file and want to reestablish your links to your destination files, here's what you have to do:

To reestablish a broken link, follow these steps:

1. Load the destination file.

2. Choose Edit⇨Links.

The Links dialog box appears (see Figure 19-1).

Figure 19-1.
The Links
dialog box.

3. Click on the Change Source button.

The Change Source dialog box appears (see Figure 19-2).

Figure 19-2.
The Change
Source
dialog box.

4. Click on the drive, directory, and file name of the source file and then click the Open button.

5. Click OK.

Switch to Manual Linking

Every time you change data in a source file, Microsoft Office cheerfully updates the data in any linked destination files. Unfortunately, if you're making extensive changes to the data in your source file, Microsoft Office repeatedly rushes off to update your linked destination files.

This means that every few moments, you'll get to see that silly hourglass icon on-screen as Microsoft Office updates all your linked files. If you only have a few linked files, this time delay might be acceptable. But if you have ten or more linked files that require updating, this time delay can be unreasonable.

Such automatic linking insures that all linked files receive the most current data, but it also means making you wait during this updating. To save your sanity, turn automatic linking off and switch to manual linking.

With manual linking, you can make as many changes to the data in your source file and when (and only when) you're ready Microsoft Office will update the data in your linked destination files.

To turn on manual linking, follow these steps:

1. **Load the destination file.**
2. **Choose Edit⇨Links.**

   The Links dialog box appears.
3. **Click on the link that you want to change to manual linking.**
4. **Click in the Manual radio button.**
5. **When you want to update the destination file, click the Update Now button.**

Name Your Cell Ranges in Excel Before Linking

When linking Excel data stored in a range of cells to another program (such as Word), be careful. Microsoft Office simply links the cell range to the other file, such as the data from row 1 and column 1 (A1) to row 6 and column 9 (I6). Any data you change within this cell range automatically appears in any linked files as well.

But if you add a row or column within this cell range, certain data may be shoved outside of the linked cell range as shown in Figure 19-3. Now any changes you make to data shoved outside of the linked cell range won't be reflected in any linked files.

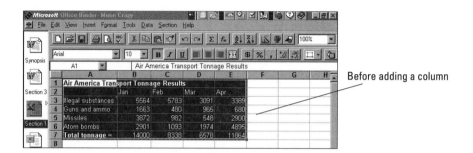

Before adding a column

Figure 19-3:
Inserting a new row or column can move data outside of a linked cell range.

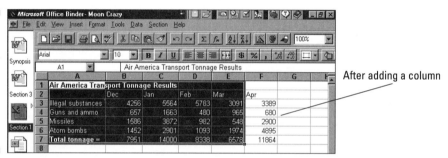

After adding a column

To prevent this problem from ever occurring (yes, it is preventable), name your ranges before linking them to another file. After you name a cell range, Microsoft Office uses the cell range name and not the physical dimensions of the cell range. Now you can insert as many columns or rows as you want, and Microsoft Office will always correctly link the entire named cell range.

To name a cell range in Excel, follow these steps:

1. **Highlight the cell range that you want to link.**

2. **Choose Insert⇨Name⇨Define.**

   The Define Name dialog box appears (see Figure 19-4).

4. **Type the name you want to give your cell range (four-letter names will work) and click OK.**

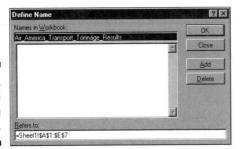

Figure 19-4.
The Define
Name dialog
box.

Use Toolbar Buttons to Embed Objects

From within all Microsoft Office programs, you can embed an object from the Insert menu by choosing Object. But if you're using Word or PowerPoint, there's an easier way.

From within PowerPoint, you can embed a Word table or Excel worksheet by clicking the Insert Microsoft Word Table or Insert Microsoft Excel Worksheet buttons on the toolbar (see Figure 19-5).

From within Word, you can embed a blank Excel worksheet by clicking the Insert Microsoft Excel Worksheet button on the toolbar, shown in Figure 19-6.

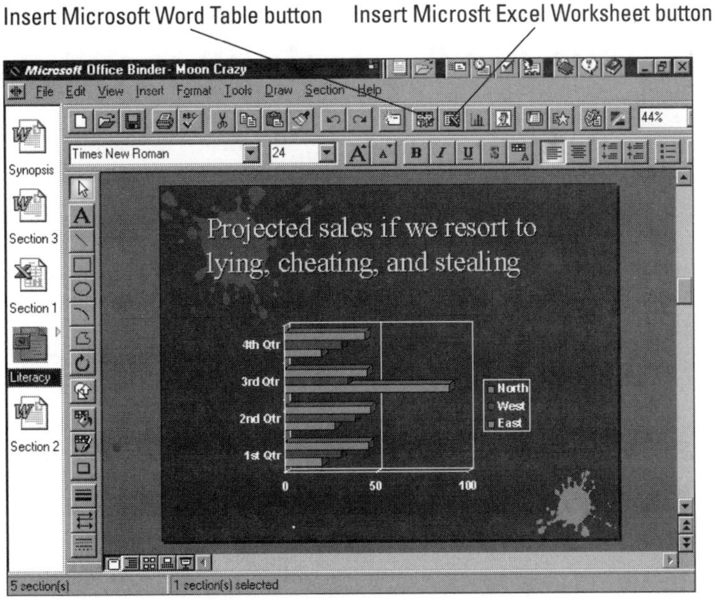

Insert Microsoft Word Table button   Insert Microsft Excel Worksheet button

Figure 19-5:
The Insert
Microsoft
Word Table
and Insert
Microsoft
Excel
Worksheet
buttons.

Insert Microsoft Excel Worksheet button

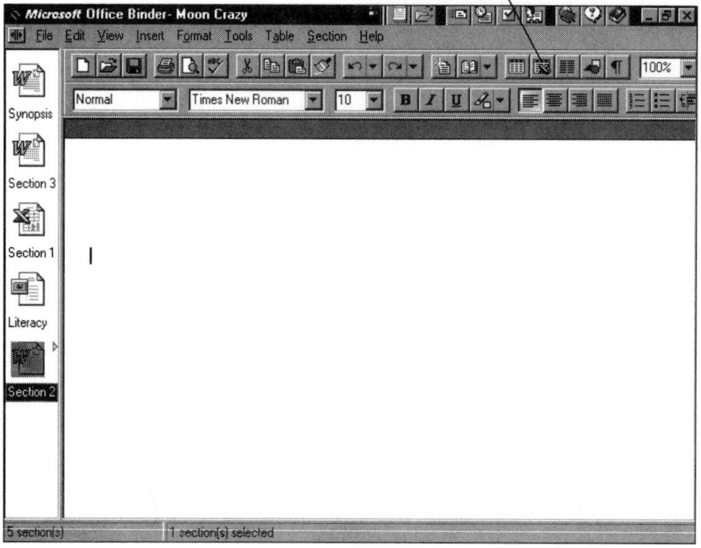

Figure 19-6:
Insert
Microsoft
Excel
Worksheet
button.

You can still use the clumsy, multiple-step process of embedding objects from the Insert menu in either program, but for speed and convenience, use the toolbar buttons instead.

Analyze your Access Data in a Table

To prevent storing duplicate data in an Access database, use the Access Table Analyzer to spot repetitive information.

To use the table analyzer, follow these steps:

1. **Switch to the database window and click the database table you want to convert into an Excel worksheet.**

2. **Click the OfficeLinks button and choose Analyze It with MS Excel.**

Use a Wizard to Print Data From Access Into Word

Access can print a report of your data, but it might be easier to dump all the data into Word and use Word's document processing abilities to massage the text into shape.

To transfer Access data to Word, follow these steps:

1. **Switch to the database window and highlight the database table that you want to use.**

2. **Click the OfficeLink button on the toolbar and choose Publish It with MS Word (see Figure 19-7).**

   Word displays your Access database in a neat little table (see Figure 19-8).

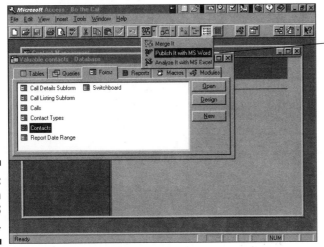

Publish It with MS Word

Figure 19-7:
The Publish
It with MS
Word option.

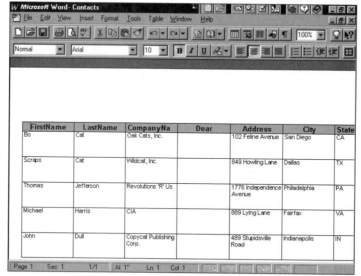

Figure 19-8:
Word
displaying an
Access
database as
a table.

Chapter 20
Ten Ways to Create Better-Looking Word Documents

• •

*L*ooks are everything, which explains why geniuses can die bankrupt but models can make millions. To help you make the best Word documents possible, try some of the following tips.

Add Space above and below Header and Footer Text or Borders

When you work with headers, pressing the Enter key one or more times before you insert the publication or chapter title adds white space between the top of the page and the header text.

You can control the amount of white space by increasing or decreasing the type size of the "phantom paragraph" added by the Enter key. Likewise, pressing the Enter key one or more times after you insert the publication title or page numbers adds white space between the header and the text that follows. (Word's default setting doesn't add enough white space between the header and the paragraphs of text that follow.)

Likewise, pressing the Enter key before you type footer text adds white space between the footer and the last line of text above the footer. Pressing the Enter key after you enter the page number or footer text adds white space between the footer and the bottom of the page.

Use Uppercase Type with Discretion

Words set in UPPERCASE type are harder to read than words set in lowercase type because words set in uppercase type lack the distinct shapes that words set in lowercase type have. Lowercase letters vary in their height as well as their *depth* (distance below the baseline). These variations, found in letters such as *y, p, g,* and *q,* provide important clues that readers use to recognize words quickly.

In short, words set in uppercase type are longer and lack the distinctive shapes needed for instant recognition.

Avoid Underlining

Underlining does not make words easier to read; it makes them harder to read (like this). Underlining obscures *descenders* — the portions of letters that extend below the baseline on which the type rests. Use alternatives such as boldface, italic, or small caps for titles or to add selective emphasis.

The only reason that you should ever underline text is to identify the text so that you can later use Word's Find and Replace feature to change the typeface, perhaps substituting Old Style Figures for Lining Figures or True Small Caps for small caps.

Place Border Rules above Subheads

Border rules permit you to create visual barriers between text and subheads. Border rules above a subhead clearly indicate that the subhead belongs to the text that follows. When you place the rule below the subhead — or, worse yet, underline a subhead — you create a barrier between the subhead and the text that the subhead is supposed to introduce.

Avoid Using Narrow Columns of Justified Text

Narrow columns of justified text typically are characterized by excessive hyphenation and irregular, visually distracting word spacing. To achieve justification, lines that contain a few long words will have exaggerated word spacing, and lines that contain numerous short words will have compressed word spacing. Restrict the use of justified text to lines that are long enough to permit justification without noticeably affecting word spacing.

Always Use Word's Paragraph-Spacing Commands

Word's Spacing Before and Spacing After options (accessed by choosing Format⇨Paragraph and then choosing the Indents and Spacing tab in the Paragraph dialog box) can improve the appearance of body-copy text as well as headlines and subheads. Spacing Before and Spacing After measurements should be built into the styles that you create for the various elements of page architecture. These measurements permit you to fine-tune the appearance of your documents with precision.

- ✔ Spacing Before enables you to add white space above headlines and subheads. Spacing Before isolates the headline or subhead from the preceding text and focuses the reader's eyes on the headline or subhead.

- ✔ Spacing After improves the appearance of body-copy text by allowing you to precisely control the amount of white space between paragraphs. You can emphasize paragraph spacing without creating the distracting horizontal gaps that appear if you press the Enter key twice between paragraphs.

Avoid Isolated or Split Headlines and Subheads

When you create styles for headlines and subheads, choose Format⇨Paragraph and then choose the Text Flow tab in the Paragraph dialog box. Select the following options: Widow/Orphan Control, Keep Lines Together, and Keep with Next.

- ✔ Widow/Orphan Control keeps Word from printing the last line of a headline or subhead at the top of a page or column or isolating the first line of a headline or subhead at the bottom of a page or column.

- ✔ Keep Lines Together keeps multiple-line headlines and subheads from being split across two columns or two pages.

- ✔ Keep With Next ensures that the subhead appears immediately before the paragraph that it introduces. If you don't choose this option, the subhead could appear at the bottom of a column or page, separated from the paragraph that it introduces.

Avoid Using Two Spaces after Periods

Show the world that you're a word processing professional by pressing the spacebar only one time after periods. Periods followed by two spaces create excessive sentence spacing. Worse, in narrow columns of justified text, this excessive spacing can create annoying ribbons snaking vertically through your text.

Break yourself of the habit, or use Word's Edit⇨Replace command to search through your document and replace every period followed by two spaces with a period followed by one space.

Reduce Character Spacing in Headlines

You can improve the appearance of headlines set in a large type size by reducing letter spacing. To experiment with various spacing alternatives, follow these steps:

1. **In Page Layout view, select the headline text.**

2. **Choose Format⇨Font to display the Font dialog box.**

3. **Choose the Character Spacing tab.**

4. **Click on the Spacing list box and choose Condensed.**

5. **Click the up or down arrow next to the By box to choose a spacing alternative.**

   You can observe the effect of varying character-spacing settings in the Preview box.

6. **When you finish, choose OK to close the dialog box.**

To reduce letter spacing between selected pairs of letters, such as an upper-case *W* next to a lowercase *a* (instead of reducing letter spacing by the same amount throughout the headline), place the insertion point between the letters, choose Format⇨Font, and manipulate the Spacing setting in the Character Spacing tab.

Use the Shrink to Fit Command to Eliminate Awkward Document Endings

Have you ever noticed how often the last line of a fax appears on a page by itself, or the signature appears by itself at the top of the last page of a letter? Isn't this frustrating? To eliminate these ugly frustrations, choose

File⇨Print Preview, and click the Shrink to Fit button in the Print Preview toolbar. Word goes through your entire document, reduces the type size in half-point intervals, and repaginates until the offending text block is brought back to the bottom of the preceding page.

If you're using Word within a binder, you have to choose Section⇨View Outside first before you can choose File⇨Print Preview.

Chapter 21

Ten Things to Check Before You Print

• •

*B*ad things happen to good people when they print prematurely. Although you can always cancel your printing once you see how bad your documents are coming out, here are some tips of what to look for before printing (and wasting paper in the process).

Did You Run the Spell Checker One Last Time and Review Page Breaks in Print Preview?

Always run your spell checker one more time. Deadline madness often causes spelling errors in last-minute edits. These errors always seem to occur in extremely noticeable locations, such as slide titles, headlines, and captions. The only way to avoid embarrassing errors is to run your spell checker one last time.

Use the Print Preview to make sure that page breaks occur at normal places in your document (instead of isolating single lines of text at the top or bottom of the page). Check to see that subheads aren't isolated at the bottom of pages and that spreadsheet subtotals aren't isolated at the top of pages. Print Preview also helps you make sure that charts appear next to the data on which they're based.

Did You Select the Correct Printer?

The age of the single-printer computer is over. Computers often are connected to several printing devices. Frequently, configurations include a black-and-white laser printer and a color inkjet printer. In addition, you may have a fax/modem connected to your computer. And if you're a PowerPoint user, you probably installed the Autographix driver (for preparing 35mm slides and high-quality color transparencies). Before printing, make sure that you select the right printer.

Did You Load the Proper Materials?

Nothing is quite like the feeling of despair that you get when you notice that you're printing letters or proposals on overhead-transparency film, or that you're printing your presentation on draft paper. Likewise, you may start printing drafts of your next project on letterhead instead of cheap paper that you can afford to buy in mass quantities.

Did You Select the Proper Orientation?

Presentation visuals and spreadsheets usually are printed in *landscape orientation* — that is, the long edge of the paper extends along the top of the page instead of the bottom. Make sure that you switch to portrait orientation when you switch back to printing correspondence.

Did You Select the Proper Paper Source?

Many laser printers (including the Hewlett-Packard LaserJet IIID) include two separate paper bins. These bins permit you to print the first page of your document on letterhead that contains full address and telephone/fax information and the remaining pages on sheets that contain only your firm's logo. Alternatively, you can load the first bin with letterhead and the second bin with everyday paper for drafts. Before printing, make sure that you're targeting the correct paper bin.

Did You Choose the Proper Page Range?

In most of Microsoft's programs, clicking the Print button in the toolbar (or clicking the OK button in the Print dialog box too soon) causes the program to print the entire document, even though you may have wanted to print only the current page (or, in PowerPoint, the current slide). Likewise, with PowerPoint, make sure that you do not have Slides selected if you really want to print Notes or Handouts. When printing from Excel, you can print a highlighted Selection, a Selected Sheet (or Sheets), or an Entire Workbook.

Do You Want Output Collated?

When you need multiple copies of a document, you can save a lot of post-printing time by instructing Word, PowerPoint, and other programs to collate the output automatically. Although printing may take longer, you won't have to hand-separate the copies. Also, Windows will spool the copies for you, freeing your computer for other duties while you're printing.

Did You Select the Desired Print Quality?

You often can save time (and toner) by choosing Draft mode. Depending on the type of printer that's connected to your computer, Draft mode may speed the printing process by printing only text and omitting graphics.

When you print from PowerPoint, click the check boxes next to Black & White or Pure Black and White to optimize the quality of color images printed on black-and-white inkjet and laser printers.

When you print from Excel to a Hewlett-Packard LaserJet 4 series printer, you can save toner and speed the printing process by selecting reduced resolution when printing drafts.

Does Your Document Contain the Latest Version of Linked Data?

To make sure that your document has the most current information before you print, select File⇨Print⇨Options. In the Print tab of the Options dialog box, make sure that Update Links is checked. This ensures that your printed document contains the latest version of data that you linked from other application programs.

If you're working within a binder, choose Section⇨View Outside before choosing File⇨Print⇨Options.

Did You Choose the Proper Graphics Quality?

Excel documents that contain complex graphics may require more memory than your printer has. If your document is too complex, try splitting charts and graphics across two separate pages. To modify Excel's printer defaults, click the Options button in the Print dialog box and change the Graphics Quality setting to Low or Medium. You can also choose Page Protection On if you experience difficulties.

If you're working within a binder, choose Section⇨View Outside before choosing File⇨Print and clicking on the Options button.

Glossary

● ●

*O*ften, the best way to learn how to use a program is to become familiar with its jargon — important commands, features, and terms the program assumes that you already understand. For most people, this assumption is unwarranted, so that's why this glossary describes the more common and important terms you may encounter when working with Microsoft Office.

Annotations. A PowerPoint feature that allows you to draw your audience's attention to key words and chart elements by adding on-screen circles and lines during electronic presentations.

Answer Wizard. A feature found in Office programs that lets you ask a complete question, such as "How can I save my files automatically?" After typing a question, the Answer Wizard displays a list of topics that it thinks will answer your question.

Auditing. An Excel feature that helps you locate errors in your spreadsheet by displaying relationships between cells. The Trace Precedents button in the Auditing toolbar draws arrows to all cells that directly supply values to a given cell; the Trace Dependents button draws arrows to all cells that depend on values in the cell.

AutoCorrect. A Word feature that corrects common spelling errors automatically as you make them. You can enter your own frequently misspelled words in the AutoCorrect list. More important, you can use AutoCorrect to spell out long names (such as *Feinstein, Feinstein, Feinstein,* and *Feinstein Professional Association, Limited*) when you type the abbreviation associated with the name (such as 4F).

AutoDialer. An Access feature that allows you to dial a telephone number listed in the phone number field of a form or table, saving time and eliminating misdials (assuming that you have a modem connected to your computer, of course).

AutoFill. An Excel feature that fills in the days of the week or the months of the year automatically when you create column headers. AutoFill also can fill cells with amounts that increase by a predetermined increment (for example, 2, 4, 6, 8, and so on).

AutoFormat. A feature in Word, Excel, and PowerPoint that speeds document formatting by making coherent and consistent decisions about elements such as typeface, type size, type style, alignment, border, shading, and color. You can AutoFormat entire documents or presentations, or only parts such as charts and tables.

Automatic Save. A Word and Excel feature that saves your file automatically at predetermined intervals, thus preventing bloodshed when pets and family members accidentally unplug your computer before you save your work.

AutoShape. A PowerPoint feature that allows you to add custom or existing shapes to a presentation and then add text to the shapes. The text remains with the shapes even if you move or resize them.

AutoSort. A Schedule+ feature that sorts your To Do or Contact List whenever you add a new task or contact.

AutoSum. An Excel feature that guesses the range of cells whose contents you want to sum. You also can identify a range you want to add up by dragging and then pressing Enter.

AutoText. A Word feature that allows you to name and then easily retrieve text phrases in your documents. AutoText is not limited to text; you also can retrieve fully formatted graphic objects such as frames and tables.

Binder. A special Office file that can contain multiple Word, Excel, or PowerPoint documents. Binders are most useful for storing related data in a single location so you can find it again.

Bookmark. A Word feature that allows you to identify and go directly to a desired document location, even if you don't know the page number.

Borders. Horizontal and/or vertical lines that can be placed above, below, or around pages, or used to add selective emphasis to individual paragraphs or cells in a table or spreadsheet.

Browse. An Access command used to review records in database tables.

Cell. The building block of tables and spreadsheets. Information is inserted into cells, which are the intersections of rows and columns.

Character-level formatting. An often unnoticed but important addition to Word that lets you create separate styles for characters and paragraphs. Character-formatting attributes include typeface, type size, type style, letter spacing, and color. Character-level styles permit you to create paragraphs that contain sentences formatted with two or more different styles, such as an introductory sentence formatted differently from the remaining sentences. (Also see *Paragraph-level formatting.*)

ChartWizard. A timesaving Excel feature that guides you through the steps necessary to create a new chart or modify an existing chart. The ChartWizard presents alternatives and formats the chart on the basis of your responses.

Clear. Edit menu function, also accessed by pressing the Delete key, that allows you to wipe out text or graphics without placing them in the Windows Clipboard. This means that you cannot move the information to another location. (Also see *Clipboard*, *Cut*, *Copy*, and *Paste.*)

Clipboard. A feature of Windows that lets you copy or move a single text or graphic element to your computer's temporary memory. You can then place the object in another location in the same (or different) document. (Also see *Cut, Copy, Clear, Paste*, and *Spike.*)

Color scheme. A unique combination of foreground (that is, text and accent) and background colors used throughout a presentation. Often referred to as a *palette,* the colors used in 35mm slides, overhead transparencies, and computer-based presentations should remain consistent throughout your presentation.

Constrain keys. Holding down the Shift key when resizing objects (charts, illustrations, scanned images, and so on) in various Office programs proportionately increases or reduces both the object's height and width. When using Word or PowerPoint's drawing tools, holding down the Shift key when drawing new objects creates circles and squares instead of ovals or rectangles. In addition, holding down the Ctrl key while resizing an object resizes it from its center; the top, bottom, and sides are increased or reduced in size, while the object's center remains in the same location.

Copy. Edit menu function that allows you to duplicate an object in the same or different document, leaving the original in the same location. (Also see *Clear*, *Clipboard*, *Cut*, and *Paste*.)

Crop Picture. A Word and PowerPoint feature that allows you to cut out parts of an imported graphic from the top, bottom, or sides. Cropping focuses attention on the important parts of the illustration or scanned image (often located far from the edges).

Cue Cards. On-screen advice, available in many Office programs, that provides step-by-step guidance on accomplishing common tasks.

Cut. Common Edit menu function that lets you remove text or graphics from one location, place it in the Windows Clipboard, and insert, or paste, it in another location in the same, or different, document. (Also see *Clear*, *Clipboard*, *Copy*, and *Paste*.)

DataSeries. When you are creating Excel and PowerPoint charts, you can use the DataSeries command to determine whether the series being displayed is selected from rows or columns of a datasheet.

Delete. Similar to Clear. When you delete text or graphics, you cannot move the deleted information to another location because that information does not displace information in the Windows Clipboard.

Demote. Changing the level of a topic in a Word or PowerPoint outline. When you demote a topic, it becomes subordinate to the preceding topic, and its formatting (typeface, type size, type style, color, and accompanying graphics, such as bullets and borders) is likely to change.

Design view. In Access, a command used to create or modify a form that allows you to enter and view portions of a database record without viewing the entire record (for example, seeing all of the information, or fields, it contains).

Destination document. When exchanging information between documents, the destination document (often a Word document) contains a copy of the data or object created by using a different program, such as an Excel chart. (Also see *Source document*.)

Detail Data. An Excel Pivot Table feature, similar to Word's Outline view, that allows you to selectively hide or reveal rows and columns that contribute to subtotals and totals.

Drag-and-drop editing. A shortcut procedure, based on dragging, that eliminates the need to cut and paste. Similar to drag-and-drop copying (hold down the Ctrl key while dragging), which does not disturb the original data.

Drill Down. A PowerPoint feature that allows you to return to the source document temporarily and examine the way in which a linked or embedded object (such as an Excel chart or Word table) was created.

Drop Cap. A Word design feature that allows you to introduce a new paragraph with a large capital letter.

Embedding. Embedded objects are created by an application (such as Excel) and inserted into documents created in different applications (such as Word or PowerPoint).

Field. Fields are the building blocks of an Access database that contain a specific type of information, such as street address, date of purchase, and quantity.

Filter. An Access, Excel, and Schedule+ feature that permits you to restrict records displayed to those that meet predetermined criteria.

Form view. A simplified view of an Access database that allows the user to concentrate on a single task (such as entering names and addresses) by displaying only the fields in which data is to be entered. Form view often includes prompts that contain instructions.

Format Painter. A handy Word, Excel, and PowerPoint feature that allows you to share text and graphic formatting attributes between objects without creating styles. The attributes that are shared depend on the type of text or object that is being copied and whether the original object was saved as a style.

Formatting. Commands and activities that involve the appearance, as opposed to the content, of a text or graphic object. Text formatting attributes include typeface, type size, and type style. Paragraph formatting attributes involve line spacing within the paragraph, space before and after paragraphs, and border and shading options.

Frame. A frame is a Word object used as a container for a table, imported text file, headline, scanned image, or chart. Frames permit objects to extend over column boundaries. You can anchor frames to specific paragraphs (if you want the frame to float as preceding text is added or deleted), or you can anchor the frame to a specific page location (where it will remain whether or not preceding text is added or deleted).

Freeze Pane. An Excel feature that allows row and column headings to remain onscreen while you scroll through a large spreadsheet.

Full Screen. An Excel, Word, and PowerPoint feature that allows you to fill your screen temporarily with a portion of a document or a complete presentation visual without menus or toolbars. This feature gives you a fresh, magnified look at your work.

Goal Seek. An Excel command that permits you to specify a desired, minimum, or maximum value for a cell and then works backward to achieve that value by modifying the values in cells.

Group/Ungroup. The Group command located in Word's Drawing toolbar and PowerPoint's Draw menu allows you to create a single object from individual text and graphic objects, allowing you to move and resize those objects as a single object. The Ungroup command (often used with imported clip art) permits you to return the object or drawing to its components so that you can eliminate unwanted elements or selectively recolor parts of the drawing.

Hidden Slide. A PowerPoint feature, active during electronic (computer-based) presentations, that allows you to create slides that will be displayed only if necessary. You can use this feature to provide supporting information and arguments that you may not need to include in your presentation.

Hyphenation. A Word feature applied to words that are too long to fit on a single line. Hyphenation breaks the word at a logical point and places the remainder of the word at the beginning of the next line. Although text type nearly always should be hyphenated, never hyphenate headlines, and try to avoid hyphenating captions.

Keyboard shortcuts. A timesaving feature that allows you to access frequently used commands (and apply styles) without clicking a toolbar button or opening a menu and navigating through dialog boxes. Keyboard shortcuts typically consist of a single letter (usually one associated with the most easily remembered word or the word that best describes the command) pressed in combination with the Shift, Ctrl, or Alt key. When applying keyboard shortcuts, the program displays a list of currently used keyboard shortcuts so that you don't accidentally erase an existing keyboard shortcut.

Legend. An Excel or PowerPoint chart feature that provides a visual, color-coded link between chart slices or bars and the data series that the chart elements represent.

Link. A method used to exchange dynamic, or changing, data between programs rather than simply pasting static copies of the original information or object. When information in the source document is modified (for example, information in an Excel spreadsheet), links inform the destination document (often a chart in a Word proposal or PowerPoint slide) that

the data has been changed. If both programs are open, the object in the destination document is updated. If the destination document is closed, Word asks you whether you want to update the information or object when you open the file.

Macro. A file containing the commands used to perform a frequently repeated function — for example, a Word macro used to eliminate unwanted spaces after periods, an Excel macro used to search for maximum and minimum values that fall in a certain range, and an Access macro used to print individual records or reports.

Merge. You can print form letters, envelopes, and labels by merging a Word document with the names and addresses contained in an Access database. You can specify the database files that will be included, and you can preview your document and letter on-screen before printing (or automatically print the document).

Microsoft Network. A new online service, containing files and technical support, that can be reached via a modem and a phone line. To access The Microsoft Network, pull down the Help menu and choose The Microsoft Network.

Microsoft Office Shortcut Bar. A customizable toolbar that makes it easy to launch or switch between all the programs included in Microsoft Office.

Normal view. A Word view, normally used while entering and editing text, that shows text formatting without headers and footers. Normal view suppresses multi-column layouts; it also indicates the size and location of imported graphics but doesn't show the graphics.

Page Layout view. A Word feature that displays formatted text and multicolumn documents as well as headers and footers. (Also see *Normal view*.)

Paragraph-level formatting. Paragraph styles that contain line spacing, text alignment, and border and background shading information. (Also see *Character-level formatting*.)

Paragraph marks. A Word feature that displays the hard returns that indicate paragraph breaks. Paragraph formatting is contained in the paragraph mark, and if you inadvertently delete the paragraph mark, the paragraph is reformatted with the typeface, type size, alignment, and line spacing of the following paragraph.

Password. An Access, Excel, Word, and Schedule+ feature that limits other users' access to sensitive documents. Passwords can protect a document from prying eyes but can also prevent you from using your own document if you forget the password too. (Also see *Read Only* and *Write Protected*.)

Paste Special. A command used in sharing information between documents. Paste Special allows you to specify whether you want to paste a picture (static image) of an object that will not change if the original document changes or whether you want to use a link, which means that the object in the destination document will change if the data in the source document is modified.

PivotTable. An Excel feature that permits you to create a worksheet table that summarizes and analyzes data in existing worksheets, providing a different view of the information contained in the original

spreadsheet. You can temporarily eliminate unwanted details, consolidate information, or sort rows and columns. You can update a pivot table at any time. The PivotTable Wizard guides you through the creation of a PivotTable.

Print Preview. A Word, Excel, and Access feature that permits you to view the way a document will look when printed. Word permits you to display up to six pages at a time, which helps you review the flow of your document.

Properties. A brief description of a file, such as its name, date of creation, and the number of times it has been revised.

QBE. Stands for *Query By Example,* an Access feature that allows you to establish query criteria by dragging fields from the top to bottom of the Query dialog box.

Query. An Excel command used to locate and display or print desired information. Also, an Access command used to locate or summarize information. *Select queries* display query results without changing the original data. *Action queries* change, update, or move the original data. *Crosstab queries* compute total values for individual rows and columns.

Question-mark pointer. A feature of many Office programs that allows you to access context-sensitive help by clicking the Help button in the Standard toolbar (or by pressing Shift+F1). When the question-mark pointer appears, click the command or feature on which you want information. In addition, in Word, clicking on a text or graphic object with the question-mark pointer displays character and paragraph formatting of text objects (or the attributes of graphic elements).

Read Only, Write Protected. A password feature that allows other users to open and read a Word document but not to modify or save their changes. This feature is useful when you are sharing instructions or procedures on a network. (Also see *Password.*)

Recolor Picture. A PowerPoint feature that allows you to harmonize the colors of an imported clip art illustration with your presentation's existing color scheme, eliminating the "tuba in a string quartet" appearance of inappropriate colors. Recolor Picture permits you to maintain visual consistency throughout your presentation.

Record. As a verb, a macro feature that saves keystrokes in a separate file; to repeat the keystrokes, you run the macro. As a noun, *record* refers to information in an Access database contained in rows. Records include fields that, together, describe an individual firm (such as name and address) or an individual transaction (such as shipping information, date and quantity ordered, and total price).

Record set. A combination of previously selected records that can be treated as a single object.

Rehearse New Timings. A PowerPoint Slide Show feature that keeps track of the time spent rehearsing each slide and displays the time spent on each slide in Slide Sorter view.

Report. An Access feature that prints a summary of information contained in a database table. Reports can be as detailed or as concise as you want.

Saved Search. An Excel feature that allows you to save a complicated search containing multiple variables so that you can

modify or repeat the search later without re-entering search criteria. The Saved Searches dialog box displays a list of Saved Searches.

Section. A single Word, Excel, or PowerPoint file that makes up part of a binder. (Also see *Binder.*)

Sheets. Multilayer Excel spreadsheets that have a common format and layout and are devoted to a single time period or product line. Sheets are contained in workbooks, and the totals can be consolidated.

Shortcut menus. An Office feature displayed by right-clicking a text or graphic object. A shortcut menu displays the commands most often used with the object (Cut, Copy, Paste, Font, Paragraph, and so on). The menu displayed differs, depending on the object you select.

Slide Master. The underlying structure that determines the appearance of a PowerPoint presentation. Slide Master elements include the position of the title and other objects (such as text charts or illustrations), repeating elements (such as the slide number and presentation date), as well as the presentation's color scheme.

Slide Show. A PowerPoint feature that allows you to review your presentation on-screen by hiding menus and toolbars. During a slide show, you can advance from one slide to another by clicking the mouse or pressing keyboard keys, or you can set up self-running presentations that advance from slide to slide automatically.

Solver. An Excel feature that permits you to enter a goal amount (or a minimum or maximum value) in a target cell and then work backward to achieve that goal by changing values in adjustable cells. You can also enter constraints that must be satisfied — for example, you cannot enter labor costs of zero to increase profits.

Sorting. Rearranging information (such as items in a list or information in rows or columns) in ascending or descending order.

Source document. Refers to the program and file containing information that is linked to, or embedded in, a document created in another program. Often, an Excel spreadsheet is the source document for a chart that appears in a Word document or PowerPoint slide.

Spike. An AutoText feature that allows you to cut, copy, or paste multiple text and graphic objects from several locations to one location. (A spike is also hardware used by railroads to keep rails from getting out of alignment.)

Status bar. An Office feature that displays a brief description of a highlighted menu command. The status bar always appears at the bottom of a window.

Style Gallery. A Word feature that permits you to preview templates (formatted document layouts) that can be applied to an existing document or serve as the basis of a new document.

Table. As used in Word and PowerPoint, refers to graphic objects containing information displayed in row-and-column format. In Excel, refers to the entire spreadsheet. In Access, refers to the structure of a database, typically containing individual records in rows and fields and categories of information in columns.

Tabs. A dialog box feature in many Office programs that permits a single dialog box to contain several layers. You can switch

among the layers by clicking the tabs to reveal a different set of formatting options. The Font dialog box, for example, contains Font and Character Spacing tabs; the Paragraph dialog box contains the Indents, Spacing, and Text Flow tabs. Word's Options dialog box contains 12 tabs.

Templates. Read-only documents that contain styles and repeating elements (such as logos, borders, and header/footer information). Templates save time by permitting you to share formatting between documents.

Tick marks. Small horizontal and vertical marks added to the horizontal and/or vertical axis of Excel and PowerPoint charts to indicate values between the gridlines (major divisions).

TipWizard. Context-specific Excel Help information that shows you how to perform common tasks as quickly and easily as possible.

Toolbar. A feature in Office programs that allows you to access frequently needed commands by clicking the buttons that represent those commands. Toolbars can be customized; you can move them around the screen and add or delete buttons.

ToolTips. Short, descriptive words and phrases that appear when you place the mouse pointer on a toolbar button. ToolTips help you identify the function that each button performs.

Undo/Redo. You can use Undo to reverse most editing and formatting changes — that is, you can restore deleted text and restore typeface, type size, and color to their original settings. Redo permits you to restore your changes, in case you're not convinced that they were as bad as you thought.

Update. A command used when information in a source document is linked to an object in a destination document. Update shares changes in the source document with objects in the destination document.

View buttons. Buttons located at the left end of Word's and PowerPoint's horizontal scroll bars that permit you to change your view of your document or presentation. Word's view buttons permit you to switch among Normal, Page Layout, and Outline view. PowerPoint's view buttons permit you to switch among Slide, Outline, Slide Sorter, Slide Show, and Notes view. (When you hold down the Shift key in PowerPoint, you can go to the Slide Master, Outline Master, and Notes Master views, which allow you to establish formats to be repeated throughout your presentation.)

Viewer. The PowerPoint Viewer is a stand-alone program that you can freely distribute to other users, allowing them to view PowerPoint presentations on their computers even if they have not installed PowerPoint. This feature permits you to distribute copies of your presentation to people who were not able to attend it.

Wizards. Word, Excel, PowerPoint, and Access include numerous wizards that interactively help you learn faster and work more efficiently. Word's wizards provide suggestions for document content. Excel's wizards help you format charts. PowerPoint's wizards help you determine the content and formatting of your presentation. Access wizards help you set up a database that will satisfy your information-management goals.

Word Count. A feature that allows you to count the words in a Word file (or part of a file).

WordArt. Word utility that allows you to modify TrueType fonts, change letter spacing, rotate and stretch clip art, add callouts to Word documents, and create logos by manipulating letters and graphics that can be saved and resized as a single object.

WordDraw. Powerful Word feature that allows you to import and modify clip art, add callouts to Word documents, and create logos by manipulating letters and adding graphic accents (such as shaded backgrounds), which can be saved and resized as a single object.

Workbook. Excel feature that allows a single file to contain several individual spreadsheets that can be consolidated. Individual spreadsheets can represent the various months of the year (consolidated into a single yearly spreadsheet) or separate departments (consolidated into company-wide totals).

Zoom. A Word, Excel, and PowerPoint feature that allows you to see as much, or as little, of your document as possible. Working at large magnification increases the accuracy with which you place text and objects. Working at small magnification provides a better view of the overall appearance of your document or presentation visual.

Index

(continued)

(continued)

(continued)

Notes

Notes

The Internet For Macs® For Dummies® 2nd Edition	by Charles Seiter	ISBN: 1-56884-371-2	$19.99 USA/$26.99 Canada
The Internet For Macs® For Dummies® Starter Kit	by Charles Seiter	ISBN: 1-56884-244-9	$29.99 USA/$39.99 Canada
The Internet For Macs® For Dummies® Starter Kit Bestseller Edition	by Charles Seiter	ISBN: 1-56884-245-7	$39.99 USA/$54.99 Canada
The Internet For Windows® For Dummies® Starter Kit	by John R. Levine & Margaret Levine Young	ISBN: 1-56884-237-6	$34.99 USA/$44.99 Canada
The Internet For Windows® For Dummies® Starter Kit, Bestseller Edition	by John R. Levine & Margaret Levine Young	ISBN: 1-56884-246-5	$39.99 USA/$54.99 Canada

MACINTOSH

Mac® Programming For Dummies®	by Dan Parks Sydow	ISBN: 1-56884-173-6	$19.95 USA/$26.95 Canada
Macintosh® System 7.5 For Dummies®	by Bob LeVitus	ISBN: 1-56884-197-3	$19.95 USA/$26.95 Canada
MORE Macs® For Dummies®	by David Pogue	ISBN: 1-56884-087-X	$19.95 USA/$26.95 Canada
PageMaker 5 For Macs® For Dummies®	by Galen Gruman & Deke McClelland	ISBN: 1-56884-178-7	$19.95 USA/$26.95 Canada
QuarkXPress 3.3 For Dummies®	by Galen Gruman & Barbara Assadi	ISBN: 1-56884-217-1	$19.95 USA/$26.99 Canada
Upgrading and Fixing Macs® For Dummies®	by Kearney Rietmann & Frank Higgins	ISBN: 1-56884-189-2	$19.95 USA/$26.95 Canada

MULTIMEDIA

Multimedia & CD-ROMs For Dummies® 2nd Edition	by Andy Rathbone	ISBN: 1-56884-907-9	$19.99 USA/$26.99 Canada
Multimedia & CD-ROMs For Dummies® Interactive Multimedia Value Pack, 2nd Edition	by Andy Rathbone	ISBN: 1-56884-909-5	$29.99 USA/$39.99 Canada

OPERATING SYSTEMS:

DOS

MORE DOS For Dummies®	by Dan Gookin	ISBN: 1-56884-046-2	$19.95 USA/$26.95 Canada
OS/2® Warp For Dummies® 2nd Edition	by Andy Rathbone	ISBN: 1-56884-205-8	$19.99 USA/$26.99 Canada

UNIX

MORE UNIX® For Dummies®	by John R. Levine & Margaret Levine Young	ISBN: 1-56884-361-5	$19.99 USA/$26.99 Canada
UNIX® For Dummies®	by John R. Levine & Margaret Levine Young	ISBN: 1-878058-58-4	$19.95 USA/$26.95 Canada

WINDOWS

MORE Windows® For Dummies® 2nd Edition	by Andy Rathbone	ISBN: 1-56884-048-9	$19.95 USA/$26.95 Canada
Windows® 95 For Dummies®	by Andy Rathbone	ISBN: 1-56884-240-6	$19.99 USA/$26.99 Canada

PCS/HARDWARE

Illustrated Computer Dictionary For Dummies® 2nd Edition	by Dan Gookin & Wallace Wang	ISBN: 1-56884-218-X	$12.95 USA/$16.95 Canada
Upgrading and Fixing PCs For Dummies® 2nd Edition	by Andy Rathbone	ISBN: 1-56884-903-6	$19.99 USA/$26.99 Canada

PRESENTATION/AUTOCAD

AutoCAD For Dummies®	by Bud Smith	ISBN: 1-56884-191-4	$19.95 USA/$26.95 Canada
PowerPoint 4 For Windows® For Dummies®	by Doug Lowe	ISBN: 1-56884-161-2	$16.99 USA/$22.99 Canada

PROGRAMMING

Borland C++ For Dummies®	by Michael Hyman	ISBN: 1-56884-162-0	$19.95 USA/$26.95 Canada
C For Dummies® Volume 1	by Dan Gookin	ISBN: 1-878058-78-9	$19.95 USA/$26.95 Canada
C++ For Dummies®	by Stephen R. Davis	ISBN: 1-56884-163-9	$19.95 USA/$26.95 Canada
Delphi Programming For Dummies®	by Neil Rubenking	ISBN: 1-56884-200-7	$19.95 USA/$26.99 Canada
Mac® Programming For Dummies®	by Dan Parks Sydow	ISBN: 1-56884-173-6	$19.95 USA/$26.95 Canada
PowerBuilder 4 Programming For Dummies®	by Ted Coombs & Jason Coombs	ISBN: 1-56884-325-9	$19.99 USA/$26.99 Canada
QBasic Programming For Dummies®	by Douglas Hergert	ISBN: 1-56884-093-4	$19.95 USA/$26.95 Canada
Visual Basic 3 For Dummies®	by Wallace Wang	ISBN: 1-56884-076-4	$19.95 USA/$26.95 Canada
Visual Basic "X" For Dummies®	by Wallace Wang	ISBN: 1-56884-230-9	$19.99 USA/$26.99 Canada
Visual C++ 2 For Dummies®	by Michael Hyman & Bob Arnson	ISBN: 1-56884-328-3	$19.99 USA/$26.99 Canada
Windows® 95 Programming For Dummies®	by S. Randy Davis	ISBN: 1-56884-327-5	$19.99 USA/$26.99 Canada

SPREADSHEET

1-2-3 For Dummies®	by Greg Harvey	ISBN: 1-878058-60-6	$16.95 USA/$22.95 Canada
1-2-3 For Windows® 5 For Dummies® 2nd Edition	by John Walkenbach	ISBN: 1-56884-216-3	$16.95 USA/$22.95 Canada
Excel 5 For Macs® For Dummies®	by Greg Harvey	ISBN: 1-56884-186-8	$19.95 USA/$26.95 Canada
Excel For Dummies® 2nd Edition	by Greg Harvey	ISBN: 1-56884-050-0	$16.95 USA/$22.95 Canada
MORE 1-2-3 For DOS For Dummies®	by John Weingarten	ISBN: 1-56884-224-4	$19.99 USA/$26.99 Canada
MORE Excel 5 For Windows® For Dummies®	by Greg Harvey	ISBN: 1-56884-207-4	$19.95 USA/$26.95 Canada
Quattro Pro 6 For Windows® For Dummies®	by John Walkenbach	ISBN: 1-56884-174-4	$19.95 USA/$26.95 Canada
Quattro Pro For DOS For Dummies®	by John Walkenbach	ISBN: 1-56884-023-3	$16.95 USA/$22.95 Canada

UTILITIES

Norton Utilities 8 For Dummies®	by Beth Slick	ISBN: 1-56884-166-3	$19.95 USA/$26.95 Canada

VCRS/CAMCORDERS

VCRs & Camcorders For Dummies™	by Gordon McComb & Andy Rathbone	ISBN: 1-56884-229-5	$14.99 USA/$20.99 Canada

WORD PROCESSING

Ami Pro For Dummies®	by Jim Meade	ISBN: 1-56884-049-7	$19.95 USA/$26.95 Canada
MORE Word For Windows® 6 For Dummies®	by Doug Lowe	ISBN: 1-56884-165-5	$19.95 USA/$26.95 Canada
MORE WordPerfect® 6 For Windows® For Dummies®	by Margaret Levine Young & David C. Kay	ISBN: 1-56884-206-6	$19.95 USA/$26.95 Canada
MORE WordPerfect® 6 For DOS For Dummies®	by Wallace Wang, edited by Dan Gookin	ISBN: 1-56884-047-0	$19.95 USA/$26.95 Canada
Word 6 For Macs® For Dummies®	by Dan Gookin	ISBN: 1-56884-190-6	$19.95 USA/$26.95 Canada
Word For Windows® 6 For Dummies®	by Dan Gookin	ISBN: 1-56884-075-6	$16.95 USA/$22.95 Canada
Word For Windows® For Dummies®	by Dan Gookin & Ray Werner	ISBN: 1-878058-86-X	$16.95 USA/$22.95 Canada
WordPerfect® 6 For DOS For Dummies®	by Dan Gookin	ISBN: 1-878058-77-0	$16.95 USA/$22.95 Canada
WordPerfect® 6.1 For Windows® For Dummies® 2nd Edition	by Margaret Levine Young & David Kay	ISBN: 1-56884-243-0	$16.95 USA/$22.95 Canada
WordPerfect® For Dummies®	by Dan Gookin	ISBN: 1-878058-52-5	$16.95 USA/$22.95 Canada

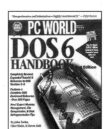

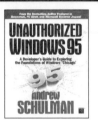

Unauthorized Windows® 95: A Developer's Guide to Exploring the Foundations of Windows "Chicago"
by Andrew Schulman

ISBN: 1-56884-169-8
$29.99 USA/$39.99 Canada

Unauthorized Windows® 95 Developer's Resource Kit
by Andrew Schulman

ISBN: 1-56884-305-4
$39.99 USA/$54.99 Canada

Best of the Net
by Seth Godin

ISBN: 1-56884-313-5
$22.99 USA/$32.99 Canada

Detour: The Truth About the Information Superhighway
by Michael Sullivan-Trainor

ISBN: 1-56884-307-0
$22.99 USA/$32.99 Canada

PowerPC Programming For Intel Programmers
by Kip McClanahan

ISBN: 1-56884-306-2
$49.99 USA/$64.99 Canada

Foundations™ of Visual C++ Programming For Windows® 95
by Paul Yao & Joseph Yao

ISBN: 1-56884-321-6
$39.99 USA/$54.99 Canada

Heavy Metal™ Visual C++ Programming
by Steve Holzner

ISBN: 1-56884-196-5
$39.95 USA/$54.95 Canada

Heavy Metal™ OLE 2.0 Programming
by Steve Holzner

ISBN: 1-56884-301-1
$39.95 USA/$54.95 Canada

Lotus Notes Application Development Handbook
by Erica Kerwien

ISBN: 1-56884-308-9
$39.99 USA/$54.99 Canada

The Internet Direct Connect Kit
by Peter John Harrison

ISBN: 1-56884-135-3
$29.95 USA/$39.95 Canada

Macworld® Ultimate Mac® Programming
by Dave Mark

ISBN: 1-56884-195-7
$39.95 USA/$54.95 Canada

The UNIX®-Haters Handbook
by Simson Garfinkel, Daniel Weise, & Steven Strassmann

ISBN: 1-56884-203-1
$16.95 USA/$22.95 Canada

Learn C++ Today!
by Martin Rinehart

ISBN: 1-56884-310-0
34.99 USA/$44.99 Canada

Type & Learn™ C
by Tom Swan

ISBN: 1-56884-073-X
34.95 USA/$44.95 Canada

Type & Learn™ Windows® Programming
by Tom Swan

ISBN: 1-56884-071-3
34.95 USA/$44.95 Canada

Windows is a registered trademark of Microsoft Corporation. Mac is a registered trademark of Apple Computer. UNIX is a registered trademark of AT&T. Macworld is a registered trademark of International Data Group, Inc. Foundations of ----, Heavy Metal, Type & Learn, and the IDG Books Worldwide logos are trademarks under exclusive license to IDG Books Worldwide, Inc., from International Data Group, Inc.

For scholastic requests & educational orders please call Educational Sales, at 1. 800. 434. 2086

FOR MORE INFO OR TO ORDER, PLEASE CALL ▶ 800. 762. 2974

For volume discounts & special orders please ca Tony Real, Special Sales, at 415. 655. 3048

DUMMIES PRESS™ PROGRAMMING BOOKS

10/31/95

COMPUTER
BOOK SERIES
FROM IDG

For Dummies who want to program...

Delphi Programming For Dummies®
by Neil Rubenking

ISBN: 1-56884-200-7
$19.99 USA/$26.99 Canada

Access Programming For Dummies®
by Rob Krumm

ISBN: 1-56884-091-8
$19.95 USA/$26.95 Canada

TCP/IP For Dummies®
by Marshall Wilensky & Candace Leiden

ISBN: 1-56884-241-4
$19.99 USA/$26.99 Canada

HTML For Dummies®
by Ed Tittel & Carl de Cordova

ISBN: 1-56884-330-5
$29.99 USA/$39.99 Canada

Windows® 95 Programming For Dummies®
by S. Randy Davis

ISBN: 1-56884-327-5
$19.99 USA/$26.99 Canada

Mac® Programming For Dummies®
by Dan Parks Sydow

ISBN: 1-56884-173-6
$19.95 USA/$26.95 Canada

PowerBuilder 4 Programming For Dummies®
by Ted Coombs & Jason Coombs

ISBN: 1-56884-325-9
$19.99 USA/$26.99 Canada

Visual Basic 3 For Dummies®
by Wallace Wang

ISBN: 1-56884-076-4
$19.95 USA/$26.95 Canada

Covers version 3.

ISDN For Dummies®
by David Angell

ISBN: 1-56884-331-3
$19.99 USA/$26.99 Canada

Visual C++ "2" For Dummies®
by Michael Hyman & Bob Arnson

ISBN: 1-56884-328-3
$19.99 USA/$26.99 Canada

Borland C++ For Dummies®
by Michael Hyman

ISBN: 1-56884-162-0
$19.95 USA/$26.95 Canada

C For Dummies,® Volume I
by Dan Gookin

ISBN: 1-878058-78-9
$19.95 USA/$26.95 Canada

C++ For Dummies®
by Stephen R. Davis

ISBN: 1-56884-163-9
$19.95 USA/$26.95 Canada

QBasic Programming For Dummies®
by Douglas Hergert

ISBN: 1-56884-093-4
$19.95 USA/$26.95 Canada

dBase 5 For Windows® Programming For Dummies®
by Ted Coombs & Jason Coombs

ISBN: 1-56884-215-5
$19.99 USA/$26.99 Canada

r scholastic requests & educational orders please
l Educational Sales, at 1. 800. 434. 2086

FOR MORE INFO OR TO ORDER, PLEASE CALL ▶ 800 762 2974

For volume discounts & special orders please call
Tony Real, Special Sales, at 415. 655. 3048

Official Hayes Modem Communications Companion
by Caroline M. Halliday

ISBN: 1-56884-072-1
$29.95 USA/$39.95 Canada

Includes software.

1,001 Komputer Answers from Kim Komando
by Kim Komando

ISBN: 1-56884-460-3
$29.99 USA/$39.99 Canada

Includes software.

PC World Excel 5 For Windows® Handbook, 2nd Edition
by John Walkenbach & Dave Maguiness

ISBN: 1-56884-056-X
$34.95 USA/$44.95 Canada

Includes software

PC World WordPerfect® 6 Handbook
by Greg Harvey

ISBN: 1-878058-80-0
$34.95 USA/$44.95 Canada

Includes software.

PC World DOS 6 Command Reference and Problem Solver
by John Socha & Devra Hall

NATIONAL BESTSELLER!

ISBN: 1-56884-055-1
$24.95 USA/$32.95 Canada

Client/Server Strategies™: A Survival Guide for Corporate Reengineers
by David Vaskevitch

SUPER STAR

ISBN: 1-56884-064-0
$29.95 USA/$39.95 Canada

Internet SECRETS™
by John Levine & Carol Baroudi

ISBN: 1-56884-452-2
$39.99 USA/$54.99 Canada

Includes software.

Network Security SECRETS™
by David Stang & Sylvia Moon

ISBN: 1-56884-021-7
Int'l. ISBN: 1-56884-151-5
$49.95 USA/$64.95 Canada

Includes software.

PC SECRETS™
by Caroline M. Halliday

ISBN: 1-878058-49-5
$39.95 USA/$52.95 Canada

Includes software.

IDG BOOKS WORLDWIDE

Here's a complete listing of PC Press Titles

Title	Author	ISBN	Price
BBS SECRETS™	by Ray Werner	ISBN: 1-56884-491-3	$39.99 USA/$54.99 Canada
Creating Cool Web Pages with HTML	by Dave Taylor	ISBN: 1-56884-454-9	$19.99 USA/$26.99 Canada
DOS 6 SECRETS™	by Robert D. Ainsbury	ISBN: 1-878058-70-3	$39.95 USA/$52.95 Canada
Excel 5 For Windows® Power Programming Techniques	by John Walkenbach	ISBN: 1-56884-303-8	$39.95 USA/$52.95 Canada
Hard Disk SECRETS™	by John M. Goodman, Ph.D.	ISBN: 1-878058-64-9	$39.95 USA/$52.95 Canada
Internet GIZMOS™ For Windows®	by Joel Diamond, Howard Sobel, & Valda Hilley	ISBN: 1-56884-451-4	$39.99 USA/$54.99 Canada
Making Multimedia Work	by Michael Goodwin	ISBN: 1-56884-468-9	$19.99 USA/$26.99 Canada
MORE Windows® 3.1 SECRETS™	by Brian Livingston	ISBN: 1-56884-019-5	$39.95 USA/$52.95 Canada
Official XTree Companion 3rd Edition	by Beth Slick	ISBN: 1-878058-57-6	$19.95 USA/$26.95 Canada
Paradox 4 Power Programming SECRETS,™ 2nd Edition	by Gregory B. Salcedo & Martin W. Rudy	ISBN: 1-878058-54-1	$44.95 USA/$59.95 Canada
Paradox 5 For Windows® Power Programming SECRETS™	by Gregory B. Salcedo & Martin W. Rudy	ISBN: 1-56884-085-3	$44.95 USA/$59.95 Canada
PC World DOS 6 Handbook, 2nd Edition	by John Socha, Clint Hicks & Devra Hall	ISBN: 1-878058-79-7	$34.95 USA/$44.95 Canada
PC World Microsoft® Access 2 Bible, 2nd Edition	by Cary N. Prague & Michael R. Irwin	ISBN: 1-56884-086-1	$39.95 USA/$52.95 Canada
PC World Word For Windows® 6 Handbook	by Brent Heslop & David Angell	ISBN: 1-56884-054-3	$34.95 USA/$44.95 Canada
QuarkXPress For Windows® Designer Handbook	by Barbara Assadi & Galen Gruman	ISBN: 1-878058-45-2	$29.95 USA/$39.95 Canada
Windows® 3.1 Configuration SECRETS™	by Valda Hilley & James Blakely	ISBN: 1-56884-026-8	$49.95 USA/$64.95 Canada
Windows® 3.1 Connectivity SECRETS™	by Runnoe Connally, David Rorabaugh & Sheldon Hall	ISBN: 1-56884-030-6	$49.95 USA/$64.95 Canada
Windows® 3.1 SECRETS™	by Brian Livingston	ISBN: 1-878058-43-6	$39.95 USA/$52.95 Canada
Windows® 95 A.S.A.P.	by Dan Gookin	ISBN: 1-56884-483-2	$24.99 USA/$34.99 Canada
Windows® 95 Bible	by Alan Simpson	ISBN: 1-56884-074-8	$29.99 USA/$39.99 Canada
Windows® 95 SECRETS™	by Brian Livingston	ISBN: 1-56884-453-0	$39.99 USA/$54.99 Canada
Windows® GIZMOS™	by Brian Livingston & Margie Livingston	ISBN: 1-878058-66-5	$39.95 USA/$52.95 Canada
WordPerfect® 6 For Windows® Tips & Techniques Revealed	by David A. Holzgang & Roger C. Parker	ISBN: 1-56884-202-3	$39.95 USA/$52.95 Canada
WordPerfect® 6 SECRETS™	by Roger C. Parker & David A. Holzgang	ISBN: 1-56884-040-3	$39.95 USA/$52.95 Canada

Order Center: **(800) 762-2974** *(8 a.m.–6 p.m., EST, weekdays)*

Quantity	ISBN	Title	Price	Total

Shipping & Handling Charges

	Description	First book	Each additional book	Total
Domestic	Normal	$4.50	$1.50	$
	Two Day Air	$8.50	$2.50	$
	Overnight	$18.00	$3.00	$
International	Surface	$8.00	$8.00	$
	Airmail	$16.00	$16.00	$
	DHL Air	$17.00	$17.00	$

*For large quantities call for shipping & handling charges.
**Prices are subject to change without notice.

Ship to:

Name _____

Company _____

Address _____

City/State/Zip _____

Daytime Phone _____

Payment: ☐ Check to IDG Books Worldwide (US Funds Only)

☐ VISA   ☐ MasterCard   ☐ American Express

Card # _____ Expires _____

Signature _____

Subtotal _____

CA residents add
applicable sales tax _____

IN, MA, and MD
residents add
5% sales tax _____

IL residents add
6.25% sales tax _____

RI residents add
7% sales tax _____

TX residents add
8.25% sales tax _____

Shipping _____

Total _____

Please send this order form to:

IDG Books Worldwide, Inc.
7260 Shadeland Station, Suite 100
Indianapolis, IN 46256

Allow up to 3 weeks for delivery.
Thank you!

IDG BOOKS WORLDWIDE REGISTRATION CARD

RETURN THIS
REGISTRATION CARD
FOR FREE CATALOG

Title of this book: Microsoft Office 95 For Dummies

My overall rating of this book: ❏ Very good [1] ❏ Good [2] ❏ Satisfactory [3] ❏ Fair [4] ❏ Poor [5]

How I first heard about this book:

❏ Found in bookstore; name: [6] _____ ❏ Book review: [7] _____

❏ Advertisement: [8] _____ ❏ Catalog: [9] _____

❏ Word of mouth; heard about book from friend, co-worker, etc.: [10] _____ ❏ Other: [11] _____

What I liked most about this book: _____

_____

_____

What I would change, add, delete, etc., in future editions of this book: _____

_____

_____

Other comments: _____

_____

Number of computer books I purchase in a year: ❏ 1 [12] ❏ 2-5 [13] ❏ 6-10 [14] ❏ More than 10 [15]

I would characterize my computer skills as: ❏ Beginner [16] ❏ Intermediate [17] ❏ Advanced [18] ❏ Professional [19]

I use ❏ DOS [20] ❏ Windows [21] ❏ OS/2 [22] ❏ Unix [23] ❏ Macintosh [24] ❏ Other: [25] _____
(please specify)

I would be interested in new books on the following subjects:
(please check all that apply, and use the spaces provided to identify specific software)

❏ Word processing: [26] _____ ❏ Spreadsheets: [27] _____

❏ Data bases: [28] _____ ❏ Desktop publishing: [29] _____

❏ File Utilities: [30] _____ ❏ Money management: [31] _____

❏ Networking: [32] _____ ❏ Programming languages: [33] _____

❏ Other: [34] _____

I use a PC at (please check all that apply): ❏ home [35] ❏ work [36] ❏ school [37] ❏ other: [38] _____

The disks I prefer to use are ❏ 5.25 [39] ❏ 3.5 [40] ❏ other: [41] _____

I have a CD ROM: ❏ yes [42] ❏ no [43]

I plan to buy or upgrade computer hardware this year: ❏ yes [44] ❏ no [45]

I plan to buy or upgrade computer software this year: ❏ yes [46] ❏ no [47]

Name: _____ Business title: [48] _____ Type of Business: [49] _____

Address (❏ home [50] ❏ work [51] /Company name: _____)

Street/Suite# _____

City [52] /State [53] /Zipcode [54] : _____ Country [55] _____

❏ **I liked this book!** You may quote me by name in future
IDG Books Worldwide promotional materials.

My daytime phone number is _____

IDG BOOKS
THE WORLD OF
COMPUTER
KNOWLEDGE

❏ YES!

Please keep me informed about IDG's World of Computer Knowledge.
Send me the latest IDG Books catalog.